Muru

Occupational Stress and Coping

C000052334

Murugan Shunmugasundaram

Occupational Stress and Coping Strategies among Police Constables

LAP LAMBERT Academic Publishing

Imprint

Any brand names and product names mentioned in this book are subject to trademark, brand or patent protection and are trademarks or registered trademarks of their respective holders. The use of brand names, product names, common names, trade names, product descriptions etc. even without a particular marking in this work is in no way to be construed to mean that such names may be regarded as unrestricted in respect of trademark and brand protection legislation and could thus be used by anyone.

Cover image: www.ingimage.com

Publisher:
LAP LAMBERT Academic Publishing
is a trademark of
International Book Market Service Ltd., member of OmniScriptum Publishing Group
17 Meldrum Street, Beau Bassin 71504, Mauritius

Printed at: see last page
ISBN: 978-613-9-45322-1

Zugl. / Approved by: KALASALINGAM UNIVERSITY, KRISHNANKOVIL-626 126, VIRUDHUNGAR DISTRICT, TAMILNADU, INDIA

OCCUPATIONAL STRESS AND COPING STRATEGIES AMONG POLICE CONSTABLES WITH SPECIAL REFERENCE TO TUTICORIN DISTRICT

Submitted by

M.SHUNMUGA SUNDARAM

Under the Supervision of

Dr. M. JEYAKUMARAN

Professor

Department of Business Administration

Kalasalingam University

FACULTY OF BUSINESS ADMINISTRATION

KALASALINGAM UNIVERSITY

ANAND NAGAR

KRISHNANKOIL – 626 126

Minutes of the Ph.D. Viva-Voce Examination of **Mr. M. SHUNMUGA SUNDARAM** (Reg. No. 200902211) held at 11.00am on 13th September, 2014 in the Conference Hall of *n*-CARDMATH, Kalasalingam University, Anand Nagar, Krishnankoil-626 126.

The Ph.D. Viva-Voce Examination of **Mr. M. SHUNMUGA SUNDARAM** (Reg. No. 200902211) on his Ph.D. thesis entitled "OCCUPATIONAL STRESS AND COPING STRATEGIES AMONG POLICE CONSTABLES WITH SPECIAL REFERENCE TO TUTICORIN DISTRICT" was conducted on 13th September, 2014 at 11.00am in the Conference Hall of *n*-CARDMATH, Kalasalingam University, Anand Nagar, Krishnankoil-626 126.

The following Members of Oral Examination Board were present:

1.	Dr. M. Jeyakumaran, Professor, Department of Business Administration, Kalasalingam University, Krishnankoil-626 126.	Supervisor & Convener
2.	Dr.K.Maran Professor & Director, Sri Sai Ram Institute of Management Studies, Sri Sai Ram Engineering College, Tambaram, Chennai-600044	Indian Examiner
3.	Dr. S.Sakthivel Rani, Asso. Professor & Head, Department of Business Administration, Kalasalingam University, Krishnankoil-626 126.	Chairman/ DRC

The candidate, **Mr. M. SHUNMUGA SUNDARAM,** presented the salient features of his Ph.D. work. This was followed by questions from the board members. The queries and clarifications raised by the Foreign and Indian Examiners were also put to the candidate. *The candidate answered the questions to the full satisfaction of the board members.*

The corrections and suggestions pointed out by the Indian/Foreign examiner have been carried out and duly incorporated in the thesis.

Based on the candidate's research work, his presentation and also the clarifications and answers by the candidate to the questions raised by the examiners, the board recommends that **Mr. M. SHUNMUGA SUNDARAM be awarded the Ph.D. degree in the FACULTY OF DEPARTMENT OF BUSINESS ADMINISTRATION.**

Dr. M. JEYAKUMARAN (Supervisor & Convener)	**Dr. K. MARAN** (Indian Examiner)	**Dr. S. SAKTHIVEL RANI** (Chairman, DRC)

ABSTRACT

Police officers operating under severe and chronic stress may well be at greater risk of error and over-reaction that can compromise their performance and public safety. The unrealistic expectations imposed by this occupational culture discourage officers from admitting feeling stressed and openly expressing negative emotions. The current study aims to analyse the occupational stress and the coping styles among the police constables in Thoothukudi District of Tamilnadu.

The research methodology of the study consists of two stages. First stage of the research is exploratory by nature and the second stage of descriptive in nature. The researcher has adopted Cluster based random Sampling Procedure (Probability) for defining the entire population area i.e., police stations and further more researcher has adopted "convenience sampling" techniques in the collection of primary data. The respondents are approached with the support of the affluent and references groups support and only voluntary respondents were included in the survey and no monetary benefits were paid as remuneration to the sample subjects.

It was found that the primary causes identified for occurrence of occupational stress among the police personnel are: when the police personnel see the criminals go free because of lack of evidence, court leniency and when a fellow officer is killed while on duty. It has also inferred that majority of the police constables get stress, when they do not get the opportunity for career advancement. Similarly, frequency of burnout and stress symptoms are observed to be more when police constables face the problem of handling the criminals, at the time of staff shortages and lack of participation in policy making decisions and also when the their fellow officers were killed in the line of duty. Due to constant stress the police personnel experiences stress - related symptoms like: loss of sexual interest or pleasure, crying easily and thoughts of ending one's life i.e., committing suicide.

The study concludes by stating that the stress is affecting them mentally and physically. It is also affecting their interpersonal relationships. Reducing occupational through from a frequent evaluation by the superiors can help them balance the distribution of workload and there by the quality of work of subordinates i.e., police constables can be enhanced.

Key words: Police Stress, Copings, Occupational Stress, Policing

ACKNOWLEDGEMENTS

My sincere thanks to our Chairman Kalvivallal Mr.T.KALASALINGAM, Illayavallal Mr.K.SRIDHARAN Chancellor, Dr.S.SARAVANA SANKAR, Vice-Chancellor Kalasalingam University, for providing opportunity to carry out the research work in our University.

DR. M.JEYAKUMARAN, my mentor and supervisor have extended his valuable guidance and motivation throughout this research, he is a big inspiration to me. His approach and kindness has motivated me to execute this research lively. It was possible to maintain quality throughout the research only because of his freedom and trust.

I extend my thanks to Dr.S.Sakthivel rani, Associate Professor, Head Department of Business Administration, Kalasalingam University, who gave all moral support behind the screen.

I dedicate all my work to my parents, wife, brothers and friends. I express my gratitude to the scarification, effort and pain they have taken in this regard.

I express my pleasure in thanking the students, friends, and my colleagues for the support and valuable suggestions for the improvement of this research. There are many others, who have helped me directly and indirectly to complete this research. I thank them whole-heartedly.

M.SHUNMUGA SUNDARAM

TABLE OF CONTENTS

Chapter I	**INTRODUCTION AND RESEARCH DESIGN**	
1.1	Introduction	1
1.2	Statement of Problem	3
1.3	Conceptual Framework	4
1.4	Scope of the Study	9
1.5	Objectives of the Study	9
1.6	Hypotheses of the Study	10
1.7	Research Methodology	10
1.8	Limitations of the Study	11
1.9	Chapterisation Schemes	12
Chapter II	**REVIEW OF LITERATURE**	
2.1	Introduction	14
2.2	Occupational Stress	14
2.3	Occupational Stress among the Policemen	34
2.4	Coping Strategies	42
Chapter III	**RESEARCH METHODOLOGY**	
3.1	Introduction	45
3.2	Importance of the Study	46
3.3	Research Methodology	48
3.3.1	Area of Study	48
3.3.2	Sampling Framework	49
3.3.3	Instrument Measurement	52

3.3.4	Reliability and Validation Measures	57
3.4	Tools Applied in the Study	59
3.5	Conclusion	60
Chapter IV	**OVERVIEW OF POLICE FORCE IN INDIA AND THE CAUSES FOR STRESS AMONG POLICE PERSONNEL**	
4.1	Introduction	61
4.1.1	Background of Police Administration in India	62
4.1.2	Role, Functions and Duties of the Police in General	63
4.1.3	Social Responsibilities of the Police	66
4.1.4	Maintenance of Essential Services	67
4.1.5	Organization at the Central and State Level	73
4.1.6	Organization at Range Level	77
4.1.7	Organization at District and Sub- District Level	78
4.1.7.1	Sub-division	81
4.1.7.2	Circles	81
4.1.7.3	Head Constable	82
4.1.7.4	Constables	85
4.1.8	Tamil Nadu Police	88
4.2.1	Introduction	94
4.2.2	Causes of Workplace Stress	95
4.2.3	Influences of Job Stress on Police Personnel	97
4.2.4	Cause of Stress	98
4.2.5	Symptoms of Physical and Emotional and Stress	102
4.2.6	Effects of Work-Related Stress and its Impact on Employee	105
4.2.6.1	Benefits of taking action to address work related stress	105
4.2.6.2	Methods of Identifying Stress	106
4.3	Conclusion	109
Chapter V	**ANALYSIS AND INTERPRETATION**	
5.1	Introduction	110
5.2	Demographic Characteristics	110
5.3	Job Profile	115

5.4	Police Personnel's Perception about Causes for Occupational Stress	117
5.5	Occurrence of stress / burnout	127
5.6	Outcome of Stress	137
5.7	Coping strategies	141
5.8	Results of Statistical Analysis and Hypotheses Testing	153
5.9	Conclusion	195
Chapter VI	**SUMMARY, FINDINGS, SUGGESTIONS AND CONCLUSION**	
6.1	Summary	197
6.2	Findings of the Study	198
6.2.1	Demographic Profile	198
6.2.2	Job Profile	199
6.2.3	Police Personnel's Perception about Causes for Occupational Stress	199
6.2.4	Outcome of Stress	199
6.2.5	Coping Strategies	200
6.2.6	Results of Hypotheses Testing	200
6.3	Implication of the Study	201
6.3.1	Suggestions to the Higher Officials	202
6.3.2	Suggestions to the Police Personnel	204
6.4	Conclusion	204
6.5	Further scope for the study	206
Reference		208
Appendices		
Appendix I		217
Appendix II		291

Table No	LIST OF TABLES	Page No
3.1	Details of Zones/Range/Cities/Dist/ Subdivision/Police Station/OP/ AWPS	49
3.2	Grade / wise classification of police force in Tuticorin District	50
3.3	Sampling framework	51
3.4	Grade / wise classification of sample police force	52
3.5	Cronbach's alpha for the model variables for police personnel's perception about causes for stress	58
5.1	Gender of the respondents	111
5.2	Age of the respondents	111
5.3	Educational qualification of the respondents	112
5.4	Religion of the respondents	112
5.5	Community of the respondents	113
5.6	Place of the residence of the respondents	113
5.7	Marital status of the respondents	114
5.8	Number of dependents of the respondents	114
5.9	Designation of the respondents	115
5.10	Years of experiences of the respondents	116
5.11	Monthly income of the respondents	116
5.12	Police personnel's perception about causes for stress (job demand)	118
5.13	Police personnel's perception about causes for stress (lack of resources)	121
5.14	Police personnel's perception about causes for stress (personal stresses / occupational stresses)	124
5.15	Police personnel's perception about frequency of stress occurrence (job demand)	128
5.16	Police personnel's perception about frequency of stress occurrence (lack of resources)	131
5.17	Police personnel's perception about frequency of stress occurrence (police stresses/occupational stress)	134
5.18	Police personnel's perception on outcome of stress /symptoms	138
5.19	Police personnel's perception on problem-focused stress coping strategies	142

5.20   Police personnel's perception on emotion-focused stress coping strategies   147

5.21   Result of ANOVA relation between job profile and police personnel's perception about causes for stress (job demand)   154

5.22   Result of ANOVA relation between job profile and police personnel's perception about causes for stress (lack of resources)   155

5.23   Result of ANOVA relation between job profile and police personnel's perception about causes for stress (police stress/occupational stress)   156

5.24   KMO and Bartlett's test for police personnel's perception about causes for stress   157

5.25   Influence of Factors in police personnel's perception about causes for stress   158

5.26   Factor analysis of association of police personnel's perception about causes for stress   160

5.26.1   Factor analysis of association of police personnel's perception about causes for stress   163

5.27   KMO and Bartlett's test for police personnel's perception about frequency of stress occurrence   164

5.28   Factors influence of police personnel's perception about frequency of stress occurrence   165

5.29   Factor analysis of association of police personnel's perception about frequency of stress occurrence   167

5.29.1   Factor analysis of association of police personnel's perception about frequency of stress occurrence   170

5.30   Paired samples test association between police personnel's perception on causes for stress & frequency of stress occurrence (job demand)   171

5.31   Paired samples test association between police personnel's perception on causes for stress & frequency of stress occurrence (lack of resources)   172

5.32   Paired samples test association between police personnel's perception on causes for stress & frequency of stress occurrence (police stresses/occupational stress)   173

5.33   KMO and Bartlett's test police personnel's perception on outcome of stress   174

5.34   Cumulative outcome of stress   174

5.35	Factor analysis of association of outcome of stress	175
5.35.1	Factor analysis of association of outcome of stress	176
5.36	The result of reliability statistics for police personnel's perception on problem-focused stress coping strategies	178
5.37	Result of ANOVA test police personnel's perception on problem-focused stress coping strategies	180
5.38	Result of ANOVA police personnel's perception on problem-focused stress coping strategies	181
5.39	KMO and Bartlett's test police personnel's perception on stress coping strategies (designation grade)	184
5.40	Cumulative police personnel's perception on stress coping strategies (designation grade)	185
5.41	Factor analysis of association of police personnel's perception on stress coping strategies (designation grade)	188
5.41.1	Factor analysis of association of police personnel's perception on stress coping strategies (designation grade)	191
5.42	KMO and Bartlett's test police personnel's perception on stress coping strategies (years of experience)	192
5.43	Cumulative police personnel's perception on stress coping strategies (years of experience)	193
5.44	Factor analysis of association of police personnel's perception on stress coping strategies (years of experience)	196
5.44.1	Factor analysis of association of police personnel's perception on stress coping strategies (years of experience)	200

Figure No	LIST OF FIGURES	Page No
1.1	Conceptual framework of the study	8
4.1	Rank structure in a state police force	76
4.2	History of Tamilnadu police	90
4.3	Causes of work-related stress	95
4.4	Typical symptoms of job stress	104
5.1	Police personnel's perception about causes for stress (job demand)	120
5.2	Police personnel's perception about causes for stress (lack of resources)	123
5.3	Police personnel's perception about causes for stress (police stresses/occupational stress)	126
5.4	Police personnel's perception about frequency of stress occurrence (job demand)	130
5.5	Police personnel's perception about frequency of stress occurrence (lack of resources)	133
5.6	Police personnel's perception about frequency of stress occurrence (police stresses/occupational stress)	136
5.7	Police personnel's perception on outcome of stress /symptoms	140
5.8	Police personnel's perception on problem-focused stress coping strategies (positive reinterpretation and growth)	145
5.9	Police personnel's perception on problem-focused stress coping strategies (acceptance of fact)	146
5.10	Police personnel's perception on problem-focused stress coping strategies (focusing on and ventilating emotions)	146
5.11	Police personnel's perception on emotion-focused stress coping strategies (seeking social support for emotional reasons)	150
5.12	Police personnel's perception on emotion-focused stress coping strategies (denial behaviour)	151
5.13	Police personnel's perception on emotion-focused stress coping strategies (turning religious)	151
5.14	Police personnel's perception on emotion-focused stress coping	152

	strategies (behavioral disengagement)	
5.15	Police personnel's perception on emotion-focused stress coping	152
	strategies (mental disengagement)	
5.16	Scree plot: police personnel's perception about causes for stress	159
5.17	Scree plot: police personnel's perception about frequency of stress	165
	occurrence	
5.18	Scree plot: outcome of stress	174
5.19	Scree plot: police personnel's perception on stress coping strategies	184
	(designation grade)	
5.20	Scree plot: police personnel's perception on stress coping strategies	193
	(years of experiences)	

PUBLICATION OF THE RESEARCH

1. **M.Shunmugasundaram**, M.JeyaKumaran, 2012. An Analysis of Causes for Stress among the Police with Special Reference to Grade II (Police Constables), Tuticorin District. *South Asian Academic Research Journal.* 118-139. ACADEMICIA 2(11): ISSN 2249-7137. Listed at: Ulrich's Periodicals Directory, **ProQuest**, U.S.A. Cabell's Directory of Publishing Opportunities, U.S.A.

2. **M.Shunmugasundaram**, M.JeyaKumaran, 2012. Occupational Stress among Grade I Police Constables. *International Journal of Research in Commerce & Management.* 2(8): 44-48 ISSN 2231-5756. Listed at: Ulrich's Periodicals Directory ©, **ProQuest**, U.S.A., **EBSCO Publishing**, U.S.A., Open J-Gate, India link of the same is duly available at Inflibnet of University Grants Commission (U.G.C.)], Cabell's Directories of Publishing Opportunities, U.S.A. & Index Copernicus Publishers Panel.

3. **M.Shunmugasundaram**, M.JeyaKumaran, 2012. A Study on Job demand stressors and coping strategies among Police Constables. *International Journal of Marketing and Management Research.* 3(10): 30-46. ISSN 2229-6883. Listed at: Ulrich's Periodicals Directory, **ProQuest**, U.S.A. (Dec. 2010), Cabell's Directory of Publishing Opportunities, U.S.A, **and EBSCO** Publishing, U.S.A.

4. **M.Shunmugasundaram,** M.JeyaKumaran **(2012)**. A study on coping strategies among Police constables. *International Journals of management, IT and Engineering (IJMIE).*2 (12):153-173. ISSN 2249- 0558. Listed At: Open Access Journal, ULRICH'S PERIODICALS DIRECTORY. Open J Gate, **EBSCO Publishing**, Scirus.com, **ProQuest**, Research GATE Scientific network, Google Scholar BETA, Scribd, Indian Management Academy, and Ulrich's Web Global Serials Directory.

5. **M.Shunmugasundaram**, M.JeyaKumaran, 2012. Occupational stress and coping strategies among grade II Police Constables. ***International Journal of Business***

Management and Economic Research **3(4): 579-589. ISSN 2229-6247.** Listed at: Cabell Publishing Inc, **EBSCO HOST**, and Google Scholar Beta.

6. **M.Shunmugasundaram**, M.JeyaKumaran, 2012. Occupational stress among female police constables reference to Tamil nadu police department. India. *Indian Streams Research Journal.* 2(9): ISSN:-2230-7850 **(Impact Factor: 0.2105).** Listed at : Google Scholar ,DOAJ , **EBSCO,** Index Copernicus, Crossref DOI, Academic Journal Database Publication Index , Scientific Resources Database , Scholarly Journals Index , National Library Of Australia-Trove, Mercyhurst University, Western Theological Seminary,Holland ,Washington University.

7. **M.Shunmugasundaram**, M.JeyaKumaran, 2012. Assessing Frequency of Occurrence of Stress in Policing. *Golden research Thought Journal.* 2(5), ISSN No: 2231-5063 **(Impact Factor: 0.1870).** Listed at : **EBSCO, USA**

CHAPTER I

INTRODUCTION AND RESEARCH DESIGN

1.1 Introduction

Stress is an important factor influencing individual efficacy and satisfaction in modern day occupational settings. Job stress is one of the most common afflictions among police personnel. Perhaps one of the most stress prone occupations is that of police profession. This is because the police department acts not only as a law enforcing agency but also as an instrument of social service, an agent of social change and the protector of the rights and duties of the people. Police personnel are often involved in dealing with criminals, VIP's security duties and collapse of other agencies of criminal justice system. Thus, it can be commented that police work is a human-service profession often regarded as physically and emotionally demanding. The evidence, however, is mixed regarding the nature of police work as inherently stressful. Researchers, police practitioners, health-care professionals, psychologists, as well as the lay community agree to the fact that police work is inherently stressful. It can be rightly stated that the entire life of police officers is full of tension and stresses.

The job profile of a police officer includes witnessing a fellow officer killed in the line of duty, killing someone in the line of duty, recovering bodies from motor vehicle accidents, witnessing domestic or community violence, and responding to cases involving child battery. Stress and burnout are usually considered to be by-products of police work. In and of itself, the nature of police work is regarded to be highly stressful and can even be described as hazardous. The daily psychological stresses that police officers experience in their work put them at significantly higher risk than the general population for a long term physical and mental health effects. The police culture does not look favorably on people who have problems. Job stress is dilemma that all of us work outside the home deal with on a daily traffic, fog, rain, bad drivers of the normal traffic and weather predictions will affect their attitude on the entire day will change roles from father, mother, wife or husband to boss, co-worker and employee.

Two major categories of potential stressors in police work emerge in the literature. First, "inherent police stressors" refers to events that generally occur in police work, and that have the potential to be psychologically or physically harmful, e.g. physical threat, violence, exposure to danger, crime and facing the unknown. Secondly, stress can be the result of the nature of the police organization and includes stressors such as management style, poor equipment, excessive paperwork, poor training and inadequate salary.

In short it could be stated that police occupational stress is a widespread problem because of its numerous negative effects on individuals and on police organization. Officers who experience high levels of occupational stress report a high incidence of physical ailments and psychological problems that affect their work performance. Specifically, they commonly have poor health, are frequently absent from work, experience burnout, are dissatisfied with their jobs and because of weak organizational commitment, they may not fully invest themselves in their work or they may retire prematurely. When individuals are overwhelmed by occupational stress they suffer from increased chronic stress, depression, heart disease, stomach disorders, alcohol and drug use and abuse, divorce, and even suicide attempts. It is therefore critical to understand the sources of police occupational stress (i.e., the stressors) and to implement strategies for reducing stressors or, if they cannot be reduced, for assisting officers in coping effectively with them. The current study aims to analyze the occupational stress and the coping styles among the police constables in Thoothukudi District of Tamilnadu.

1.2 Statement of Problem

Occupational stress research has an impressive history with more than three decades of sound studies that show clear correlations between certain organizational factors and stress. However, as best as can be determined, there are very few quantitative studies that measure the impact those stressors may have on police performance in Indian context. Occupational stress among police personnel can reduce productivity, encourage absenteeism, lower morale, and increase conflict with others, cause physical and emotional problems and poor satisfaction in life. Part of the problems may be that defining performance has been a challenge for many years and there is no consensus among scholars how to operationalize the concept. Compounding the problem is the definition of stress and the instruments used to measure it in police work. This has led researchers to move away from generic stress scales and into domain-specific scales that measure the unique characteristics of policing. The present study represents a focused interest in stress research in that it seeks to isolate specific self-reported organizational stressors that may negatively impact police performance, as well as analyze the extent to which the coping techniques have been adopted by the policemen. The researcher believes that of all occupations police work could be considered, highly stressful. Establishing the levels of stress police personnel experience and the coping strategies they apply would benefit intervention effort to address the problem i.e., stress management or say, reducing stress levels.

1.3 Conceptual Framework

Everyone today experiences a fairs hare of stress, irrespective of personal characteristics, environment and social conditions. The nature of police work is acknowledged as highly stressful and particularly hazardous. According to Mostert and Joubert (2005), the negative effects of job stress on employees and their work are such that it is necessary to explore the processes involved when job stress is studied.

The concept of stress was first introduced in the life sciences by Hans Seyle (1956). The term "stress" is applied to the total transaction between the stressor and coping resources in the interaction together, over time, so that one may speak of system being "under stress" or a particular situation being stressful. Hans Seyle defined stress as "the non-specific response of the body to any demand". The presence of stress among policemen is felt, but not recognized as the major enemy. Media reports of police brutality, indiscipline and mismanagement are a harbinger of the job. Social change, economic conditions, the total criminal justice system and the demands made on policemen's time with their families, all contribute towards the stress.

The policies and procedures of the police administration department in India are directly controlled by the state head (Chief Minister) and it is autocratic in nature. It has been a known fact that local government systems existing in a particular state may cause discontent and dissatisfaction among police personnel along with frequent transfer, suspension / suppression, delayed promotions, non-grant of leave on time and departmental inquiries.

Various meaning for police

"Polite obedient loyal intelligent courageous and encouraging"

"Protection of life in civil establishment"

"Police officers lobbying in common effort"

"Protectors of law in community economy"

"Protection of life and investigating criminal's establishments"

"Protection of law in case of emergency"

Police personnel of different ranks differ both quantitatively and qualitatively in their experience of stress. The subordinate officers had the highest scores on stressors such as job boredom, over load of work and lack of praise and relatively high scores on noxious physical environment, communication quality, and decision latitude and role ambiguity. Based on these understanding the current study aims to focus on the nature, causes and stress coping styles of subordinate (i.e., low rank) police officers - constables.

"Job stress" refers to a situation wherein job-related factors interact with a worker to change (i.e., disrupt or enhance) his or her psychological or physiological condition such that the person (i.e., mind and body) is forced to deviate from normal functioning. Stress among policemen would manifest in the form of fatigue, depression, inability o concentrate, irritability and impulsive behavior. These danger signals are quite common among the policemen. And these policemen are often viewed as rude and highhanded. However, outsiders may not appreciate the extreme conditions under which they lead their lives. Stress also has a negative effect on the health of the policemen. It makes them more susceptible to physical ailments. Both physical and mental illness renders the employee unfit for work. It has an adverse effect on job satisfaction and reduces job performance.

Kop and Euwema (2001) found that organizational factors are the most salient stressors in police organizations. According to Schaufeli and Enzmann (1998) organizational stressors are divided into two groups: job demands and lack of resources. Job demands refer "to the required sustained physical or mental effort aspects of the job" and can, therefore, be associated with certain physiological and psychological costs, e.g. meeting deadlines, attending work in shifts, working over-time, excessive paper work and handling crisis- situations. Job resources are aspects of the job that may be functional in achieving work goals, reducing job demands and the expected physiological and psychological costs, and stimulating personal development, e.g. adequate equipment, good supervision, adequate salary, recognition and sufficient personnel.

According to Lazarus and Folkman (1984) occupational stress takes place when job demands exceed the person's adaptive resources. Therefore stress refers to the temporary adaptation process that is accompanied by mental and physical symptoms, and is caused by a disturbance in the equilibrium between job demands and the ability of the worker to respond to the demands. When job demands are too high to cope with, stress reactions are likely to occur. The term "coping" is used reference to perceptual, cognitive or behavioral responses that are used in managing, avoiding or controlling situations that could be regarded as difficult and coping as a term could be used to refer to the strategies or results. As a strategy, "coping" refers to the different methods that a person may use in managing his/her circumstances. Moreover, "coping "also refers to the eventual outcome of this strategy on the person. "Non-coping" is defined as efforts that have failed to cope, accompanied by various physical and psychosocial disturbances, which result in increased stress. Non-coping also results in higher levels of depression and anxiety.

Police job demands that he should leave the personal issues of his life behind before entering his work environment. The policemen have to be able to give his 100% job attention to be a successful part of the team. This alone can be stressful because it can sometimes be very difficult when his personal life is complex or especially difficult at any given time. Bringing personal problems or attitudes to the coworkers can be detrimental to the attitudes of all those around them.

The coping type that a person uses is in part dependent on the person's appraisal of the situations which are amenable to change. Some studies have suggested that cognitive appraisal of a situation can be associated with coping strategies. This suggests that coping strategies will change according to context and can be important in determining health outcomes. Discussion of the previous studies has highlighted the nature of occupation stress that affected the police officers at lower ranks. Based on this understanding, the concept of the current study is framed.

EXHIBIT: 1.1

CONCEPTUAL FRAMEWORK OF THE STUDY

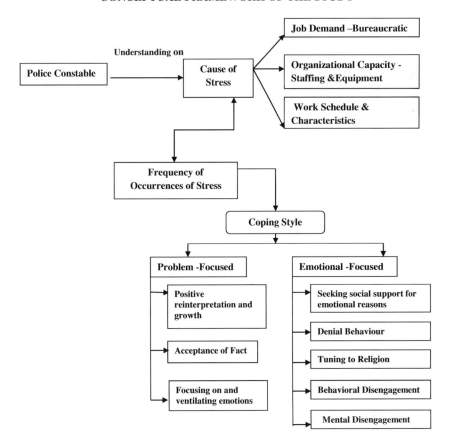

Source: Developed for the study

1.4 Scope of the Study

The overall goal of the study is to explore the major personal and cognitive factors with occupational stress, and to identifying the relationship between amount of stress, causes and stress coping strategies. The current study will be useful to a wide spectrum of police officials, policy makers and authorities in understanding the nature and causes of occupational stress faced by the police constables and it may help to frame strategic visions to overcome their stress.

1.5 Objectives of the Study

Based on the concept discussed above the following objectives were constructed for the effective conduct of the study.

- To study the socio-economic status and job profile of the police officers in the study area.

- To evaluate the police officers' perception about the nature of occupational stress faced by them.

- To measure the frequency of occurrence of occupational stress among the police officers.

- To analyze the gap between police officers' perception about their occupational stress and its occurrence frequencies.

- To study the stress coping styles adhered by the police officers and suggest suitable techniques to reduce their stress levels.

1.6 Hypotheses of the Study

The following hypotheses are framed to justify the objectives constructed.

- There exists no association between job profile of the police officers' and their perception about their occupational stress.

- There exist no similarities in the police officers' perception about their occupational stress.

- There exist no similarities in the police officers' perception about occupational stress occurrence frequency.

- There exists wide gap between the police officers' perception about their occupation stress and its occurrence frequencies.

- Stress coping styles adhered to by the police officers differ from one to another, based on their designation grade and work experiences.

1.7 Research Methodology

The research methodology of the study consists of two stages. First stage of the research is exploratory by nature and the second stage is descriptive in nature. This study is based on the police constables in Thoothu kudi district. For this study, a multistage random sampling technique was used for the selection of sample. The researcher has adopted Cluster based random Sampling Procedure (Probability) for defining the entire population area i.e., police stations and furthermore the researcher has adopted convenience sampling techniques for the collection of primary data. The respondents are approached with the support of the affluent and reference group's support and only voluntary respondents' were included in the survey and no monetary benefits were paid as remuneration to the sample subjects.

From the base data collected about the Tamilnadu Police statistics with reference to Thoothukudi district, it has been observed that there are 1467 police constables at present working in Thoothukudi of whom 1169 are men and the rest, 298, are female constables and further it has been observed that 35.11 per cent of them are group under. Grade III officials, 47.92 per cent grade II and the remaining 16.79 per cent Grade II police constables. These 1467 police personnel are taken as the research subjects. The two police out posts were not included for the study. A pilot survey was conducted with a sample of five police stations and thirty sample subjects with the support of well-structured questionnaire based on the responses collected and necessary changes were made in the for the large sample collection. A sample of 660 police personnel were targeted for the pilot survey. Out of the 660 questionnaire distributed to the sample police personnel based on the recommendation of affluent and references groups referral. Only 600 questionnaires were collected at the end of the data period. Thus the sample was restricted to 600 police personnel who are in the position of "constable" were considered a sample population for the study. Chapter III provides an elaborate discussion on the research methodology adopted in the current study.

1.8 Limitation of the Study

The researcher takes all possible care to avoid shortcomings and errors in the collection of data. All possible care and skill have been exercised to derive fair conclusions based on the findings of the study. In spite of all the efforts taken by the researcher in this regard, the present study is subject to the following limitations.

1. One of the primary limitations of the present study is that the data are to be collected only from the respondents of Thoothukudi district. Thus, the results are location specific and therefore the conclusions drawn may not be applicable to a different district having different stressor factors.

2. Since the researcher had collected primary data through self-administered questionnaire, the results may be biased on the respondents' honesty and how they perceived their attitudes towards the variables used in this study.

3. Thirdly, since this study was based on a cross-sectional research design as it covers three different grades of police constables, caution about causality must be taken into account when drawing conclusions about associations. Also the male predominance in the study population made it difficult to study gender-related patterns.

1.9 Chapterisation Schemes

The framework of this research exercise has been structured to gain insights into the above purpose and thus includes five chapters, namely, the Introduction, Literature Review, Research Methodology, Theoretical Overview of Study Subject, Analysis and Discussion, Summary, Findings, Suggestion, Conclusion, and Future Research. The thesis of the study is organized into six major chapters. A brief outline of each of them is given below:

Chapter I: The introductory chapter I deal with the introduction of the study. It includes the introduction, statement of the problem, significance of the study, objective, hypotheses, and limitations of the study and organization of chapters.

Chapter II: Second chapter focuses on the reviews of the relevant literature in this field carried out by various researchers in the past.

Chapter III: Third chapter provided a detailed discussion of the research methodology adopted by the researcher for the effective conduct of the study. It contains information on the research design, data collection tools and analysis techniques.

Chapter IV: Fourth chapter titled "Overview of Police Force in India and the Causes for Stress among Police Officials" contains discussion about the nature of police force function in India and the reasons and causes for the stress among police personnel.

Chapter V: Fifth chapter deals with analysis and Interpretation of data collected from the study region.

Chapter VI: Sixth chapter summarizes the findings of the study, suggestions and conclusions of the study.

CHAPTER II

REVIEW OF LITERATURE

2.1 Introduction

In the present paper an attempt has been made to document some of the relevant works conducted on the subject under study.

2.2 Occupational Stress

Dhillan T K Sharma (1992)[1] examines the amount of experience role stress among three levels of management upper, middle and lower. The analysis reveals a significant effect of hierarchical level of management on overall role stress and its five dimensions, with the lower level mangers perceiving the maximum amount of role stress followed by middle and upper level managers.

McCafferty (1992)[2] attributes suicide of police members due to stressors at work. Factors that may contribute to distress include authoritarian structure, lack of participation in decision-making, poor inter-personal relationships with supervisors, lack of administrative support, unfair discipline, unfair promotion and the nature of police work. The irregularity of working hours, poor working conditions and the experience of constant fear and trauma contribute to making police members more susceptible to suicide. Working in shifts, low salaries and the dangers involved in the police job seem to be related to stress and suicidal tendencies.

Srivatsava et.al (1994)[3] compares organizational role stress and job anxiety among three groups of employees in a private sector organization. Results show that middle level manager faced greater stress and anxiety when compared with top level manager and workers.

In a recent re-examination of Jackson and Schuler's meta-analysis of role stress research, Beehr (1995)[4]pointed out that 11 of the 15outcomes examined were psychological or emotional strains (e.g. job dissatisfaction and tension). It may be that including outcomes that are valued by the organization in role stress research has a practical advantage. Research based solely on individually valued states may provide managers a weak rationale for reducing role stress; they may ask how reduced role stress benefits the organization as well as the individual.

Stewart Collins (1995)[5] research article focused upon the impact of environmental stress and demands on social work. Stress is experienced as an individual phenomenon by social work lecturers, but is considered within a structural and an institutional context. In particular, it is examined against the background of recent developments in higher education generally, such as the Higher Education Funding Council quality assessment visits and the research assessment exercise. In recent years, there have been significant alterations to the shape of social work education with the establishment of the DipSW (Diploma in Social Work), its modification and review, and the development of Post Qualifying Consortia. Classic features of stress have been imposed on social work lecturer particularly by their institutions and other organizations, leading to a lack of control, an imbalance of demands over resources, role overload and role conflict. These stressors impact negatively upon interpersonal relationships with colleagues and students. Some suggestions are made for improving the structural and especially the organizational coping resources available to social work lecturers in order to assist them to develop more effective responses to stress.

Mokowska (1995)[6] attempted to identify psychosocial determinants of stress and wellbeing in occupationally active women. The significance of the work related stressors was evidently greater than that of the stressors associated with the family function, although the relationship between family functioning, stress and well – being was also significant.

Sahu and Misra (1995)[7] attempted to find out the relationship between life stress and burn out. Results indicate that female teachers experienced more stress due to their employment hours, occupation and family responsibilities, such as childcare and weekly housework, significantly affect self-reported health status of employed Latinos.

Satyanarayana (1995)[8] investigated stressors among executives and supervisors. The analysis of the data revealed that role erosion, personal inadequacy, resource inadequacy, and role stagnation were identified as dominant contributors of role stress in executives and supervisors. Kumar (1989) studied the relationship between role-stress, role-satisfaction and role efficacy using a sample of lower and middle level executives from different functional areas of an oil company. The major findings indicated that marketing executives experienced maximum role stress in comparison to finance, production and personnel executives. Personnel executives obtained lowest scores on total role stress.

Pandey (1995)[9] examined the relationship between role stress and role efficacy using a sample of personnel of Indian Railways. The findings of the study indicated that coefficients of correlation between the first dimensions of role efficacy namely, centrality and all the 10 dimensions of role stress were found to be negative. The second dimension of role efficacy i.e. integration, was correlated negatively and significantly with all the dimension of role stress except role erosion. Creativity, the third dimension of role efficacy was found to have non-significant but positive correlations with all dimensions of role stress except role overload and self-role distance. The relationship of inter-role linkage with role stress was found to be negative in seven cases but was not statistically significant.

Sexena (1996)[10] evaluated the life satisfaction and perceived happiness as function of family structure and employment of women. She studied family and employment of women in India as indicators of life satisfaction and happiness. Results of the study reveal that non-working women experience greater life satisfaction than working women and happiness was greater among non-working women than working women.

McCreary et.al (1996)[11] whose empirical study focused on the masculine gender role stress, present a theoretical construct that describes the stress created in men when they feel they are not meeting society's expectations from masculinity, or when the situation forces men to act in feminine-typed ways. The stress produced by these feelings or actions are thought to be related to negative psychological outcomes for men, but should be unrelated to well-being for women. The present study investigated the validity of the masculine gender role stress construct, especially with regard to the assumption that masculine gender role stress is related to negative psychological outcomes for men more than for women. Participants were a group of mostly Caucasian undergraduates. Results indicated that masculine gender role stress was related to depression, hostility, and anxiety, but to the same degree for both men and women. These findings suggest that, if MGRS include in the list of abbreviations is a valid construct, then researchers need to explore other ways in which this type of stress can negatively affect men, but not women.

Dollard and Winefiels (1996)[12] say that theoretical models of occupational stress are important because they suggest a focus for intervention, and inform practice. The gap between research and practice was exposed most recently by Burke (1993) claiming "little awareness of research findings by practitioners (managers, consultants, clinicians), little intervention activity being undertaken at the organizational level, little research being undertaken to determine the effectiveness of individual level interventions, and only modest use of work research findings for intervention and policy development" (p. 85). This paper discusses the issue of intervention, and examines values, assumptions and the politics of applied research. A critical review of the evaluation studies of individual vs. organizational level interventions is undertaken and finally the problem of occupational stress as a national and international issue is considered.

According to Nel and Burgers (1996)[13] the SAPS is no longer a cohesive body and has ceased to be an organization that protects, supports and prescribes to the members. Individual officials feel abandoned by this new structure and find their present circumstances anxiety-provoking. The new community policing requires that members of the police are accountable to the community. The openness to public opinion about the quality of their work performance creates additional pressure.

K Harigopal (1997)[14] in his book titled "Organizational Stress: A Study of Role Conflict" examined role conflict in all its dimensions and also provides an overall comprehensive model. The genesis of conflict, in both the objective and subjective realms, with factors that moderate it are discussed in addition to the resolution of conflict. The book also surveys relevant research work. It will be useful in designing managerial training programmes in interpersonal conflict management, team building, supervisory leadership, designing workflow processes and team structure.

Rodwell et.al's (1998)[15] research article explores the nature of organizational communication in the human resource management context. An analysis of survey data collected from employees of an Australian information technology company found that employee perceptions of teamwork, communication, employee job satisfaction, commitment, and stress significantly predicted self-rated performance. Unexpectedly, communication was found to be negatively related to performance. Analysis of the pattern of relationships indicates that while the direct relationship between communication and performance is negative, the role of communication is one of enhancing teamwork, job satisfaction, and commitment. The article relates the findings to the "communication met myth" which assumes that more communication is necessarily good.

S E Pandi (1998)[16] conducted a study on a sample of 450 employees of BHEL, hardware and explore the relationship between personality dimension of industry and their perceived organizational role stress. The findings of the study indicates that psychoticism reality and neuroticism stability dimensions found positively associated with industry perceived organizational role stress, whereas extra version, intra version dimension is found negatively associated with perceived OPS.

Biswas (1998)[17] examines the effects of six life style stressors i.e. performance, threat, boredom, frustration, bereavement and physical or organizational commitment. Job involvement and perceived organizational effectiveness across job levels (managers, supervisors and workers). Data were collected from 160 employees belonging to nine different organizations located near Vidalia. Findings suggest that performances threat and frustration stressors are significant predictors of organization commitment whereas none of stressors predict job involvement than supper in forces and works. Workers report significantly higher performance stress than managers and supervisors.

Mohan V. Chauhan D (1999)[18] in his empirical work comment that optimum stress is essential for performing well in one's job. It acts as a drive and can be called Eustress. But once stress exceeds a certain limit it can cause burnout and detrimentally affect work performance. The present study was conducted on 174 middle level managers from Government (50), public (76) and Private (48) sectors. There were 137 males and 37 females. Overall, the latter were very less in number. These managers were administered Organizational Role Stress (ORS) Scale by Udai Pareek. A t-test was done to find sex differences, if any, on the 10 subscales of ORS and the total score. None of the t-ratios were significant; as such the data were pooled. Simple ANOVA were done for all the 10 subscales and total ORS scores to test the differences amongst the three sectors. The results showed that there were only two significant F-ratios-for Role Erosion and Self-Role Conflict. The managers of Public Sector experienced the maximum Role Erosion and Self Role Conflict, followed by Government and the private sector. The private sector seems to have a better work climate which is giving enough forward orientation in one's job role and also less amount of intra-personal conflictual situations. This can have implications for improvement of work climate in Government and Public Sector.

Pestonjee and Singh (1998)[19] investigated the type-A pattern of behavioral disposition on the relationship between role stresses and state- trait anxiety. The findings revealed that stresses, type-A behavior, state and trait anger were correlated positively and most of the coefficients of correlation were statistically significant.

Sharon Conley and Sherry A. Woosley (2000)[20] have commented that educational researchers have long been concerned with role stress among teachers. In education, research on the consequences of such role stress for teachers has largely concerned outcomes valued by individuals such as job satisfaction and reduced stress. Less research has focused on examining the effects of role stress on outcomes valued by the organization, such as employee commitment and employee retention. In examining the role stress-outcome relationship, research suggests the importance of taking into consideration the work orientations of individuals as possible moderators of the role stress-outcome relationship. The role of communication is one of enhancing team work, job satisfaction and commitment first whether role of stresses– role ambiguity, role conflict, and role overload – are related to two individually and two organizationally valued states and second, whether teachers' of higher-order need strength moderates these role stress-outcome relationships. The study found that role stresses relate to individually and organizationally valued outcomes among both elementary and secondary teachers.

Rutledge, John Edvard (2001)[21] studied organizational role stress in two small law enforcement agencies. A total of 86 officers were surveyed as part of this study. The objectives of the null hypothesis are to examine compare the self-reported existence of role stressors that exist within the agencies and between the agencies. The research found that there is a difference between the agencies new questions and from the study as to the nature and cause of the organizational stress differences that warrant further research.

Other forms of stress can come from management. All of those not in management positions know we can do it better. We have better ideas, better plans and would change as much as we could. We create that stress upon ourselves. We should see our own ideas as helpful suggestions to be brought in work group meetings as a way to promote a better situation for all involved. Management is a difficult position to have in any place of employment. The police have to handle all of the office politics, personal issues and be able to work well with those above and below cadres. It is a delegate balance that put you in the middle everyday he goes to work. Managing requires that not only to take orders; the police have to issue them too. Stress will come from knowing some of the orders the police give will not make him a popular person. Management is not a popularity contest though and the personal feelings again have to put aside in order to achieve the ultimate goal. To be successfully in charge of people that will do the job that is given them to do the best of their ability whether or not they agree with it.

Kop and Euwema (2001)[23] found that organizational factors are the most salient stressors in police organizations. According to Schaufeli and Enzmann (1998) organizational stressors are divided into two groups: job demands and a lack of resources. Job demands refer to the required sustained physical or mental effort aspects of the job and can therefore be associated with certain physiological and psychological costs, e.g. meeting deadlines, shift work, working overtime, excessive paper work and handling crisis situations. Job resources are aspects of the job that may be functional in achieving work goals, reducing job demands and the expected physiological and psychological costs, and stimulating personal development, e.g. adequate equipment, good supervision, an adequate salary, recognition and sufficient personnel.

Andrea Kohan and Dwight Mazmanian (2003)[24] in this study assessed officers' perceptions of daily work experiences (operational and organizational) and the nature of their associations with burnout and pro-organizational behavior (organizational citizenship behavior [OCB]). The moderating and mediating effects of dispositional affect and coping style were also considered. Findings showed that (a) appraisals of negative experiences (hassles) depended on frequency of exposure to the different facets of work, whereas positive organizational experiences (uplifts) were perceived as being more uplifting than operational ones; (b) burnout and OCB were more strongly associated with organizational experiences than with operational ones; and (c) only problem- and emotion-focused coping moderated, but did not mediate, associations, suggesting that chronic exposure to stressful events may act independently of disposition and that both coping styles may be beneficial.

According to the Journal of Management in Engineering report (2004)[25] there is accumulating evidence that stress levels among construction professionals are increasing and that this is manifesting itself in the form of unsafe working practices, higher turnover, lower morale, and poorer performance. However, there has been no research into the influence of gender on stress levels in the construction industry. This is despite evidence that the underrepresentation of women may produce higher levels of stress among this part of the workforce. To redress this deficiency, this paper investigates whether there are differences in sources and levels of stress between male and female professionals in the construction industry. The results indicate that overall, men experience slightly higher levels of stress than women. Although there are common sources of stress for both men and women, there are also some differences. In particular, men appear to suffer more stress in relation to risk taking, disciplinary matters, and implications of mistakes, redundancy, and career progression. In contrast, the factor that causes most stress for women were opportunities for personal development, rates of pay, keeping up with new ideas, business travel, and the accumulative effect of minor tasks. These differences reflect women's traditional and continued subjugation in the construction industry.

According to Wendy R et.al (2004)[26] recent researches on reported work stress indicates that stress may not always be deleterious for an individual or organization. Research in this area, however, has not yet examined a variety of work outcomes, the mechanism by which stress leads to such outcomes, and the moderators of this effect. In the present study the authors have hypothesized that two types of reported stress (challenge- and hindrance-related) have a divergent relationship with work outcomes (relating to desirable and undesirable outcomes, respectively) and a similar (positive) relationship with psychological strain. The authors also hypothesis felt challenge as a mechanism through which challenge stress relates to desirable outcomes and job control as a moderator of the effect. Results from a heterogeneous sample of university staff employees (N=461) supported many of the hypotheses. The two types of stress differentially related to work outcomes yet both positively related to psychological strain. In addition, felt challenge mediated the relationship between challenge-related stress and work outcomes, yet the effect of challenge-related stress did not depend on job control.

Davies Rinis study (2005)[27] explain how stress is becoming a high management priority to the extent that the Health and Safety Executive has updated its management standards for workplace stress and has developed an associated online toolkit. The authors explored the consequences of failure to deal with work-related stress among employees before focusing on the signs of work-related stress in the nature of work performances, regression, withdrawal, aggressive behavior, physical sings and other out-of-character behavior. Reports of a pilot study on new stress management guidelines for the health and safety consultation revealed the constantly-changing nature of business and inadequate communication about change as a leading cause of work place stress.

Bhuian et al., (2005)[28] comment that employees who experience role ambiguity tend to perform at lower levels than employees who have a clear understanding of job requirements and what is expected of them.

Randall et al., (2006)[17] in their research article had opined that the costs of occupational stress are rising and employers increasingly need to address occupational stress, prevention and rehabilitation issues. However, there is a relative lack of understanding about implementing strategies within specific organizational contexts. Extant literature indicates a need for integrated prevention and rehabilitation strategies that address specific organizational climates that contribute to stress. The Queensland Police Service (QPS) is one policing organization facing significant occupational stress issues requiring organizational solutions. The article describes a Participatory Action Research case study, the aim of which is to develop an occupational rehabilitation system within the QPS to address identified stress issues. A combination of background information, interview and focus group data are being used to determine stress issues and provide potential solutions to specifically address the needs of the QPS. The findings of this study emphasize the importance of participant involvement in identifying issues and generating solutions, as well as demonstrating the value of taking a systemic approach. The findings suggest that the use of the Participatory Action Research approach is invaluable in promoting the long-term success of the QPS.

Clarke E (2006)[29] in his research article titled " Pressure Soars Stress Management" had studied and considered the influence of stress in the workplace on the health of employees and determine the extent to which human resource management (HRM) techniques can be applied by companies to relieve stress in their employees. The findings of the study states that manager's behavior can help to minimize the impact of work related stress.

Bordia at el., (2006)[30] in their research work titled "Rumors and stress during organizational change" found that the majority of respondents reported negative rumors and that those who reported negative rumors suffered greater levels of stress than those who reported either positive rumors or no rumors . The authors concluded by stating that the research offers tentative support for the idea that rumors can be seen as verbal symbols of the psychological climate within an organization.

H.L. Kaila (2007)[31] conducted qualitative study of 140 female managers, interviewed in 81 organizations in order to review trend of problems faced by women managers, the ways in which the problems affect them and the coping strategies used by them to overcome their problems. In-depth personal interviews were conducted with the help of a structured questionnaire using open-ended questions. The narratives of managers have provided a broad base in understanding managerial life and profession of women. The implications are underlined for better organizational health and performance. This paper is an extract from a larger study.

Ritu Lehal (2007)[32] the study includes two important variables related to behavioral science viz. Organizational role stress (ORS) and Job satisfaction (JS). It includes the whole State of Punjab and 200 executives (men and women) from both public and private sector units. The study reveals that in case of ORS and JS both, the results of public sector are better than private sector. Further in public sector, female executives are more stressful than males. But in the case of JS, in the same sector, female executives are more satisfied with their jobs. The correlation analysis brings to light that there is a strong but negative relationship between two variables. The 't' test also confirms the significance of studying the two variables together.

R. Ravichandran and R. Rajendran (2007)[33] in their empirical research work made an attempt to investigate the various sources of stress experienced by higher secondary teachers. A sample of 200 higher secondary teachers was randomly selected. They were administered Teacher's Stress Inventory developed by Rajendran, which measures eight independent factors of sources of stress. The result of one way ANOVA indicated that the personal variables: sex, age, educational levels, years of teaching experience and types of school, play a significant role in the perception of various sources of stress related to the teaching profession.

Drawing from Karasek's job demands control model, Wong et.al (2007)[34] empirical study investigated how perceived amount and clarity of interdependency in managers' jobs affect role stress, and the extent to which job control moderates these relationships. Results show that amount of interdependency was positively associated with role conflict, and clarity of interdependency was negatively associated with role ambiguity. There was also support for the job demands control model as greater job control reduced role ambiguity when clarity of interdependency was low. Although higher job control produced lower role ambiguity when both clarity and amount of interdependency were low, higher job control did not produce lower role ambiguity when clarity of interdependency was low and amount of interdependency was high, suggesting that the buffering value of job control on reducing role stress is contingent on the task interdependencies that managers confront.

Ongori Henry and Agolla Joseph Evans (2008)[35] Human resource practitioners, counselors, professionals and managers in various organizations are concerned about the impact of occupational stress in organizations. Occupational stress affects employee turnover, productivity and firms' performance. Managers in various organizations are in dilemma over what interventions need to be employed to minimize the costs associated with occupational stress. It is therefore, essential to understand the causes, symptoms and effects of occupational stress on organizational performance. The data used for this study were generated by convenience random sampling of employees working in public sector organizations in Botswana. The findings from this study show that occupational stress affects employees in several ways and is a major source of employee's turnover in many organizations. Suggestions have been made to inspire managers to understand and develop appropriate interventions to manage and minimize stress in their organizations.

The study led by Associate Professor Tony LaMontagne from the McCaughey (2008)[36] has found that nearly 21000 Victorians suffer depression due to high job demands and low control over how the job gets done or job strain. They found that working women were more likely to suffer depression than men, and job stress is likely in lower skilled occupations. In his findings he found that improving job control, moderating demands and providing more support from supervisors and co-workers makes a difference.

Rashmi Shahu and S.V. Gole (2008)[37] comment that occupational stress is commonly acknowledged to be a critical issue for managers of private manufacturing companies. This study attempts to fill part of this void in literature by examining the relationship between manufacturing firms. The study's findings suggest that higher stress levels are related to lower performance whereas higher job satisfaction indicates higher performance. The main objective was to see if there was any relationship between job performances job satisfaction and job stress & to preface model for the same. The research was assessed by using various instruments.

Salleh et.al (2008)[38] made an empirical research which provides an insight of the causes of stress among employees in the furniture manufacturing company in Malaysia. Overall the study indicated that 35.85per cent of the respondents feel they are stressful at work. The main sources of stress were unrealistic objectives, the issue of incompetent boss, time pressure and deadlines. From the study, the five major predictor of stressors found in the furniture industries are support, adaptability, job security, conflict, and integrity. These are all the potential elements affecting job stress. In addition, integrity has an inverse relationship and highest correlation towards stress. In order to stay competitive and cost effective, the management in the furniture industry has to be sensitive towards employee's perception. In the era of hyper competitiveness, every effort should be made to maximize our resources in order to stay competitive. Human resources are one of the strategic company resources which can help a company to move ahead of others. Individuals, particularly the organizational leaders need to take initiative to learn about themselves and their careers, to pick up new skills, to develop self-motivation and acquire the expertise needed to make decisions. The breakdown of integrity among employers and employees can be a major cause of stress if not carefully monitored.

Singh and Singh's (2008)[39] study was designed to investigate the relationship as well as the impact of Emotional Intelligence (EI) on to the perception of role stress of medical professionals in their organizational lives. It was conducted on a sample size of 312 medical professionals consisting of 174 male and 138 female doctors working for privately managed professional hospital organizations. The findings of the study indicate no significant difference in the level of EI and perceived role stress between genders, but significantly negative relationships of EI with organizational role stress for both the gender and the medical professionals as a whole. The study also found EI of both the gender and the medical professionals as a whole to predict significant amount of variance in the total variance in their perceived role stress. The findings of the study have been discussed and interpreted in the light of research findings of other researchers. The findings of the study have got important in academic as well as practical implications and that have been clearly stated. The authors hope that the findings of the study will provide much more respite to the HR professionals of hospital organizations in India to effectively manage the medical professionals.

Eric G. Lambert et.al (2008)[40] Correctional institutions rely on staff to accomplish a variety of tasks and objectives to ensure the safety and security of society. A significant body of research has focused on characteristics and attitudes of correctional staff to uncover positive work outcomes. One area that rarely appears in the correctional literature is organizational citizenship behavior (OCB), which refers to those prosaically work behaviors in which employees engage that reflect extra effort and benefit the organization. This study examined the influence of work environment variables (i.e., organizational commitment, job stress, and job involvement) and individual-level characteristics on OCB. The results indicate that organizational citizenship behavior is affected by both organizational commitment and job stress. Findings are discussed in terms of possible policy implications for correctional organizations as well as the need to examine further the reciprocal nature of the employee/employer relationship.

Sibnath Deb et.al (2008)[41] found that traffic constables play a very significant role in controlling the traffic system especially in the metropolitan cities despite several limitations. The broad objective of the present study was to understand the job-related stress of traffic constables, causal factors behind the same, coping strategies as well as other problems faced by them in discharging their duties efficiently and perceived solution. A group of 68 traffic constables under Kolkata Police were randomly selected from 11 Traffic Guards. Data were collected by using a standardized psychological scale entitled 'Occupational Stress Index' and a ''Semi-Structure Questionnaire'. The study disclosed that 79.4% of the traffic constables were stressed (76.5% moderately and 2.9% highly) because of a number of factors like inadequate rest, lack of communication with the family members, long duty hours, inadequate leave, political pressure, excessive number of vehicles on the road, hot weather, non-cooperation from public, lack of coordination among colleagues, seeing too many accidents on the road, problems at home and so on. The most common coping strategies adopted included sharing problems with the colleagues, family members and friends, becoming workaholic, accepting the reality, watching TV, being optimistic about future, exercise and so on. They also face some other problems like lack of manpower, offensive language from public, non-cooperation from higher authorities, lack of infrastructure and unnecessary case pressure. They suggested some solutions for addressing the problems faced by them like reduction of duty hours, recruitment of more staff, salary hike, proper interaction among all categories of staff, removal of internal politics, strict enforcement of discipline in the department, use of Euro II vehicles and so on.

Triantoro Safaria and Ahmad bin Othman (2010)[42] observed in their papers which commend Globalization brings change in all aspects of human life, including in how job and organization operate. All of these changes create much strain and stress not only among employees at business organization, but also among university academic staff. The dean of faculty or department at university has important role in buffering the effect of job stress among their academic staff by giving support, motivation, and creating policy to reduce job stress. This study aims to examine the role of leadership practices on job stress among Malay university academic staff. Design of this study is to survey research with quantitative approach. As much as 124 questionnaires from 500 questionnaires were completed. Then data from questionnaire was analyzed in two step process. First step, data were analyzed using multiple regressions. Second, the result of regression analyses was tested and confirmed with structural equation modeling method. All data will be processed using SPSS 15 and Amos 18 program. The result of multiple regression and structural equation modeling suggests that four dimension of leadership practices show unique pattern of relationship with four dimensions of job stress. The multiple regression analysis find a significant relationship between challenging the process and inspiring a shared vision dimension of leadership practices with behavioral, emotional, cognitive and physiologic stress responses. Whether modeling the way dimension of leadership practices is significantly a predictor of emotional and cognitive stress responses. In step two, the significant relationship between exogenous and endogenous above was tested using structural equation modeling (SEM). The result of SEM analysis just confirm four exogenous variables that significantly have relationship with endogenous variable, and those are challenging the process with behavioral, and emotional stress responses, modeling the way with cognitive stress response, and inspiring a shared vision with physiologic stress responses. Overall, the proposed model achieves a fit model with empirical data. The mechanism of relationship among exogenous and endogenous variable had discussed in the research paper.

Karena J. Burkel and Jane Shakespeare- Finch (2011)[43] this article present data from a longitudinal study of adjustment to policing, specifically examining the role played by exposure to traumatic events prior to entry to the profession. This study aims to explore the impact of a prior traumatic experience on the appraisal of potentially traumatizing events experienced within the policing context. Seventy-eight police constables were followed from point of entry until the completion of 12 months of operational duties. The results suggest the experience of a traumatic event prior to joining the police may facilitate positive emotional outcomes from exposure to adverse events on the job. This article is the first to examine the impact of prior traumatic events on adjustment to the demands of policing in a longitudinal context and suggests that the experience of prior traumatic events can have a positive impact on officer's capacity to adapt to the challenges of the police role.

Kamble SV and Phalke DB (2011)[44]In their research police work is widely considered to be among the most stressful occupations. There is increased prevalence of cardiovascular diseases risk factors and type 2 diabetes among policemen in many countries. There is limited data on health status of policemen in India. Hence a cross-sectional study was conducted during the period April 2007 to

September 2007 at three police stations in Rahata taluk of Ahmednagar district. Study was done to assess the level of stress and source of stress among policemen and to study the stress as a risk factor for hypertension, diabetes, obesity and depression. All available 90 policemen were interviewed and their occupational stress was assessed by occupational stress index. Clinical examination and necessary investigations were done. Depression among them was diagnosed with the help of Hamilton depression rating scale. Majority of policemen (88.89%) were having moderate level of stress. Role overload and responsibility for person were moderately stress producing factors among all ranks. Stress score was significantly high among overweight (137), diabetes (142), hypertensive (137) and depressed (118) policemen. Thus occupational stress is the risk factor for development of obesity, diabetes, hypertension and depression.

2.3 Occupational Stress among the Policemen

Bhaskar (1982)[45]in his study explored the relationship between behavioral, psychological and health effects and experience of job stress among police.

Martocchio and O'Leary (1989)[46]conducted a meta-analysis of studies investigating the relationship between gender and occupational stress and concluded that there were no differences in experienced stress between males and females. International studies showed that police officers report varying amounts of work stressors on the basis of rank (Brown & Campbell, 1990; Brown, Cooper & Kirkcaldy, 1996; Kaufmann & Beehr, 1989), race and ethnicity (Violanti & Aron, 1995), and gender (Wexler & Logan, 1983). Cooper & Bramwell (1992) indicated that potential sources of stress varied between different sub-cultures and status groups within the same organisation.

Suresh (1992) also found the need of research for extending the findings of his study to police officers in divergent regional and cultural context.

Bernie L. Patterson (1992)[47] surveyed nearly 4,500 police, correctional, and probation and parole officers and it provided a unique opportunity for cross-occupational comparisons of perceived job stress among criminal justice personnel. The questionnaire included a modified version of Spielberger's Police Stress Survey. Results revealed that police and probation/parole officers demonstrated an apparent curvilinear relationship between time on the job and perceived stress. However, the trend was more linear when only line officers of both groups were considered. Correctional officers, as a group, did not show a curvilinear pattern, although line correctional officers did. The reasons for these patterns are discussed.

B Kirkcaldy's study observed (1993)[48] Scores of 30 police officers on the Occupational Stress Indicator differed from British norms on organizational structure and climate, home and work interface, and relations with others. Officers showed internal control and individual influence. Through managed time and home support, officers coped with stress. Scale scores were inter-correlated.

Tripathi et al. (1993)[49] gave a scope for a larger and more representative sample in future studies in police. His study was based on four districts to UP state. Terry & Calan (1997) showed that those higher in the organizational hierarchy experience higher levels of perceived stress.

A number of determinants of emotional exhaustion have been defined by Cordes and Dougherty (1993)[50] with the three most important ones being work overload, role conflict and interpersonal relationships. Work overload is defined as "the perception of too much work to accomplish in the time available" (Powell, 1993, p. 53), which is suggestive of the existence of a mismatch between the person and the job. Role conflict is the second source of emotional exhaustion and may occur when an individual has certain job expectations which may be in conflict with individuals already within the organisation. Trying to reconcile these differences can lead to frustration and emotional exhaustion (Jackson, Schwab, & Schuler, 1986). Personal expectations can also add further to emotional exhaustion. Having unrealistic expectations of the job that one has newly undertaken and coming to the realization that these expectations are not met, further adds to this frustration (Philip, 2004). The third source of emotional exhaustion is interpersonal relationships, especially when the relationships are very intense and emotional.

Gulle et al. (1998)[51] conducted a study that explored inherent and organizational stress in the South African Police Service. It included 91 Police members ranging in ages for 21 to 53 years with the sample consisting of 85 males and 6 females. This study indicated that in comparison to American stressors, which were all inherent in the nature of the job, South African police stressors were among the more organizationally-oriented. Violanti & Aron (1994) found the South African sample displaying a greater degree of stress than the USA sample. The way in which the SAPS operate creates stress in addition to the inherent pressure already existing as a result of the nature of police work. The study also found that excessive paperwork, insufficient person power, fellow officers not doing their job, inadequate or poor quality equipment and inadequate salaries were cited among the stressors which occurred most frequently within the police.

According to Spielberger, Vagg & Wasala (2003)[52] stress is recognized as a complex process that consist of three major mechanisms: sources of stress that are encountered in the work environment, the perception and appraisal of a particular stressor by an employee, and the emotional reactions that are a response to perceiving a stressor as threatening. Spielberger's State-Trait (ST) model of occupational stress focuses on the perceived severity and frequency of occurrence of two major categories of stressors, i.e. job pressures and lack of support (Spielberger et al., 2003). Stress resulting from work is described as the mind-body arousal resulting from physical and/or psychological job demands. If a stressor is perceived as threatening then the person may react with anger and anxiety and this leads to the activation of autonomic nervous system. If the reaction continues to be severe, the resulting physical and psychological strain may cause adverse behavioural consequences.

Basson (2005)[53] reported that police units involved with family violence, child abuse and sexual offences had 254 vacancies (20% of total number of jobs). The average number of criminal cases managed by each detective vary from 32 (Northern Cape) to 52 (Eastern Cape), with a national average of 43, whereas the ideal is that each detective should not investigate more than 18 cases. Therefore police members (detectives in particular) experience high job demands (Pienaar & Rothmann, 2006).

Pienaar and Rothmann (2006)[54] found in a study of stress among 2145 police members that race had a significant impact on the experience of occupational stress in the SAPS. Although all the race groups experienced higher levels of stress due to lack of support e.g. salary, promotion and recognition (compared to other occupational stressors), in comparison with Blacks and Colored, Whites and Indians experienced a greater intensity and frequency of stress. The results are reported to have been influenced by the implementation of police equity in the police. Rank was reported to have also impacted significantly on the experience of occupational stress in the police. In comparison with other ranks, constables experienced stress less frequently because of job demands and lack of support and also experienced stress less frequently because of job demands, crime-related stressors and lack of support. It was also acknowledged that constables were not exposed to the demands and lack of support to the same extent and length as other police officers. Gender impacted significantly on occupational stress with females experiencing crime-related stressors less intensely and frequently than their male counter-parts. Pienaar & Rothmann (2006) contends that "the fact that females are less operationally involved also explains why they experienced crime-related stressors less intensely and frequently" (p.76).

According to Alexander (1999)[55] in addition to the stressful work events and situations experienced in law enforcement such as traumatic incidents, some officers experienced additional environmental factors as a result of their gender or race, which in turn influenced cultural differences in coping and social support. Studies which have been conducted among non-police samples indicate that gender differences are associated with the number and types of traumatic incidents as well as psychological reactions to such incidents (Kessler, Sonnega, Bromet, Hughes & Nelson, 1995; Violanti & Lauterbach, 1994).

Martin, McKean, and Veltkamp (1986)[56] reported that female officers reported exposure to more traumatic incidents such as natural disasters, suicide, child and spousal abuse than did their male counterparts. Their suggestion was that perhaps female officers were more exposed to such incidents and not more exposed to stressful events and situations, and that gender differences in psychological reactions are related to the degree of identification with the victim, frequency of exposure to victims, and coping styles.

According to Edwards and Holden (2001)[57] other interpretations of suicidal behavior in women focus on suicide as a coping response. It has also been suggested that traditional gender socialization may hinder women from choosing healthy, active coping strategies when faced with difficult situations (Stillion & McDowell, 1996). Wilson (1981) characterizes attempted suicide as a means of coping with stress for those individuals who have few resources. She suggests that women have fewer resources than do men in terms of economic power, autonomy, self-concept, and power over others. Women may attempt suicide as a way of telling those around them that they are having difficulty coping as a result of limited sources of influence.

Patterson (2001)[58] conducted a study that examined the influence of demographic characteristics on exposure to traumatic incidents among police officers and focused on family violence, child abuse, and situations requiring the use of force as frequently occurring incidents. Traumatic incidents where family members and children were involved were the most frequently occurring traumatic events for police officers in the sample, followed by situations where police officers and other individuals were at risk of being seriously injured or killed in primarily non-family related situations.

A comparison was made between the results of this study and Violanti and Aron (1994)[59] findings in which officers ranked situations such as battered children, high speed car chases, use of force, and aggressive crowds as among the most stressful situations.

Ortega et al. (2007)[60] explored the relationship among demographic factors such as personality, tenure and gender; occupational stress; coping strategies; well-being; organizational commitment; and job satisfaction. The aim of the study was to estimate the relationship between the above-mentioned variables, and to test whether such relationships were supported by the sample. The sample comprised of 1, 535 police officers from a British police force; 20.78% of whom were female. The results of the study showed that only personality and tenure were significantly related to occupational stress and coping; and gender, age and rank did not show a meaningful relationship with any of the variables. It was also found that personality was significantly associated with feelings of being worn out and no significant direct association was found between coping strategies and well-being factors. It was also reported that the results were suggestive of a significant direct relationship between personality traits and the type of coping strategies police officers use.

Kroes (1985)[61] on the other hand, found that bad administration policies, job conflict, moonlighting, under load-overload work, shift work and line-of-duty situations, courts, and negative public image are some important factors and stressors which affect police family life negatively.

Buker and Wiecko (2007)[62] conducted a survey research on civilian officers, police officers, and mid-level supervisors (a total number of 811 respondents) working for the Turkish National Police Organization. They found that the organizational factors are the most stressful ones among other causes of stress. Moreover, there are differences in some stressors depending on the size and structure of the department.

Gul (2008)[63] studied law enforcement officers' depression on their profession and examined the stressors in policing. He found that officers that make violent arrests were more likely to feel negative/depressed about their work. In addition, he found that officers who attended a police funeral were more likely to feel negative/depressed about their profession and Afro-American officers were less likely to feel negative or depressed about their jobs than whites. Finally, patrol officers were more likely to feel negative/depressed about their work compared to other ranks.

Sever and Cinoglu (2010)[64] found in their study that highly stressful officers are 4 times more likely to commit domestic violence. Further, they found that gender matters in domestic violence, as the male officers are more inclined to commit domestic violence compared to female officers. Finally, when officers are involved in negative and critical situations at work, they are more likely to act violently at home.

Priyanka Sharma (2013)[65] in her empirical study had commented that police is recognised as the most stressful professions on the earth because of the multiple factors. The nature of work, prolonged working hours, critical incident exposure, strict organizational policies which form the climate of an organisation contribute to the stress levels in a big way. Such organizational conditions constitute the climate, the positive climate thus created have positive impact on the psyche of the people working in an organisation similarly vice versa is also true. This attempts to explore the impact of organizational climate at stress levels. Besides this its impact on both the sexes and personnel's working at different hierarchical levels is also explored. There is a significant relationship between perceived organizational climate and stress level of the group of police personnel but insignificant relationship exists between perceived organizational climate and stress for the police personnel at different hierarchical levels. The author found no significant relationship between perceived organizational climate and stress for both the sexes.

2.4 Coping Strategies

According to Lazarus and Folkman (1984)[66] occupational stresses take place when job demands exceed the person's adaptive resources. Therefore stress refers to the temporary adaptation process that is accompanied by mental and physical symptoms, and is caused by a disturbance in the equilibrium between job demands and the ability of the worker to respond to the demands. When job demands are too high to cope with, stress reactions are likely to occur. The term "coping" is used in reference to perceptual, cognitive or behavioural responses that are used in managing, avoiding or controlling situations that could be regarded as difficult (Folkman & Lazarus, 1984; Moos, 1994; Zeidner & Endler, 1996) coping as a term could be used to refer to the strategies or results. As a strategy, coping refers to the different methods that a person may use in managing his/her circumstances. In coping as a result, reference is made to the eventual outcome of this strategy for the person. Non-coping is defined as efforts that have failed to cope, accompanied by various physical and psychosocial disturbances, which result in increased stress (Callan, 1993). Non-coping also results in higher levels of depression and anxiety (Carver, Sheier & Weintraub, 1989).

According to Folkman and Lazarus (1985)[67] when a person believes that the situation cannot be changed, emotion-focused coping is the most likely to be used. It has been recognised that coping strategies of police officers are limited (Ortego, Brenner & Leather, 2007) and that the results of studies that have been conducted imply that police officers tend to use maladaptive emotion-focused behaviours for the immediate reduction of stress (Evans & Coman, 1993; Richmond, Wodak, Kehoe & Heather, 1998; Violanti, Marshall & Howe, 1985).

According to Endler and Parker (1990)[68] found that the response of an individual to a situation can be a critical component in determining the impact the event will have. The type of coping style may act as a buffer between a stressful situation and a negative outcome (Lazarus & Folkman, 1984). Zeidner and Saklofske (1996) postulated that when a situation is remediable, an adaptive response would consist of problem-solving strategies. Suls and Fletcher (1985) conducted a meta-analysis of coping strategies and concluded that, in comparing what they termed "attention" (i.e. problem-focused and emotion-focused) strategies and avoidance strategies, little evidence pointed to the superiority of one strategy over the other. However, over the short-term, emotion-focused coping was associated with more negative outcomes than was avoidance, and problem-focused coping was the most advantageous to use.

Carver et al. (1989)[69] describe five varieties of problem-focused coping:

1. *Active coping*. This consists of the process of taking steps towards the removal or alleviation of the stressor and its effects. It includes initiating direct action, increasing one's efforts, and attempting to use a coping attempt in a step-by-step manner.

2. *Planning*. This refers to thinking about how to cope with the stressor. It involves thinking about various ways which could be used to solve the problem.

3. *Suppression of competing activities*. This means putting other projects on the background, and trying to avoid becoming distracted by other events in order to deal with the stressor.

4. *Restraint coping*. This involves waiting until the right opportunity to solve a problem and avoiding acting prematurely. The person's behavior is focused on dealing effectively with the stressor.

5. *Seeking social support for instrumental reasons*. This deals with looking for advice, help or information.

Five varieties of emotion-focused coping are also discussed by Carver et al. (1989).

1. *Seeking social support for emotional reasons*. This involves reaching out to others for moral support, sympathy and understanding.

2. *Positive reinterpretation and growth*. This is aimed at managing stress emotions rather than the stressors themselves by reinterpretation.

3. *Denial*. This is the refusal to believe that the stressor exists or trying to act as though the stressor isn't real.

4. *Acceptance*. The acceptance of a stressor as real and engaging in an attempt to deal with the situation.

5. *Turning to religion*. This entails focusing on religion to facilitate emotional support, positive reinterpretation and active coping.

The following are distinguished by Carver et al. (1989) as coping strategies that are less used:

1. *Focusing on and ventilating emotions*. Including focusing on a stressful situation and expressing feelings about it.

2. *Behavioural disengagement*. Involves ignoring and avoiding stressors and becoming more helpless and powerless.

3. *Mental Disengagement*. The excessiveness of sleeping or daydreaming to escape from stressors.

4. *Alcohol-disengagement*. The use of substances to manage stress.

CHAPTER- III

RESEARCH METHODOLOGY

3.1 Introduction

Research is a logical and systematic search for new and useful information on a particular topic. It is an investigation of finding solutions to scientific and social problems through objective and systematic analysis. It is a search for knowledge, that is, a discovery of hidden truths. Here knowledge means information about matters. The information might be collected from different sources like experience, human beings, books, journals, nature, etc. A research can lead to new contributions to the existing knowledge. Only through research it is possible to make progress in a field. Research is done with the help of study, experiment, observation, analysis, comparison and reasoning.

In this chapter the research design and methodology have been outlined. The research design focuses on the following aspects:

- The purpose of quantitative and qualitative research
- The design of the interview schedule as a research instrument.
- A discussion of the selected questions used by the researcher.
- A motivation for selection of the respondents used.

The research design emphasizes the merits in quantitative research as far as data collection is concerned; recording procedures and the instrument of research is concerned.

Quantitative research (empirical) approach was adopted to carry out this study, particularly the survey design. The reasons for the adoption of this approach are given below. There is the cause and effect relationship in the study. To make a generalization from a sample of a population is an efficient way of collecting information from a large number of respondents, Statistical techniques can be used to determine validity, reliability, and statistical significance, because they are standardized. They are relatively free from several types of errors. They are relatively easy to administer and there is an economy in data collection due to the focus provided by standardized questions. The nature of the survey is cross-sectional, because it is possible to obtain the desired information at a time.

3.2 Importance of the Study

Occupational stress among police is often viewed as an unlucky, but expected part of police work. Police men are like real heroes, but most of the people are unaware of the amount of stress that police personnel face every day. Police work involves protection of life, safeguarding property through vital patrol techniques, enforcement of laws and ordinances in the place for which the Police station is responsible. Police who are out in the street, every day during their duty struggle throughout. They are the first line of protection for the society against the criminals. During their duty, unexpectedly they may encounter situations involving major crisis without any warning. There are several factors like 24 hours availability and administration problems involved make policing a most stressful job.

Police occupational stress is a widespread problem because of its numerous negative effects on individuals and on police organizations. Officers who experience high levels of occupational stress report a high incidence of physical ailments and psychological problems that affect their work performance. In particular, they suffer from poor health, frequently absent themselves from work, experience burnout, dissatisfied with their jobs and because of weak organizational commitment, they may not fully invest themselves in their work or they may retire prematurely. When individuals are overwhelmed by occupational stress they suffer from increased chronic stress, depression, heart disease, stomach disorders, alcohol and drug use and abuse, divorce, and even suicide attempts. It is therefore critical to understand the sources of police occupational stress (i.e., the stressors) and to implement strategies for reducing stressors or, if they cannot be reduced, for assisting officers in coping effectively with them.

This study explores the major causes of stress and amount of stress faced by police constables. Police Constable is the lowest police grade in India, but they are the prime victims of stress. Several inspectors and constables have died of heart attacks while on duty. Constables are feeling that they work under great pressure and their job is demanding and uncertain, also, public expectations from the police are high. During festival timings, constables often work for more than36 hours at a stretch. This may take a heavy charge on their health. Stress can cause hypertension, joint pains, high blood pressure, diabetes as well as paralytic strokes and heart attacks. They also experience lack of concentration, resulting in their making errors while passing orders or taking important decisions. Besides the routine work, constables often face stressful situations because of harassment from superiors. The overall goal of the study is to explore the major personal and cognitive factors with occupational stress, and identify the relationship between amounts of stress, causes and the relations between the socio demographic factors.

3.3 Research Methodology

The research methodology of the study consists of two stages.

Stage I: First stage of the research is exploratory by nature. This is done in two phases. The initial phase is to undertake detailed secondary data search about occupational stress, causes and effects of stress on police personnel. This forms the desk research work where the reviews of available secondary literature for the study were collected. This exploratory search forms the basis for preparing the questionnaire for the next stage.

Stage II: A descriptive research has been carried out at the second stage by applying a survey method. Data for the study were collected from police constables both men and women working in Thoothukudi District, Tamilnadu. The tool used for data collection was a well-structured questionnaire.

3.3.1 Area of Study

Thoothukudi is a port town situated in the Gulf of Mannar about 125Km.North of Cape Comorin and 720km south of Thoothukudi. The town is a fast growing industrial area of South India. Realising the importance of the town, the Department of Town and Country Planning notified Thoothukudi Town and its surrounding 29 villages as Local Planning Area and constituted theThoothukudi Local Planning Authority to guide and control the development in an orderly manner. Since a caste has strong roots in Tamilnadu, it leads to many communal riots among the prominent communities in Thoothukudi and other sub-classes. In addition, there are many civil crimes, social crimes and social and cultural activities keep the police personnel busy around the clock, causing heavy stress. Based on the prominence of the study area and its socio-cultural activities this area is considered for the conduct of the study.

3.3.2 Sampling Framework

This study is based on the police constables in Tuticorin district. The research concentrated on eight sub divisions comprising 55 police stations i.e., 48 local and armed forces stations and seven (7) all women stations. The eight taluks are Tuticorin, Thiruchendur, Sathankulam, Srivaikundam, Ottapidaram, Kovilpatti, Ettayapuram and Vilathikulam. The study included both police and armed force personnel as the sample subjects. At present the district has 1467 police constables at different grades, Table: 3.1and Table: 3.2 depict the distribution of police stations based on the zonal distribution and the constables deputed in the Thoothukudi District.

TABLE: 3.1
DETAILS OF ZONES/RANGE/CITIES/DIST/
SUBDIVISION/POLICE STATION/OP/ AWPS

Zone	Range	Cities/ Districts	Sub.Div	P S	OP	AWPS
South & Madurai	Madurai	Madurai	7	44	0	5
		Virudhunagar	7	48	1	6
	Dindigul	Dindigul	7	36	0	6
		Theni	5	30	3	4
	Ramnad	Ramanathapuram	7	41	1	6
		Sivagangai	5	36	3	5
	Tirunelveli	Tirunelveli	9	60	5	7
		Thoothukudi	8	48	2	7
		Kanniyakumari	4	33	2	4

Source: Handbook on Police Department, 1.1.2012.
Key: Sub.Div (Sub-Division), PS (Police Station), OP(Out Post), AWPS (All Women Police Station)

For this study, a multistage random sampling technique was used for the selection of sample. The researcher has adopted Cluster based random Sampling

Procedure (Probability) for defining the entire population area i.e., police stations and further researcher has adopted convenience sampling techniques in the collection of primary data. The respondents' are approached with the support of the affluent and references groups support and only voluntary respondents' were included in the survey and no monetary benefits were offered as remuneration to the sample subjects.

TABLE: 3.2
GRADEWISE CLASSIFICATION OF POLICE
FORCE IN TUTICORIN DISTRICT

Gender	Grade II Police Constables	Grade I Police Constables	Grade III Police Constables	Grade II Armed Police Constables	Grade I Armed Police Constables	Grade III Armed Police Constables	Total
Male	235	175	469	208	44	38	1169
Female	132	22	3	128	8	5	298
Total	367	197	472	336	52	43	1467

Source: Handbook of Police Department, Tamilnadu Police, Government of Tamilnadu, As on 1.1.2012

The size of a population is a critical factor in making sampling choices. One should have knowledge of the size of the population before making sampling choices. From the base data collected about the Tamilnadu Police statistics deputed in Thoothukudi district, it has observed that there are 1467 police constables at present working in Thoothukudi of which 1169 are men and rest of the 298 are female constables and further it has been observed that these police constables are grouped as 35.11 per cent Grade III officials, 47.92 per cent grade II and 16.79 per cent Grade II police constables. These 1467 police personnel are considered as the research subjects. The two police out-posts were not included for the study. A pilot survey was conducted with a sample of five police stations and thirty sample subjects with the support of well-structured questioner, based on the responses collected required changes were made in the questionnaire the large sample collection. A sample of 660 police personnel were targeted for the filed survey. The sample framework of the study is discussed in the following Table: 3.3 and 3.4.

TABLE: 3.3
SAMPLING FRAMEWORK

Gender	Actual Police Force	Percentage	Sample Police Force	Percentage
Male	1169	80.00	526	79.69
Female	298	20.00	134	20.31
Total	1467	100	660	100

Source: Computed from Handbook of Police Department, Tamilnadu Police, Government of Tamilnadu, As on 1.1.2012

The sampling technique used was convenience sampling and data collection is through well-structured interview schedule.As per James H. McMillian (1996) a convenience sample is a group of subjects selected because of availability, often this is the only type of sampling possible especially in geographical area-based study, where the target group of population is only available for study, and the primary purpose of the research may not be to generalize but to better understand relationships that may exist. Similarly Roscoe (1975) proposed that a sample size of >30 and <500 are appropriate for most research. Based on this concept the sampling frameworks of the study are constructed.

Based on the proportionate distribution of police constables, a sample of 45 per cent was chosen, that included 526 men and 134 lady police constables. The stratified data of the police constables based on their grade i.e., Head constable (Grade III: 35.15 per cent), Constable (Grade I: 16.97 per cent) and Entry Level Constable (Grade II: 47.88) is presented in the following table.

TABLE: 3.4
GRADEWISE CLASSIFICATION OF SAMPLE POLICE FORCE

Gender	Grade II Police Constables	Grade I Police Constables	Grade III Police Constables	Grade II Armed Police Constables	Grade I Armed Police Constables	Grade IIIArmed Police Constables	Total
Male	106	78	211	94	20	17	526
Female	58	10	1	58	4	3	134
Total	164	88	212	152	24	20	660

Source: Handbook of Police Department, Tamilnadu Police, Government of Tamilnadu, As on 1.1.2012

Out of the 660 questionnaire distributed to the sample police personnel based on the recommendation of affluent and references groups' referral only 600 were collected at the end of the data period. Most of the police personnel hesitated to fill the required data, there were partially filled questionnaire which were sixty in all. These partially filled questionnaire were deducted from the actual population of samples, it included those distributed to 38 Grade III constables and 22 Grade II constables. Thus the sample was restricted to 600 police personnel in the grade of "constable" were considered as sample population for the study.

3.3.3 Instrument Measurement

The questionnaire is an often used as observational device for collecting personal data and opinion it provides a way to collect personal information from subjects that may not be readily obtainable using other methods. Questionnaire must provide for structured responses and must be carefully developed, and revised to obtain valid data. The current study has 70 queries which were duly grouped into 15 questions:

- Demographic and social information was collected from participants regarding their age, gender, educational qualification, and religion, and community, place of residence, marital status and number of dependents. In total eight questions were included in this section.

- Job Profile contains information about designation grade, years of experience and monthly income. In total three questions were posed in this sub-section.

- Police constables' perception about causes for occupational stress was assessed with 44 queries in the 12th question. The variables are grouped into three categories i.e.,

  ❖ Job demand includes 18 causes which are listed as follows *"assignment of disagreeable duties, assignment of new or unfamiliar duties, performing tasks not in job description, periods of inactivity, assignment of increased responsibility, competition for advancement, frequent changes from boring to demanding activities, shift work, delivering a death message or bad news to someone, attending to incidences of domestic violence, reorganization and transformation within the organization, killing someone in the line of duty, handling, having to handle a large crowd/mass demonstration, a forced arrest or being physically attacked, having to go to court, having to deal with the media and seeing criminals go free (for example because of lack of evidence, court leniency)"*.

  ❖ Followed by the second segment which contained queries related to lack of resources (14 causes): *"lack of opportunity for advancement, fellow workers not doing their job, inadequate support by supervisor, lack of recognition for good work, inadequate or poor quality equipment, inadequate salary, difficulty getting along with supervisor, insufficient personnel to handle an assignment, lack of participation in policy-making decisions, poor or inadequate supervision, noisy work area, insufficient personal time (e.g., coffee breaks, lunch), poorly motivated co-workers and staff shortages"* and

❖ Third category included queries on police stresses/occupational stress (12 causes):*"working overtime, dealing with crisis situations, experiencing negative attitudes toward the organization, making critical on-the-spot decisions, personal insult from customer/consumer/colleague, frequent interruptions, excessive paperwork, meeting deadlines, covering work for another employee, conflicts with other departments, too much supervision stressful job-related events and a fellow officer killed in the line of duty"*.

- The question number 13 probe queries on the occurrence of stress/burnout. The three dimensions considered significant for causes of stress in the previous query number 12 i.e., Job Demand, Lack of Resources and Police stresses/Occupational Stress are used to measure the frequency of stress occurrence among the sample police constables.

- Outcome of the stress i.e., symptoms of stress is enquired in the 14th question. A set of 15 variables were constructed with the help of three point scale: *"Loss of sexual interest or pleasure, Thoughts of ending your life, Poor appetite, Crying easily, A feeling of being trapped or caught, Blaming yourself for things, Feeling lonely, Feeling lovable, Feeling blue, Worrying or stewing about things, Feelings no interest in things, Feeling hopeless about the future, Disbelief in Others, Quarreling with family members and Feeling of insecurity".*

- Stress coping styles practiced by the police constables are assessed in the 15th question of the study. Based on the conceptual discussion made in the chapter I of this study the stress coping style of police constables are grouped into two categories, i.e. problem focused and emotion-focused. Problem focused coping styles contain 28 queries grouped into three styles: Positive reinterpretation and growth (12), Acceptance of fact (9) and Focusing on and ventilating emotions (7). Emotional focused coping styles contain 25 queries grouped into five styles: Seeking social support for emotional reasons (8), Denial behaviour(3), Turning to religion (4), Behavioral disengagement (5) and Mental disengagement (5).

- Each of the statements enquires under the head positive reinterpretation and growth perception: *"I force myself to wait for the right time to do something, I put aside other activities in order to concentrate on this, I think about how I might best handle the problem, I admit to myself that I can't deal with it, and quit trying, I try to see it on a different light to make it seem more positive, I try hard to prevent other things from interfering with my efforts at dealing with this, I do what has to be done one step at a time, I give up the attempt to get what I want, I try to come up with the strategy as to what to do, I focus on dealing with the problems and it is necessary to let other things slide a little, I concentrate on efforts on doing something about it and I just give up trying to reach my goal".*

- The acceptance of fact styles included an introspective queries like: *"I try to grow as a person as a result of the experience, I get used to the idea that it happened, I say to myself this isn't real, I make sure not to make matters worse by action to soon, I make a plan of action, I learn to live with it, I take direct action around the problem, I accept that this has happened and that can't we changed and I accept the reality of the fact that it happened".*

- Queries on the focusing on and ventilating emotions are grouped as: *"I sleep more than usual, I let my feelings out, I turn to work or other substitute activities to take my mind, I thought for something good happening, I talk to someone to find out more about the situation, I learn shooting from experience and I think hard about what step to take".*

- The emotional stress coping style of seeking social support for emotional reasons are listed as: *"I ask about how I feel, I try to get emotional support from friends or relatives, I try to get advice from someone about what do to, I get sympathy and understanding from someone, I talk to someone who could do something about the problem. I reduce the amount of effort I am putting to solve the problem and I discuss my feelings with someone".*

- Emotionally denial behaviour is listed as: *"I refuse to believe it has happened, I take additional action to try to get rid of the problem and I withhold anything about it until the situation permits".*

- In certain studies researchers had identified turning religious are significant stress coping strategies of army or police officials, the strategies is cross examined in the current study with the support of the following queries: "I put in my trust in god, I pray more than usual, I try to find comfort in my religion, I seek god's help".

- Behavioral disengagement is asses with the support of the following set of queries: *"I upset and let my emotion out, I restrain myself from doing anything so quickly, I go to movies or watch TV to think it, I act as though it hasn't even happened and I get upset and am really aware of it"*
- Mental disengagement has a negative impact on the health and well- being of the police personnel, the current study assesses whether the sample subjects are addicted to some of these behaviours: *" I drink alcohol or drink drugs, in order to think about it less, I pretended that it has not really happened, I feel a lot of emotional distress and I find myself expressing those feeling a lot, I keep myself from getting distracted by other thought or activities and I daydream about things other than this".*

3.3.4 Reliability and Validation Measures

The reliability of an indicator can be defined as its overall quality, i.e. its consistency and its ability to give the same results in repeated measurement. The most outstanding feature of reliability is the test-retest correlation of the specific measure under scrutiny. It is well-known that minor differences in circumstances and technical features of the specific questionnaire used, affect the reported causes for stress, its level of occurrence and coping strategies. Correspondingly, the test-retest correlation for most single-item measures is presented in the following table.

TABLE: 3.5
CRONBACH'S ALPHA FOR THE MODEL VARIABLES
POLICE PERSONNEL PERCEPTION ABOUT CAUSES FOR STRESS

General Variables	Number of items	Range	Cronbach's alpha
Causes of Stress			
Job demand	18	1-3	.989
Lack of resources	14	1-3	.974
Police stresses/occupational stress	12	1-3	.985
Frequency of Stress Occurrence			
Job demand	18	1-3	.870
Lack of resources	14	1-3	.665
Police stresses/occupational stress	12	1-3	.610
Outcome of Stress			
Outcome of Stress	15	1-3	.763
Stress Coping Styles			
Seeking social support for emotional reasons	8	1-4	.670
Positive reinterpretation and growth	12	1-4	.668
Denial behaviour	3	1-4	.664
Acceptance of fact	9	1-4	.659
Turing to religion	4	1-4	.661
Focusing on and ventilating emotions	7	1-4	.661
Behavioral disengagement	5	1-4	.667
Mental disengagement	5	1-4	.668

Source: Computed from Primary Data

The most widely used measure to assess the internal consistency of constructs is Cronbach's alpha. The generally agreed upon value of Cronbach's alpha is 0.70, although it may decrease to 0.60 in case of exploratory research (Hair et al. 2006; pp.137). In this research the reliability measure for the whole scale is 0.744 which is acceptable. Again the reliability for all the constructs is shown in Table 3.5; the values for all the constructs range between 0.610- 0.989, which is acceptable. Hence, construct reliability in this research is satisfactory. The result of Cronbach's alpha draws a significant amount of correlation between the variables tested. The validity of a test is the extent to which differences in scores reflect differences in the measured characteristic. Predictive validity is a measure of the usefulness of a measuring instrument as a predictor. Proof of predictive validity is determined by the correlation between results and actual behavior. Construct validity is the extent to which a measuring instrument measures what it intends to measure.

The primary data for this research were collected through a structured questionnaire to answer the research questions and objectives. The structured questionnaire consists of five distinct sections, each of which contains queries pertaining to personal and professional of the police personnel, their perception towards causes of stress, its frequency of occurrence and stress coping styles. The secondary data needed for the study were sourced from various magazines, journals, internet and thesis works. The data collected are analysed and tabulated with help of SPSS package version 19.

3.4 Tool Applied in the Study

The data collected through the questionnaire were classified and tabulated for analysis in accordance with the outline laid down for the purpose of justifying the objective and the hypotheses framed at the time of developing research design.

1. The frequency distribution of the variables has helped the researcher to calculate distribution value of variables tested.

2. Weighted arithmetic means and Likert's Summated scales helped in interpreting the averages, police personnel's perception about occupational stress, frequency of its occurrences and stress coping styles.

3. One-way ANOVA test was applied to measure the association between job profile of the police officers and their perception about their occupational stress.

4. With the support of Rotation Factor analysis existing similarities in the police officers' perception about their occupation stress, its occurrence frequency and outcome of stress were established by the researcher. The same test is applied to segregate the data based on the stress coping styles adhered to by the police officers in different grades and work experiences, based on their designation.

5. Paired 't'test is applied to measure the existing gap between the police officers' perception about their occupation stress and its occurrence frequencies.

6. Reliability and F test were applied to measure and test the stress coping styles adhered to by the police officers in different grades and work experiences, based on their designation.

3.5 Conclusion

The entire hypothesis test in this study has been carried out at 5 percent level of significance. The following chapter IV contains theoretical description of the study subject and Chapter V draws detailed empirical discussion on data analysis and inferences made by the researcher.

CHAPTER IV

OVERVIEW OF POLICE FORCE IN INDIA AND

THE CAUSES FOR STRESS AMONG POLICE PERSONNEL

The current chapter is grouped into two sections. Section one contains a theoretical overview on the role of police force in India and the section the study draws a theoretical discussion on the causes for stress among police personnel and the means to cope with overcome the stress.

Section I

Overview of Police Force in India

4.1 Introduction

In the field of administration, police men have an important role to play. In India, Police force is the coercive arm of the State, which is entrusted to perform the basic duty of the State, that is, maintenance of law and order. Therefore, law and order administration has acquired significance at the Central, State, Range, District and Sub-District level in rural and urban areas. Rapid growth of population, industrialization, urbanization and growing political consciousness lead to law and order problems. Agrarian and tribal revolts, political, caste and communal violence, labour and student unrest and terrorism are indications of law and order problems. In all societies, particularly in developing societies, these conflicts and tensions are inevitable and many manifest in different forms. Freedom and independence will not have meaning unless these basic issues are properly attended. In this Unit, an attempt will be made to study the organisation of police at various levels; and critical issues that confront the Police Administration.

Police are one of the most ubiquitous organizations of the society. The policemen, therefore, happen to be the most visible representatives of the government. In an hour of need, danger, crisis and difficulty, when a citizen does not know, what to do and whom to approach, the police station and a policeman happen to be the most appropriate and approachable unit and person for him. The police are expected to be the most accessible, interactive and dynamic organisation of any society. Their roles, functions and duties in the society are natural to be varied and multifarious on the one hand; and complicated, knotty and complex on the other. Broadly speaking the twin roles, which the police are expected to play in a society are maintenance of law and maintenance of order. However, the ramifications of these two duties are numerous, which result in making a large inventory of duties, functions, powers, roles and responsibilities of the police organisation.

4.1.1 Background of Police Administration in India

In all societies, organizations were established to protect the life and liberties of people since the dawn of civilization. With the passage of time, complexities in the nature of societies have led to the creation of modem police. In the European context the term 'police' refer to a 'force for the city' and the police officer was known as Nagarpal, which means protector of the city and governance based on Dharma and Danda. Dandaneeti was an important ingredient of Statecraft. Manu talked about the prevention and detection 'of crime and also a system of collecting intelligence during the Vedic period. Vedas refer to different kinds of crimes and punishments for the criminals. During the Mauryan and Gupta periods, policing was undertaken systematically. Kautilya's Arthashastra gives a vivid picture of the nature of police organisation and their functions. During Mughal period, law and order administration was under the charge of Fauzdars. They were assisted by Thanedars who were in charge of Police Stations. He was also responsible for revenue functions. The office of the Kotwal was fairly important, as he was the chief of city police. His functions included patrolling the city at night, collection of intelligence, prevention of crime and social abuses and regulation of jails. During the British period, the police system that existed under the Mughals was allowed to continue with certain reforms to meet the changing needs.

The present Indian police system is based on the Police Act of 1861. Under this act the police were made subordinate to the Executive Government. Later, several changes were brought about in the structure as well as functioning of the police system. But the basic structure and characteristics as enshrined in the police act of 186 1 continued to dominate over the police system in the country. By the time India attained independence in 1947; the Police Administration had developed into one of the best systems. After independence, the Government of India felt that the system was capable of facing new challenges and was also well developed to help the new Government to maintain stability.

4.1.2 Role, Functions and Duties of the Police in General

As per (n) Sec (57), Model Police Act 2006 The role and functions of the police in general are:
(a) To uphold and enforce the law impartially, and to protect life, liberty, property, human rights, and dignity of the members of the public;

(b) To promote and preserve public order;

(c) To protect internal security, to prevent and control terrorist activities, breaches of communal harmony, militant activities and other situations affecting Internal Security;

(d) To protect public properties including roads, railways, bridges, vital installations and establishments etc. against acts of vandalism, violence or any kind of attack;

(e) To prevent crimes, and reduce the opportunities for the commission of crimes through their own preventive action and measures as well as by aiding and cooperating with other relevant agencies in implementing due measures for prevention of crimes;

(f) To accurately register all complaints brought to them by a complainant or his representative, in person or received by post, e-mail or other means, and take prompt follow-up action thereon, after duly acknowledging the receipt of the complaint;

(g) To register and investigate all cognizable offences coming to their notice through such complaints or otherwise, duly supplying a copy of the First Information Report to the complainant, and where appropriate, to apprehend offenders, and extend requisite assistance in the prosecution of offenders;

(h) To create and maintain a feeling of security in the community, and as far as possible prevent conflicts and promote amity;

(i) To provide, as first responders, all possible help to people in situations arising out of natural or man-made disasters, and to provide active assistance to other agencies in relief and rehabilitation measures;

(j) To aid individual, who are in danger of physical harm to their person or property, and to provide necessary help and afford relief to people in distress situations;

(k) To facilitate orderly movement of people and vehicles, and to control and regulate traffic on roads and highways;

(l) To collect intelligence relating to matters affecting public peace, and all kind of crimes including social offences, communalism, extremism, terrorism and other matters relating to national security, and disseminate the same to all concerned agencies, besides acting, as appropriate on it themselves.

(m) To take charge, as a police officer on duty, of all unclaimed property and take action for their safe custody and disposal in accordance with the procedure prescribed.

(n) To train, motivate and ensure welfare of police personnel.

4.1.3 Social Responsibilities of the Police

Sec (58) Model Police Act 2006 every police officer shall:

(a) Behave with the members of the public with due courtesy and decorum, particularly so in dealing with senior citizens, women, and children;

(b) Guide and assist members of the public, particularly senior citizen, women, children, the poor and indigent and the physically or mentally challenged;

(a) individuals, who are found in helpless condition on the streets or other public places or otherwise need help and protection;

(b) Provide all requisite assistance to victims of crime and of road accidents, and in particular ensure that they are given prompt medical aid, irrespective of medico-legal formalities, and facilities their compensation and other legal claims;

(c) Ensure that in all situations, especially during conflict between communities, classes, castes and political groups, the conduct of the police is always governed by the principles of impartiality and human rights norms, with special attention to protection of weaker sections including minorities;

(d) Prevent harassment of women and children in public places and public transport, including stalking, making objectionable gestures, signs, remarks or harassment caused in any way;

(e) Render all requisite assistance to the members of the public, particularly women, children, and the poor and indigent persons, against criminal exploitation by any person or organized group; and

(f) Arrange for legally permissible sustenance and shelter to every person in custody and making known to all such people's provisions of legal aid schemes available from the Government and also inform the authorities concerned in this regard.

(g) Preserve, promote and protect human rights and interests of weaker sections, backward classes, poor, weak and the downtrodden.

4.1.4 Maintenance of Essential Services

As per Sec (58), Model Police Act 2006, when the State Government declares any specified service to be an essential service to the community, it shall be the duty of the police to maintain the essential services and every police officer must obey any order given by any officer superior to him in connection with the service specified in the declaration by the government.

i. Senior Police Officer Performing Duties of a Subordinate Officer

A senior police officer may perform any duty assigned by law or by a lawful order to any officer subordinate to him, and may aid, supplement, supersede or prevent any action of the subordinate by his own action or that of any person lawfully acting under his command or authority, whenever the same shall appear necessary or expedient for giving more complete or convenient effect to the law or for avoiding any infringement thereof.

ii. The Inventory of Police Duties, Functions & Jobs

In the light of above mentioned description of police work and functioning, an inventory of police duties, functions and jobs can be prepared in the following manner:

1. Investigation related duties and jobs
2. Crime prevention and preservation of peace and security
3. Crime detection work
4. Order maintenance and security jobs
5. Enforcement of Social Legislation, Minor, Major and Special Acts
6. Collection of Intelligence
7. Democratic and election related duties
8. Natural calamities, disaster management and emergency duties
9. Maintenance of Police Records
10. PRO duties
11. Assistance to other departments
12. Miscellaneous duties and functions

1. Investigation related duties and jobs

This would include police functions like:

(a) Crime registration

(b) Guarding, protecting visit to the scene of crime

(c) Lifting, handling and packing of exhibits and sending them to various places like the PS, SP office, FSL and other places calling witnesses and serving notices to them.

(d) Calling witnesses and serving notices to them

(e) Arresting criminals and suspects

(f) Search and seizure proceedings during an investigation

(g) Interrogation of suspects, witnesses and criminals

(h) Collection and recording of various types of evidences i.e. oral, documentary and expert opinion etc.

(i) Taking criminals to courts for police/judicial custody and trial

(j) Raids for various purposes.

2. Crime prevention and preservation of peace and security

This would include:

a) Gast and patrolling, including nakabandi, performing picket and ambush jobs, checking vehicles and frisking passengers

b) Surveillance and checking of bad characters

c) Preventive arrests

d) Collection and transmission of criminal intelligence.

3. Crime detection work

The crime detection job profile would include:

(a) Collection of information/intelligence about criminals of various types and taking notes from the CIG.

(b) Creation of mukhbirs/informers and creating contacts with the members of criminal tribes and other segments of society so as to obtain useful information with regard to the detection of various property and other offence

4. Order maintenance and security jobs

This profile would include among other things the following tasks:

a) Surveillance, watch and action to be taken during peaceful processions, demonstrations and strikes of various types like murder, dacoit, robbery etc.

b) Action to be taken on agitating and unruly mobs. This would include pushing off agitators, stopping them with improvised barricades and effective intervention to contain mobs under the instructions of senior officers and the use of force whenever needed

c) Protection of vital installations during the spate of crimes and emergencies of various types

d) VIP security and performance of various duties during VIP visits in different capacities

5. Enforcement of Social Legislation, Minor, Major and Special Acts

Performance of this role would require the police:

a) To know the significance and importance of various social legislations like Child Marriage Restraint Act, Protection of Civil Rights Act, anti-dowry, guest-control and other social legislations which provide a positive and adequate push to social change in a development-oriented society like India. The role of a constable in the implementation of these acts has to be an integral part of the job profile of the constabulary.

b) To know the significance and importance of various local, special and minor acts along with the role of constabulary in the effective execution of the various provisions thereof.

6. Collection of Intelligence

Police are required to collect intelligence about:

a) Any incident of law and order

b) Political activities

c) Labor activities

d) Student activities and agitations thereof

e) Communal tensions and events

f) Employees' associations and strikes by them

g) Criminal activities

h) Miscellaneous activities and events tending to destroy peace and tranquility.

7. Democratic and election related duties

In order to perform their role adequately the police must know:

a) Importance of elections

b) Types of elections

c) The role of police in ensuring the conduct of free, fair and impartial elections

d) Various duties of a constable during different types of elections.

8. Natural calamities, Disaster and emergency duties

Various jobs like saving life and property, providing shelter, rehabilitation, evacuation of people from crisis situations and their transportation during:

a) Fires

b) Floods

c) Famines

d) The spread of an epidemic

e) The breakout of war or external aggression

f) Internal disorders like communal riots, struggle between various classes, castes and sects and other clashes.

9. Maintenance of Police Records

This would include:

(a) Proper handling of the record

(b) Upkeep and maintenance of the record

(c) Preparation, destruction, revision and modification of the record of various police units.

10. PRO duties

Police are the most visible and effective PROs of the police department. They should thereof understand

a) The importance of PCR and its present state in the area of their operations and functions and

b) The role of constables in improving PCR and police image.

11. Assistance to other departments

This would include assistance to

(a) The education department during examinations, students, and employees' strikes and other situations of disorder,

(b) The revenue department and loaning organizations for recovery of loans revenue collection etc.,

(c) The departments like banks and municipalities for guards etc for the removal of encroachments etc, and

(d) The other departments as and when the need arises.

12. Miscellaneous duties and functions

This would include:

a) Ceremonial duties

b) Discharging regulatory duties and regulation of traffic and traffic management duties.

c) Comprehension of the norms of loyalty, commitment, neutrality and impartiality in the discharge of one's functions

d) Obligation and commitment to the Govt. and to the police organization

e) Contribution of constables during anti-dacoit operations, raids, emergencies, rounding up of and controlling of goonda and anti-social elements

4.1.5 Organization at the Central and State Level

Article 246 (entry 2, List 11, Seventh Schedule) of the Indian Constitution enumerates police as a State subject. Police Administration, therefore, is a State responsibility. This does not, however, minimize the role of Central Government in .Police Administration. The Constitution itself enumerates a long list of subjects like All India Services, preventive detention, HRMs, ammunition, passports etc. in the union list. The Central Government's role in Police Administration is related to making laws on subjects included in Union and Concurrent lists and making amendments to the basic police laws like Indian Penal Code, the Code of Criminal Procedure, Evidence Act, etc. Administration of the States, policing the Union Territories, management of Indian Police Service, matters relating to arms and ammunition are also the responsibility of the Central Government. The Ministry of Home Affairs and the Department of Personnel plays the administrative and coordinating role. In maintenance of law and order, whenever required, the Central Government provides aid and assistance to the States. To discharge this function, the Central Government maintains a network of line and staff units all over the country. The Central Reserve Police Force, Border Security Force, Railway Protection Force, Central Industrial Security Force are some of the reserve units.

Similarly Central Forensic Institutes, Police Wireless and Sardar Vallabhbhai Patel Police Academy are the staff units at the Central level. These apart, there are Central Bureau of Investigation (CBI) and Central Intelligence Bureau (CIB) also to aid the Central Government. These agencies, under the control of the Central Government provide assistance to the State Police Organization in the fields of law - and order, security and administration of justice in the country. Rules and regulations have been formulated for the operation of these agencies in the States. There are occasions when these rules are violated leading to tensions between the Central and State Governments.

At the State level, the Police Administration is more or less uniform throughout the country. The Chief Minister or Home Minister is largely responsible for policy and supervisory functions. The Home Department coordinates and supervises the Police Administration in the State. It acts as a link between Central and State Governments. But the Director General of Police (DGP) who is the Head of the State Police undertakes the real work. His office is called the Office of the

IGPIDGP popularly called Chief Office. This office collects information and feeds it to the Government; advises political decision-makers like the cabinet and the ministers; supervises and controls line agencies. It organizes training and acts as a clearinghouse of special police services. The IGP/DGP aids and advises the Government and exercises general supervision and control over the police department. He exercises administrative, personnel, and financial power. He provides leadership to the Police Administration in the State. He is assisted in his duties of IGP by the Deputy Inspector General of Police (DIGS) and Superintendents of Police (SPs) and other staff. They Head the specialised branches like intelligence department, crime branch, transport department, training, armed forces, general administration, law and order etc. The organisation of police will become more evident by the following chart.

EXHIBIT: 4.1

RANK STRUCTURE IN A STATE POLICE FORCE

**Home Minister / Home
secretary**

↓

Director General of Police
Or the **Inspector General of Police** (in a union territory)
(Head of the State/office or the Chief (office)

↓

Deputy Inspector General of Police
(Head of the range office)

↓

Superintendent of Police
(Head of the district police office)

↓

Deputy Superintendent of Police
(Generally called the **Sub-Divisional Police Officer** (SDO)
(Head of the sub-divisional office)

↓

Inspector of Police
(Head of the circle office)

↓

Sub-Inspector
(Head of the Police Station, generally called the **Station House Officer)**

↓

Asst. Sub-Inspectors

↓

Head Constable

↓

Police Constables

The real police work takes place in the districts and below. Before we discuss the field organization, let us have a cursory view of police organization at the range level into which the State police organization is divided.

4.1.6 Organisation at Range Level

Many States are too big to be administered effectively and 'efficiently from a central point. It is not possible for the Head of the police that is the police chief or the DGP/IGP to keep in touch with the functioning of the entire organisation. Therefore, the police organisation in a State is divided into ranges for operational convenience. This is above the district and below the State level. Deputy Inspector General of Police Heads each range. Each police range comprises a few districts. The number of districts in each range varies from 2 to 8 depending upon the size of the district, population, and importance of the district.

The DIG functions as a staff officer to the State police chief and as a line officer to the district police. His functions include periodic inspections, receiving and processing reports and returns from districts, and issuing instructions to the district police functionaries. A major function of the range DIG is to coordinate the activities of district police and also take measures for inter-district co-operation. He is personally responsible for the enforcement of discipline among the police personnel under his charge. He exercises power of transfer and discipline over certain categories of personnel. He keeps a watch on the crime situation in the district particularly over grave offences like dacoit, murder etc. He also exercises control, over police funds. The range of DIG'S functions, thus, includes personnel management, budgetary control and coordination. He is responsible for the maintenance of efficiency and discipline of his staff. He ensures uniformity of procedure and securing co-operation between the police functioning in the districts within his range. He has to ensure harmonious relations between the police and the executive magistracy.

There are some criticisms about a range becoming a mere post office. It is criticized to be functionally superfluous. Some feel that inspite of range offices the workload of the State level offices has not been reduced and in fact it has been on the increase. The National Police Commission recommended that DIG of the range should play a positive role in functioning of the districts under his control. He should act as coordinating authority between districts in his range and with those of the adjacent ranges. It also recommended that he/she should be a sensitive judge of public opinion and play an important role in planning and modernization of the force. The commission felt that to be effective, the range of DIG should not have more than five districts under his control. It also recommended that for adequate supervision, territorial Inspector General of Police should be appointed in large States. They should not have more than 15 to 20 districts or 4-5 ranges under his charge. The Armed Battalions of the range should also be placed under the operational charge of the territorial IGP. They should be delegated administrative, financial, disciplinary and other power. This will reduce the workload on the DGP and enable him to concentrate on higher matters of policy and administration

4.1.7 Organisation at District and Sub- District Level

District is an important unit of the public administrative structured in the country. Almost all the State Government offices are located in the district. In Police Administration also district plays a pivotal role. All the laws and rules passed by the police are transformed into action at this level. District Police Organisation is responsible for the effective maintenance of law and order and control of crime.

Police Administration at the district level is carried out by the chief of the district police, called Superintendent of Police, who is responsible for the maintenance of law and order, and other law enforcement activities. Technically, Superintendent of Police functions under the overall control of the Collector. He and his subordinate officers, in practice, enjoy operational autonomy in the discharge of their functions. The Collector as a District Magistrate is broadly responsible for preventive aspects; and the police are responsible for the control of crime, maintenance of law and order, etc. Police Administration below the district level is organised into divisions; divisions into circles; and circle into Police Stations. The organisation and working of Police Stations, marginally, varies between urban and rural areas.

District Police work under the Superintendent of Police. He is always a member of the Indian Police Service and wields a great amount of power and prestige in the district. He is accountable to the Head of the range police that is Deputy Inspector General of Police for the maintenance of law and order in his district. He is also responsible to the Director General of Police at the State Headquarters. The Superintendent of Police (S.P) is responsible for the efficiency, morale and discipline of the police force in the district. He collects information about various aspects from the entire district and communicates the same to the State Government along with his own assessment.

The Superintendent of Police is primarily responsible for the maintenance of law and order, and prevention of crime. He is empowered to take preventive measures to ensure peace in the district. He has to make adequate police arrangements during fairs and festivals as well as elections and agitations. If he apprehends untoward situations, he can advise the Collector to promulgate prohibitory orders and even to clamp curfew. He controls crime by patrolling, investigating and taking preventive measures. He also supervises the operations of crime and special branches working under him. He has many personnel and organisational responsibilities like adequate Supply of arms, vehicles, uniform etc. He also has responsibilities regarding matters of training, promotion and discipline of the staff, maintaining financial property etc. He is the link between police organisation and people's representatives at the district level. He maintains cordial and friendly relations with people. In the district where important urban centers are located, he has responsibilities of regulating traffic and receiving VIPs. Thus, the SP occupies a pivotal and a powerful position not only in the district police organisation but also in the District Administration itself. The Additional Superintendent of Police assists him. The later helps him in his day-today general administration. Deputy Superintendents of Police, Circle Inspectors of Police, Sub-Inspectors of Police, and Head Constables and Police Constables assist him in the enticement of law and order at various levels. To assist him in undertaking his functions professionals and technical units are also placed at his disposal.

The organisation at the district level broadly consists of two wings namely the District Police Office (DPO) and the Field Organisation. The general administration of the entire police in the district is carried by the DPO. It works under the SP or ASP, who is in-charge of the office administration and also exercises general control and supervision. The office administration is carried out by several sections like crime and statistics, crime bureau, audit and accounts, equipment and stores, etc. The DPO can be considered as the secretariat of the police and the nerve center of the Police Administration in the district. Generally, the accommodation and facilities at the DPO are not adequate. One find ill-equipped and overstaffed office; insufficient accommodation; and inadequate lighting and ventilation in these offices. To provide special assistance to the police, a number of field units function at the district level. The district armed reserve, the home guards, the women police, crime bureau, special branch finger print unit, dog squad, transport unit are some of the field units supporting the district Police Administration

4.1.7.1 Sub-division

For operational convenience, the district police organisation is divided into a number of sub-divisions. Police sub-division is a unit where police work is coordinated and controlled. It is an intermediary link between police circles, Police Stations and the district police office. The police sub-division is under the charge of a Deputy Superintendent of Police or Additional Superintendent of Police. They are generally called Sub-Divisional Police Officers. The main work of the sub-division is to look into law and order matters, and discipline among the police force and other related matters at the sub-divisional level. A number of reports and registers relating to crime, security and other administrative aspects are maintained in the Sub-divisional office. The Sub-Divisional Officers are responsible primarily for the maintenance of law and order and crime control; collection and communication of intelligence; submission of periodic reports to the Superintendent of Police, Inspection of Police Stations and Circle Offices. They also have an important public relations role to perform. They act as a link between the Superintendent of Police and the Sub- Inspectors and Inspectors.

4.1.7.2 Circles

Sub-Divisions are further divided into police circles, which is a link between Police Stations and sub-division. This is the third tier in the district police organisation. Sometimes, the police circles are coterminous with taluka; sometimes with blocks; and sometimes they may not be in conformity with either of them. As there are no rules governing the formation of police circles, they vary size from State to State and even in the State from circle to circle. The number of Police Stations in each police circle is determined on the basis of crime, population, area, topography, etc. - Each circle may have **3** to 10 Police Stations. The Circle office facilitates smooth administration at the field level

Inspector of Police is the Head of police circle. He is responsible for the maintenance of law and order, and control of crime. He has to promote discipline among the policemen. He guides, advises, and supervises the work of Police Stations and the men working there. He also investigates grave crimes with the assistance of supporting staff. As is the case with the divisional office, several registers and records are maintained at the circle level. They include communication register, case diary, circle information book, annual review of crime, crime charts, criminal intelligence file, etc.

The Police Station is the lowest tier in the police organisation. It is here that the actual work of the police is undertaken. It is the basic and primary unit, which is responsible for the maintenance of Law and order, prevention and control of crime and protection of life and property of the community.

4.1.7.3 Head Constable

Head Constables are mainly employed to be in charge of general duty in police stations, as station writer, as officer in charge of out post and guards, armed reserves, in charge of beat areas in rural and town police stations. He acts as SHO in the absence of Sub-Inspector and Asst. Sub-Inspector. He is authorized to hold inquests and make investigation when asked by the Sub Inspector to do so.

He will work with Constables and help them to understand instructions, catechism and drill and help them, to perform duties allotted by SHO. He will be in charge of guard or escort when deputed. He will visit villages in the station jurisdiction when deputed for a specific purpose and will work as HC in charge of a particular beat area. He will attend to court work under the orders of SHO, and will investigate cases when deputed by the SHO and to assist the IO in investigation. He will conduct enquiries into petty complaints and will take care of arrested persons kept in police station. He will take care of reception and proper behavior with the persons coming to police station and to attend telephone calls. He will remain present in the police station in the absence of Sub-Inspector unless called away in an emergency

Head Constable shall normally be assigned the duties of station writer. He will perform the ministerial work of the station under the direction of SHO. In the absence of SI or ASI, he will allocate urgent duties to the Constables and be in charge of station property including arms and ammunition and carry out the routine work of the station. In the absence of the SI, ASI and other senior, HC, he will function as station house officer; take steps for registration and investigation of cases reported under his charge. He may also be employed by SHO to go on night rounds and may occasionally be kept in charge of beat area. He is also responsible to watch the arrested persons kept in police station and proper reception to persons visiting police station and also for answering telephone calls when SHO, SI, or ASI are not present in police station.

The head constables form the main strength of investigating team. They assist the team leader in the investigation of cases especially in preserving, and collecting the clues like finger prints, foot prints, materials, photograph etc. and also in collection of information, process service, pursuit of clues and arrest of accused and recovery of property, assisting in searches and seizures, surveillance of specially marked persons, holding inquests where directed, securing the presence of witnesses, perform, court duty to assist prosecutor when SI or Inspector are not able to be present, any other work connected with the investigation of crimes.

Head Constable or Asst. Sub-Inspector is generally assigned a beat approximately covering 2000 households and around 10,000 populations in cities and towns and a group of villages in rural areas. He shall, with the help of constables provided, be responsible in that area for prevention of all offences, surveillance over criminals and bad characters, collection of information and intelligence, affecting crime, security and law and order, service of beats by night and day, preventing and dealing with public nuisances, maintaining order and incidence control, associate with citizen committees and keeping the SHO informed of all happenings, ensure discipline and conduct of constables of his charge, and conducting such enquiries as are entrusted to him.

HC may be kept in charge of small and rural out post. The duty of outpost in charge is to supervise the work of constables in his charge, see to the proper performance of all duties attached to the outpost and maintain the prescribed records. He should submit a copy of the outpost general diary daily to the mother police station. Therefore whenever the information of cognizable offence is received in the outpost, he shall forward it to the mother station for registration of FIR after issuing a receipt for the same to the complainant. He will also enter the substance of the report in the outpost general diary. However the complainant is entitled for a copy of the FIR from the mother police station free of cost. The officer in charge of an outpost may without intervention of the officer in charge of a police station, take action in such of the offences as can be legally taken by SI, ASI or HC as per the rank of officer-in-charge. The officer in charge of outpost shall on receipt of a complaint or information of a crime or serious occurrence, take such immediate action as may appear necessary i.e. proceeding and preserving the scene, rendering medical assistance to victims, arrest of accused persons etc.

In the absence of the regular SHO, the senior officer present shall assume charge of the station. Senior constable present shall also be deemed to be the officer in charge in the absence of higher ranks as per section 2(O) of Cr.P.CWhenever a guard is detailed for treasury or jail or for security of a minister of a government, a Head Constable shall be kept in charge of the guard. A Head Constable from reserve police will be deputed to be at the disposal of Sessions Judge, to maintain order in the court when there is a criminal trial. Wherever it is warranted, the SHO shall make security arrangements commensurate with the situation with the permission and consultation of the District and Sessions Judge or other Judicial Officers.

4.1.7.4 Constables

A Constable has maximum interface with public. As the most accessible person for public, he is expected to protect the needy, rescue people from danger, apprehend offenders and assist in securing prompt help and justice. Some of the important roles assigned to him are organizing and securing community participation, activating him in prevention and detection of crime and maintenance of law and order. Another main role of the Constable is, performance of all tasks connected with beat area and thereby help in prevention of offence and breach of peace. The constable on traffic duty has the task of regulating traffic. All constables in their dealings with public should inspire confidence in the efficacy of police to protect them. The police image is directly proportionate to their good conduct and behaviour in the public as they are the persons who are basically and directly in touch with them. At all costs they must avoid ill treatment either to the victims or to the accused as a first step to build the better police image. The main duties of civil Constables are;

A. To perform duties in beats, patrols and pickets and to keep surveillance over history sheeted and other potential criminals as per orders.

B. Collection of information and intelligence relating to crimes and criminals, subversive, terrorist and anti- social elements in their areas primarily and communication of the same to the authorized superiors.

C. Developing cordial relations with local citizen committees/voluntary organizations and knowledge of households in the beat area and convey information relating to persons and events that cause or likely to cause law and order situation or wide spread disturbances.

D. Keep in touch with local disputes, caste/communal overtones and inform SHO.

E. Assistance to investigating officers in the matter of arrests, recoveries, searches, identification and securing of witnesses or verification of information and execute warrants and serve summons promptly, escort prisoners, arrested persons, escort injured or dead to the hospital, guard of prisoners in custody and all station property.

F. Help and assist in dealing with Floods, Earthquakes, Fires, Accidents, Epidemics etc. and put in responsible efforts to save lives and property and to perform allotted duties in Fairs, Festivals, Bundhs, Agitations, Riots, Large Assemblies, Elections, Bandobust and security duties.

G. To preserve and guard the scene of occurrence until necessity ceases.

H. To behave courteously with all sections of public and treat poor people, children, women, aged and all weaker sections of society with consideration, sympathy and helpful attitude.

I. To be regular and punctual in his duties, catechism, physical training and weekly parades.

J. To work as data entry operators in Computers and in the areas of reprography, photography and cartography wherever they have necessary skill.

K. To meet the common people in his beat on a regular basis and maintain rapport with the public representatives.

L. To visit the victims of crime and keep they updated about the investigation of their cases, except where the identity of the victims needs to be kept secret or where the victim wants no interference.

M. To keep a list of senior citizens living alone and visit them occasionally.

N. To keep a list of vital installations and places of worship and maintain watch over the same.

O. To keep a track of any brewing social, religious or sectarian conflict/ unrest.

P. To keep a watch on the movement of foreigners in his area.

Q. To make entries in the prescribed register and forms and maintain records entrusted to him particularly those relating to beat area.

R. Any other duties allotted by SHO or other superior officers or elsewhere in this manual.

The entire preventive work of the police depends on the efficiency, commitment, professionalism and integrity of the beat area policeman. The Constable allotted to a beat should realize that his participation in the community even in a small measure is essential for successful policing. Professionalism and integrity but not power and authority shall command respect and bring in a large measure of co-operation from general public.

4.1.8 Tamil Nadu police

The Tamil Nadu Police Force is the law enforcing agency of the state of Tamilnadu, India. It is over 150 years old and is the fifth largest state police force in India. Tamil Nadu has a police population ratio of 1: 632. The administrative control of Tamil Nadu Police vests with the Chief Minister of Tamil Nadu who holds the portfolio of Home Minister. The supervision and coordination of Police is done by the Home Department, Govt. of Tamil Nadu. The force is headed by Mr. K. Ramanujam, IPS who is currently the Director General of Police (Law & Order). He is assisted by the Additional Director General of Police (Law & Order), currently Mr. S. George, IPS. For administrative purposes, Tamil Nadu is divided into four zones- North, South, West and Central. Each Zone is headed by one Inspector General of Police. The zones consist of Ranges and Cities headed by city police commissioners, DIGs (Deputy Inspector General of Police) and SPs (Superintendent of Police).

All the equipment for the TNP is manufactured indigenously by the Indian Ordnance Factor by the controlled by the Ordnance Factor Board, Ministry of Defence, and Government of India.

- Rifles: AK-47, Ishapore 2A1 rifle, Lee-Enfiled, INSAS Rifle, FN FAL
- Handguns: All Glock variants.
- Weapon systems: Ordnance Factor Tiruchirappalli made advanced shotguns and grenade launchers.

There are nine metropolitan cities in Tamil Nadu: Chennai (Greater Chennai Police), Madurai, Coimbatore, Tiruchirappalli, Salem, Tirunelveli, Vellore, Tiruppur and Erode.

Each of the cities has a City Police force, headed by a Commissioner of police. There are thirty two police districts in Tamil Nadu, each headed by a Superintendent of Police. In each City and District, the Commissioner of Police / Superintendent of Police has, besides the civil police force, an armed reserve of police personnel. One Director Inspector General of Police supervises the work of 2-3 districts, which constitute a Police Range. There are eleven ranges in Tamil Nadu. Tiruppur, Erode and Vellore are recently formed Cities and they are still under the control of the respective district police authorities.

The special units of Tamil Nadu Police perform specific functions related to security, intelligence, criminal investigations and support services. They are as follows: Armed Police or Tamil Nadu Special Police, Civil Defense and Home Guards, Civil Supplies, CID, Coastal Security Group, Crime Branch, CID,

Economic Offences Wing, Operations - T.N. Commando Force & Commando
School, Prohibition Enforcement Wing, Railway police, Social Justice and Human
Rights, Special Branch, CID including Security, Technical Services and Special
Task Force.

The Tamil Nadu police have various distinctions and honors to its credit. It
has the largest strength of women police personnel in the country, the highest
number of women police stations in the country, the first women police battalion of
special police, the first women Commando Force in the Country, the first
established Finger Print Lab in the World, the first Integrated Modern Police
Control Room in the country and has the greatest number of computers against
other police departments in the Country. It can be noted that the overall number of
crimes registered has come down steadily over the years.

EXHIBIT: 4.2
HISTORY OF TAMILNADU POLICE

Year	Description
1659	Pedda Naik engaged by the British to Guard the town of Madraspatanam with the assistance of peons. The system was the remnant of the 'Kaval' organization.
1770	Board of Police constituted by the then Governor Josios DuPre to deal with removal of public nuisance, & maintenance of public health and order.
1771	Governor Stratton appointed " Kotwal" or overseer of markets to control prices of commodities in the market and to make the tradesmen "behave".
1780	Post of Superintendent of Police was created to supervise the markets and to reduce the prices of provisions.
1782	Comprehensive plan for the Police prepared by S.Popham to promote health and to prevent impositions and frauds.
1791	Institution of Kotwal Police abolished, on complaints of extracting more money than was due from merchants. Office of "Poligar" (synonymous with "Pedda Naik") restored.
1806	Walter Grant became the first regularly appointed Superintendent of the City Police with three Police Magistrates.
1815	Thomas Harris, Superintendent of Police, Madras, formulated - the city pattern of policing, divided the area into eight divisions for effective control.

1829 – 32	On the recommendation of George Norton, Advocate General, Madras City was divided into four Districts namely Black Town District, Triplicane District, Vepery District and St. Thomas District (Santhome).
1834	Francis Kelly and Vambaukkam Raghavachariar became the first Indians to be inducted as Police Magistrate and Dy. Supdt. Of Police.
1856	Police Act XII was passed by Legislative Council of the Governor General. J.C Boudlerson became the first Commissioner of Police under the new Act.
1858	W. Robinson, a covenanted civil servant was appointed Chief Commissioner of Police (IGP). The proposal submitted by Robinson formed the basis of the present day district Police.
1859	Act XXIV marks the beginning of Modern Madras Police. The Act was also the forerunner for the Police Commission set up by the Government of India in 1906.
1865	Free Masons Lodge Building "Perfect Unanimity" (Present Police Headquarters) taken on lease by the Police for a rent of Rs.90/- p.m.
1874	Madras Presidency Police bought the Police Headquarters Building for a sum of Rs.20, 000/-. An additional sum of Rs.10, 000/- was spent on expansion and repairs.
1884	Formation of Malappuram Special Police to deal with periodical outbreaks of Muslim fanaticism by Moplahs.
1895	Finger Print Bureau was established in Madras.
1902	The Madras City with an area of 29 sq. miles and population of 5, 09,346 was divided into two ranges - Northern range in the immediate charge of Dy. Commissioner of Police and the Southern Range under the direct control of Commissioner of Police himself assisted by a Chief Superintendent. H.A. Stuart, Inspector General of Police, Madras Presidency was appointed Secretary of All India Police Commission.
1905	Police Training School was strengthened and equipped to train the new cadre of Sub-Inspectors who were to replace the old Station House Officers (who were Head Constables).
1906	Criminal Investigation Department was established. F.Fawcett was appointed as DIG.
1909	The King's Police Medal was instituted for Gallantry and Distinguished Service.
1912	Presidency Police Sports inaugurated.
1919	Diwan Bahadur Parankusam Naidu was appointed as Commissioner of Police - the first Indian to occupy the post. P.B. Thomas, I.P., became the first Police Officer to be appointed as Inspector General of Police to head the Police Department.
1921	Malabar Special Armed Police was formed in the wake of Moplah rebellion.
1923	H.G. Stokes appointed as Special Officer for re-organisation of Armed Reserves and Special Police Parties. MSP equipped with "Marconi" wireless sets. First Police Organisation to use wireless for operations in Madras State.

1928	The CID was divided into Special Branch and Crime Branch
1929	Madras City Police re-organized with functional divisions of Crime, Law and Order and Traffic
1931	Statutory rules for the Madras Police Subordinate Service come into force.
1935	"Village Vigilance Committees" constituted to enlist public Co-Operation.
1946	Police Wireless commissioned. Capt.D.R. Clamp appointed as first Police Wireless Officer.
1947	T.G. Sanjeevi, from Madras became the first Indian to occupy the Post of Director, Intelligence Bureau, and New Delhi.
1951	Madras Police Dog squad was formed. Madras became the pioneer in India after Independence to use dogs in the prevention and detection of crime.
1956	Police Radio Office established. Single Digit Finger Print Section was established in the Finger Print Bureau
1957	Headquarters of the MSP (Tamil Nadu) was shifted to Thiruchirapalli.
1959	Centenary year of Tamil Nadu Police.
1960	Police Research Center (PRC) was formed.
1961	Dog squad established at Madurai. Government sanctioned to establish State Forensic Science Laboratory
1963	City Police Hospital at Madras (Originally formed as a dispensary) was converted as a full-fledged Hospital. Home Guards was created to assist police.
1963	H.A. Stuart, Inspector General of Police, Madras Presidency was appointed Secretary of All India Police Commission.
1971	"Police Computer Wing", Madras was established. Tamil Nadu was the first State to start Computerization. Tamil Nadu Police Commission set up under the Chairmanship of Thiru Gopalswamy Iyengar. Special Cell CID was formed to deal with extremist's activities. This was later known as Q' Branch CID.
1973	Women Constables and Women SI recruited in Tamil Nadu Police for first time.
1976	Police Transport Workshop cum training school, Avadi started functioning. Security Branch was constituted in CID.
1979	Post of Director General of Police was created to head the Police Department E.L. Stracey I.P. was the first Director General of Police of Tamil Nadu.
1981	Tamil Nadu Police Housing Corporation was formed.
1984	Forest Cell CID, Madras was formed.
1985	Rising of T.S.P. VIII and T.S.P IX Battalions.
1987	Regional Police Transport workshop was opened at Trichy

1989	Tamil Nadu Police Housing Corporation merged with TN Housing Board. Police Commission appointed under the Chairmanship of former Chief Secretary Thiru Sabanayagam . Dr.R. Rajagopalan I.P.S., appointed as the Member Secretary of the Commission. Control Room was opened in the Directorate of Civil Defence.
1991	Uniformed Service Recruitment Board was constituted for the recruitment of personnel in the non-gazetted category for the uniformed departments -Police, Prison and Fire Services. Once again the TN Police Housing Corporation Started Functioning as a separate entity.
1992	Special Security Group established. First Women Police Station, was opened at Thousand Lights, Chennai, headed by an Woman Inspector. Subsequently Women Police Stations were opened in all districts.
1993	Separate establishment for Human Rights was formed. Special task Force was formed
1994	Coastal Security Group, first of its kind in the country constituted to strengthen the security of 1000 km-long Tamil Nadu coast line.
1995	Chief Office Shifted to "Government House", Government Estate, and Chennai. First phase of the Pilot Project on Computerization of Police Stations was introduced in 4 Police Stations.
1997	Swift Action Force (SAF) formed to deal with communal riots.
2001	In the new Millennium, Tamil Nadu Police has a Strength of 91,341.There are 11 Police ranges, 32 police Districts including 2 railway Districts,6 commissionerates,189 Sub Divisions,287 Circles and 1276 Police Stations including Women Police Stations.
2002	"Police Personnel Grievance Redressal Day" was conducted by Hon'ble CM. Four Zones created, each headed by an IGP with headquarters at Chennai, Coimbatore, Trichy and Madurai.
2003	One Mobile Police Station and 80 Highway patrol vehicles introduced to improve highway surveillance and reduce accidents. 117 police Clubs opened all over the State.
2004	"Woman Police Battalion of Tamilnadu Special Police "formed -the first such battalion in India. STF succeeded "Operation Cocoon" in which the notorious bandit Veerappan was killed. "Integrated Modern Police Control Room" opened at Chennai City.
2005	Merging of Chengai East District with the Commissionerate of Chennai city Police. The greater Chennai Police now has a jurisdiction over 588.7 Sq.Kms, with 156 Police Stations, the largest Commissionerate in the country. A new building for State Crime Records Bureau(SCRB) inaugurated. The SCRB building is a State-of-the-art facility for the Finger Print Bureau, Police Computer Wing, Modus Operandi Bureau and Statistical Wing.
2006	Asia's Largest and Modern Prison called Puzhal Prison was inaugurated.
2007	Sesquicentennial (150Years)1856-2006 of the Chennai Police Celebrated.
	Ariyalur District was newly formed, bifurcating the erstwhile Perambalur District. Hyundai Motors Ltd., Presented 100 Hyundai Accent Cars as a goodwill gesture to augment the Chennai City Patrolling fleet. Thus Chennai Police is the only force in the country having a fleet of sedans.
2008	Tamil Nadu Police Celebrated Sesquicentennial (150 Years). The Chennai Police has been bifurcated as Chennai City Police Commissionerate and Chennai Sub- Urban Commissionerate. The Tamil Nadu Police Academy has been inaugurated at Oonamancheri, Vandalur, and Chennai. The DGP, Tamil Nadu launched the redesigned Tamil Nadu Police Official Website with e-Governance facility.

2009	01.07.09 National Security Guard hub was opened at Chennai. 01.09.09 Senior IPS officer Ms Letika Saran IPS became the first woman DGP in Tamil Nadu Police. 18.10.09 Hon'ble CM M.karunanidhi unveiled a new Police Memorial at DGP office to commemorate the police personnel who laid down their lives while discharging duty.
2010	An Organized Crime Intelligence Unit (OCIU) starts function under the Intelligence Wing of the Tamil Nadu police. 13.01.10 Ms Letika Saran IPS., an officer of 1976 batch, has taken over charge as DGP (law and order), Tamil Nadu. Tamil Nadu's first woman director general of police (DGP) and the second woman in the country to head a state police force.23.09.10 New annexe building opened at DGP office.
2011	27.07.11 Anti-Land Grabbing Special Cells. In G.O.Ms.No.423, Home (Pol-XI) Dept., dt.28.07.2011 Govt. have sanctioned the formation of 36 Anti Land Grabbing special cell in the state with one cell each at the State Police Headquarters, all Commissionerrates and all districts except Karur, Thiruvannamalai and Nagapattinam for a period of one year on temporary basis. In those 3 districts, district crime branch will handle the investigation of Land Grabbing cases. **24.08.11 Chennai-Suburban Police commission rates merged**. In G.O.Ms.No.471, Home (Pol-XIV) Dept., dt.24.08.2011 Govt. have ordered to merge Chennai suburban Police with Chennai city Police and formed Greater Chennai Police. The Greater Chennai Police commissionerate is divided into four L & O zone viz.East zone (27 Police stations), West zone (35 Police stations), North zone (30 Police stations), and South zone (37 Police stations). **3.09.11 Police Rifle and Pistol/Revolver Shooting Competition 2010.** The 11 th All India Police rifle and Pistol, Revolver Shooting competition 2010 was held at Commando Force shooting range othivakulam Kanchipuram district in Tamil Nadu from 2011-08.09.2011.

Section II
The Causes for Stress among Police Personnel

4.2.1 Introduction

Stress at work is a relatively new phenomenon of modern lifestyles. The nature of work has gone through drastic changes over the last century and it is still changing at whirlwind speed. They have touched almost all professions, from an artist to a surgeon, or a commercial pilot to sales executive. With change comes stress, inevitably. Professional stress or job stress poses a threat to physical health. Work related stress in the life of organized workers, consequently, affects the health of organizations. Job stress is a chronic disease caused by conditions in the workplace that negatively affect an individual's performance and overall well-being of his body and mind. One or more of a host of physical and mental illnesses manifests job stress. In some cases, job stress can be disabling.

4.2.2 Causes of Workplace Stress

Job stress may be caused by a complex set of reasons. Some of the most visible causes of workplace stress are:

EXHIBIT: 4.3
CAUSES OF WORK-RELATED STRESS

Sl. No		Some potential causes of work related stress include
1.	Task design	• A mismatch between qualifications/experience and the demands of the job. • Fragmented or meaningless work • Lack of variety
2.	Work load or work pace	• Lack of control over work methods, pace and rate • Work overload or under load • High work rate or time pressure
3.	Role in the organisation	• Role or task ambiguity or uncertainty people are unsure about what they are doing • Role conflict • Responsibility beyond the individual's capacity to cope
4.	Work context	• Hazardous work • Poor communication on workplace issues • Dealing with difficult clients/customers • Violence or threat of violence
5.	Physical work environment and equipment	• Poor workplace layout • Lack of space • Excessive noise • Inadequate equipment
6.	Degree of control	• Low participation in decision-making • Lack of control over work methods and scheduling of work
7.	Organizational function and culture	• Poor management of organizational change • Poor communication within the workplace • Rigid work practices people unable to work out their own solutions to the day to day problems they encounter in the workplace • A non- supportive work culture where concerns and requests are dismissed
9.	Work schedule	• Shift working disruption to body processes • Inflexible work schedules • Unpredictable working hours

		• Long or unsociable working hours
10.	Management of work	• Poor leadership • Supervision arrangements • Performance management arrangements • Inadequate information, instruction and training
11.	Employment status	• Job insecurity • Career uncertainty or stagnation • Lack of reward, recognition, status • Low social value of the work
12.	Relationship at work	• Bullying and harassment • Poor relationships with co-workers and supervisors • Interpersonal conflict • Physical or social isolation • Lack of opportunity to be consulted • Lack of social support

i. **Job Insecurity:** Organized workplaces are going through metamorphic changes under intense economic transformations and consequent pressures. Reorganizations, takeovers, mergers, downsizing and other changes have become major stressors for employees, as companies try to live up to the competition to survive. These reformations have put demand on everyone, from a CEO to a mere executive.

ii. **High Demand for Performance:** Unrealistic expectations, especially at the time of corporate reorganizations which sometimes lead to unhealthy and unreasonable pressures on the employee, can be a tremendous source of stress and suffering. Increased workload, extreme long working hours and intense pressure to perform at peak levels all the time for the same pay, can actually leave an employee physically and emotionally drained. Excessive travel and too much time away from family also contribute to an employee's stressors.

iii. **Technology:** The development of technology like computers, pagers, cell phones, fax machines and internet has resulted in heightened expectations for productivity, speed and efficiency, increasing pressure on the individual worker to constantly operate at peak performance levels. Workers working with heavy machinery are under constant stress to remain alert. In this case both the worker and their family members live under constant mental stress. There is also constant pressure to keep up with technological breakthroughs and improvisation, forcing employees to learn new software all the times.

iv. **Workplace Culture:** Adjusting with workplace culture, whether in a new company or not, can be intensely stressful. Making oneself adapt to the various aspects of workplace culture such as communication patterns, hierarchy, dress code if any, workspace behavioral patterns of the boss as well as the co-workers, can be a lesson of life. Maladjustment workplace cultures may lead to subtle conflicts with colleagues or even with superiors. In many cases office politics or gossips can be major stress inducers.

v. **Personal or Family Problems:** Employees going through personal or family problems tend to carry their worries and anxieties to the workplace. When one is in a depressed mood, his unfocused attention or lack of motivation affects his ability to carry out job responsibilities.

4.2.3 Influences of Job Stress on Police Personnel

Police job tends to be regarded as inherently stressful because of personnel risk of exposure to confrontations and violence and day to day involvement in a variety of traumatic incidents. As a result high levels of stress related disorders may be prevalent in this population. Increased demands of work impinging upon home life, lack of consultation and communication with the higher authorities in the organization, lack of control over workload, inadequate support have been identified as the potential factors responsible for the stress in the policemen.

On an average policemen work twelve hours every day and often put in 36 hours at a stretch during VIP bandobusts and festivals. Unlike other jobs, the policemen start the day with bad news. There is only negative feedback in terms of how many murders, robberies and rapes had taken place the previous night. Working throughout the day in such an atmosphere produces adverse psychological effects. Moreover long working hours, irregular eating habits, sleepless nights, shift duties and disturbed personnel life produces stress in the policemen's life and they become vulnerable to various disorders. To alleviate the stress the policemen tend to stick to the unhealthy habits like drinking liquor or chewing tobacco and suffer from many adverse effects of these habits. Unable to cope with the stressful condition, some of them also commit suicide.

Various studies have reported significantly high prevalence of stress related disorders like hypertension, diabetes and coronary heart disease among the policemen and found police occupation as a prominent risk factor for coronary heart disease.

4.2.4 Cause of Stress

Police stress arises from several features of police work. Alterations in body rhythms from monthly shift rotation, for example, reduce productivity. The change from a day to a swing, or graveyard, shift not only requires biological adjustment but also complicates officers' personal lives. Role conflicts between the job—serving the public, enforcing the law, and upholding ethical standards—and personal responsibilities as spouse, parent, and friend act as stressors. Other stressors in police work include:

- Threats to officers' health and safety.
- Boredom, alternating with the need for sudden alertness and mobilized energy.
- Responsibility for protecting the lives of others.
- Continual exposure to people in pain or distress.
- The need to control emotions even when provoked.
- The presence of a gun, even during off-duty hours.
- The fragmented nature of police work, with only rare opportunities to follow cases to conclusion or even to obtain feedback or follow-up information.

Administrative policies and procedures, which officers rarely participate in formulating, can add to stress. One-officer patrol cars create anxiety and a reduced sense of safety. Internal investigation practices create the feeling of being watched and not trusted, even during off-duty hours. Officers sometimes feel they have fewer rights than the criminals they apprehend. Lack of rewards for good job performance, insufficient training, and excessive paperwork can also contribute to police stress.

The criminal justice system creates additional stress. Court appearances interfere with police officers' work assignments, personal time, and even sleeping schedules. Turf battles among agencies, court decisions curtailing discretion, perceived leniency of the courts, and release of offenders on bail, probation, or parole also lead to stress. Further stress arises from perceived lack of support and negative attitudes toward police from the larger society. (Most public opinion surveys, however, show strong support for and positive attitudes toward police.)

Stress also stems from distorted and/or unfavorable news accounts of incidents involving police. The inaccessibility and perceived ineffectiveness of social service and rehabilitation agencies to which officers refer individuals act as further stressors.

Women and minority officers face additional stressors. They are more likely to face disapproval from fellow officers and from family and friends for entering police work. Supervisors, peers, and the public question women officers' ability to handle the emotional and physical rigors of the job, even though research indicates women can do so. The need to "prove themselves" to male officers and to the public constitutes a major stressor for women officers.

Stress contributes not only to the physical disorders previously mentioned, but also to emotional problems. Some research suggests that police officers commit suicide at a higher rate than other groups. Most investigators report unusually high rates of divorce among the police personnel. Although some maintain that researchers have exaggerated the divorce rate among police, interview surveys demonstrate that police stress reduces the quality of family life. A majority of officers interviewed reported that police work inhibits non-police friendships, interferes with scheduling family social events, and generates a negative public image. Furthermore, they take job pressures home, and spouses worry about officers' safety. Systematic studies do not confirm the widely held belief that police suffer from unusually high rates of alcoholism, although indirect research has established a relationship between high job stress and excessive drinking. Finally, officers interviewed cited guilt, anxiety, fear, nightmares, and insomnia following involvement in shooting incidents.

In the past, departments either ignored officers with problems or dealt with them informally by assigning them to desk jobs. During the 1950s, some departments began to formalize their responses, usually by incorporating officer-initiated Alcoholics Anonymous groups made up exclusively of alcoholic officers. In the 1970s, departments instituted "employee assistance" programs to deal with problem officers, particularly those suffering from alcoholism. These programs have expanded into a broad range of responses to police stress. Some programs focus on physical fitness, diet, relaxation, and biofeedback to cope with stress.

Some of the most visible causes of workplace stress include:
Job insecurity, high demand for performance, technology, workplace culture, personal or family problems etc.Job related stress is likely to become chronic because it is such a large part of daily life and stress in turn reduces a worker's effectiveness by impairing concentration, causing sleeplessness and increasing the risk for illness, back problems, accidents and loss. Work stress can lead to harassment or even violence while on the job.

i.   By all definitions, the profession of policing has a prestigious place in all professions. Police personnel are a kingpin in the entire system of public administration. Almost all cultures of the civilized world have considered their teachers in a very high esteem. They are very often been given names like "Master" "Mentor" and "Guru". To achieve this status teachers throughout the history of civilization have come up to the expectations of the world around them. Most thinkers and philosophers of the past who are still remembered, because they had their disciples and students.

ii.   Time has changed and the societies and culture have drastically diversified, but the tasks of a teacher are primarily the same, which is the transfer of knowledge to the next generation. With change in cultural norms and traditions in the societies there has been a drastic change in the expectations from a teacher. Some of these changes have limited the measures which a teacher in the past could exercise in disciplining a student and some have put additional burden on teachers with respect to their preparation of lessons and adopting and maintaining their policing styles. This is because most of the school systems prefer to maintain uniformity in all their branches.

iii. Policing has now become a very demanding occupation with a lot of stresses for a teacher who has a lot of deadlines to meet and a lot of responsibilities to shoulder besides policing a student with new means of and ragogy.

4.2.5 Symptoms of Physical, Emotional and Stress

The signs of Job stress vary from person to person, depending on the particular situation, how long the individual has been subjected to the stressors and the intensity of the stress itself. Typical symptoms of job stress can be. The police service has the highest level of stress and maximum consequences.

Many studies have been conducted for understanding the level of stress among police personnel and most of them have revealed alarming negative effects of stress on these personals. Prolonged or repeated exposure to work related stress or even a single serious occurrence can cause adverse health effects and reduce a person's capacity to perform at work. Work related stress is a health and safety hazard that can have negative effects on both the individual and the organisation, for the individual, negative effects can include:

i.   **Mental health:** Including post-traumatic stress disorder, depression and anxiety, difficulty with decision making, forgetfulness.

ii. **Physical health:** Including headaches, indigestion, tiredness, slow reaction times, and shortness of breath, musculoskeletal disorders and cardiovascular disease.

iii. **Emotional health:** Including irritability, excess worrying, and feeling of worthlessness, anxiety, defensiveness, anger and mood swings.

iv. **Behavioral:** Include changes in performance, social withdrawal, and impulsive behaviour, increased consumption of alcohol, nicotine or recreational drugs.

EXHIBIT: 4.4

TYPICAL SYMPTOMS OF JOB STRESS

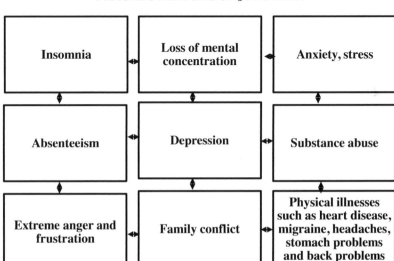

Police officers play a very significant role for maintaining law and order in the society despite all the shortcomings and limitations in the police department especially concerning he infrastructural facilities, work force shortages and periodic training. Police officers are supposed to implement all the criminal laws for which they work round the clock and/ or without any leave/ break, which cause tremendous mental pressure and physical exertion on them. As a result, sometimes a few of them may have violent outbursts and/or take leave without any prior notice. Police officers are at high risk of experiencing exposure to psychologically straining situations and potentially psycho-traumatic experiences.

4.2.6 Effects of Work-Related Stress and its impact on Employer

Job stress poses a significant threat to employee health and consequently to the health of an organization. It is important for both employees and employers to recognize and understand stress and its causes. Often employers confuse job challenges and job stressors. Most employees view job challenge as a motivating factor, which enables them to grow within their positions. This motivation has the potential to produce positive results for both employee and employer. However, when challenges become demands, employee often resort to the fight or flight response to the situations. The negative effects on the organisation can include:

1. Reduced productivity, performance or quality of service.
2. Lower levels of job satisfaction and morale
3. Increases in absenteeism or sickness absence
4. Increase in conflict and impact on quality of relationships
5. Increase in injury. Illness and lost time
6. Increased staff turnover

4.2.6.1 Benefits of taking action to address work related stress

Implementing measures to prevent work relates stress can benefit both individuals and the workplace by:

1. Creating a positive working environment
2. Increasing job satisfaction and morale
3. Decreasing staff turnover rates
4. Reducing accidents and incidents
5. Improving communication
6. Increasing productivity

7. Establishing sound decision making processes

8. Decreasing injury, illness and absenteeism

9. Improving customer/client satisfaction

10. Improving staff and customer loyalty

Such benefits can be achieved by implementing preventive measures that address the risk factors or causes of stress depending on the issues identified in the assessment process.

1. Setting clear accountabilities and goals for staff

2. Planning workload to match potential demands

3. Ensuring that everyone understands their role in the organization

4. Improving skills of managers and supervisors

5. Reviewing communication and consultation strategies

6. Providing positive feedback and encouragement for work well done

4.2.6.2 Methods of Identifying Stress

Identification is the first step towards correction; with this belief in mind it is strongly advised that a teacher should understand the implications of stress on his personal health and social life. The best way to identify stress easily is to remain active in his social circle and readily accept any recent psychological or behavioral change observed by others.

It is also possible to keep a track of stressors' changes by maintaining a self-checklist that will help in establishing changes in ideas and opinions over a period of time. This will show a clear picture of how the work place environment have affected an individual thinking gradually and with the help of their friends, colleagues and relatives, stressors can change the effects of stress on their life.

i.   **Self- Analysis:** The best way is to keep a check on your own health, attitude and behavior. Any change in these should be noted and necessary remedial measures should be taken immediately to overcome this situation. The self-stress checklist given in appendix 1 can be a helpful aid in determining the change in attitude which can be useful for determining the own state.

ii. **Mutual Analysis:** Another way is to maintain close liaison with other colleagues and discuss the irritants that are creating problems or are likely to create stress for the police personal. This is one way to identify and eradicate the issues which are likely to become the cause of stress beforehand. The faculty members or an organization of teachers can benefit the affected teacher with each other's experience.

iii. **Organizational Role:** The organization can also play a positive role in helping their police personal in identifying the causes of stress. Problems such as isolation and disruptive behavior on the part of police person and can conveniently handle at the top level by the management amicably without putting the staff in a stressful situation.

iv. **Remedial Measures:** Some elements of stress are intrinsic while others are situational in the police job. The police personal have to understand how to cope with those which are intrinsic, while the situational ones can be managed with experience and common sense.

v.   **Individual Measures:** When a person decides to adopt the policy as career profession, he or she during the training phase must realize the demands of this profession in terms of effort involved and in terms of time investment.

The workload of police officer will always be great and everything will always be bracketed by a very tight time schedule. A police officer has to be punctual and able to meet the deadline without fail. Police officers will have to always face the criticism of common public and faces different set of problems. Sensible police personnel must know where to draw a line to prevent his social and personal life from being absorbed by his professional life. Though it is very difficult to leave the stresses in the office and not let it affect their personal life, but there are methods which can help police personnel to reduce these effects.

vi. **Adopt a Hobby:** It is very important for a police officer to have a hobby which is totally different from their professional teaches at school. Music, gardening, hiking and painting are a few examples of hobbies which a may adopt. These can give them an outlet and take their minds off from the problems that they face at school. This is one way of getting the day's stress off from their minds.

vii. **Adopting Healthy Habits:** It is very important for a police person to maintain a healthy lifestyle. Cutting back on bad habits like:

   ❖ Reduce caffeine intake will help their stay focused and reduce stress

   ❖ Eat breakfast as it is the most important meal of the day as it will help them stay healthy

   ❖ Avoid junk snacks and eat right food.

❖ Should not let their life just roll by itself. Set realistic goals in life and then pursue them.

❖ Make it a point to visit the guidance counselor, as it can help them to identify any underlying psychological or behavior problem related to workplace stress.

❖ Worrying unnecessarily can be a big source of stress. So cut back on worrying as that will reduce individuals' stress.

❖ Learn and practice anger management techniques as it will help in managing stress.

4.3 Conclusion

Theoretical overview of Indian police services and stress faced by the police personnel and its coping strategies has been discussed in this chapter. Based on these theoretical discusses the following chapter provided an empirical discussion on police personnel's perception towards causes for stress, its frequency of occurrence and its coping strategies.

CHAPTER V

ANALYSIS AND INTERPRETATION

5.1 Introduction

Job stress is one of the most common afflictions among police personnel. Stress, leading to suicides and homicides, is one of the major problems facing the police personnel. Tough working conditions, lack of basic amenities, long working hours, physical separation from the family, tight controls and rigidly stratified hierarchies have been considered the reasons for the high level of stress. However, no formal study has been conducted to actually ascertain the various causes of stress in the Tamilnadu police force. The present study uses the inputs provided by the personnel, of various ranks in the force, at the field level to understand the causes of stress. The study also discusses various ways to reduce stress by means of analysis the stress coping strategies adopted by the police personnel, so as to improve the physical and psychological health of the police personnel and to improve the overall efficiency of the force. The data collected were analyzed in the light of the objectives of the present study by employing appropriated statistical method. The obtained results after analyzing the data are submitted in this chapter.

5.2 Demographic Characteristics

Demographic variables such as gender, age, rank, and tenure have also been found in association with occupational stress and choice of coping strategies among police officers. The demographic parameters of Police Officers of Tamil Nadu in Thoothukudi district is briefly discussed in this sub-section of the study.

TABLE: 5.1
GENDER OF THE RESPONDENTS

Sl. No	Gender	No. of Respondents	Percentage
1.	Male	481	80.17
2.	Female	119	19.83
	Total	600	100

Source: Primary Data

The above table indicates that out of 600 police constables surveyed, 80.17per cent of the total constables are Male and the rest of 19.83per cent of the total constables are female.

TABLE: 5.2
AGE OF THE RESPONDENTS

Sl. No	Age	No. of Respondents	Percentage
1.	20-29 years	299	49.80
2.	30-39 years	191	31.80
3.	40-49 years	94	15.70
4.	50-59 years	16	2.70
	Total	600	100

Source: Primary Data

The above table clearly indicates that, 49.80 per cent of the police constables are in the age group of 20-29 years and 31.80 per cent of the respondents are between 30-39 years, followed by, 15.70 per cent of the respondents are in the age group of 40-49 years and the rest of 2.70 per cent of them are between the ages of 50-59 years.

TABLE: 5.3
EDUCATIONAL QUALIFICATION OF THE RESPONDENTS

Sl. No	Educational Qualification	No. of Respondents	Percentage
1.	School level	97	16.20
2.	UG	417	69.50
3.	PG	78	13.00
4.	Professional	8	1.30
	Total	600	100

Source: Primary Data

The above table narrates that,69.50 per cent of the total constables are under graduates,16.20 per cent of the total constables had school level education, 13per cent of the total constables had post graduate level education and the rest of 1.30 per cent of the total constables are professionals.

TABLE: 5.4
RELIGION OF THE RESPONDENTS

Sl. No	Religion	No. of Respondents	Percentage
1.	Hinduism	462	77.00
2.	Islam	100	16.70
3.	Christianity	38	6.30
	Total	600	100

Source: Primary Data

From the above table, it is clearly inferred that, 77 per cent of the respondents are Hindus, 16.70 per cent of the constables were Muslims and the remaining 6.30 per cent of the total constables were Christians.

TABLE: 5.5

COMMUNITY OF THE RESPONDENTS

Sl. No	Community	No. of Respondents	Percentage
1.	Other castes	280	46.70
2.	Backward castes	143	23.80
3.	Most backward castes	48	8.00
4.	Scheduled castes	129	21.50
	Total	600	100

Source: Primary Data

The above table depicts that,46.70 per cent of the total constables belonged to other castes, 23.80 per cent of the total constables belonged to backward castes, 21.50 per cent of the total constables belonged to Scheduled castes and the rest of 8 per cent of the total constables were most backward castes.

TABLE: 5.6

PLACE OF THE RESIDENCE OF THE RESPONDENTS

Sl. No	Place of residence	No. of Respondents	Percentage
1.	Rural	433	72.20
2.	Urban	167	27.80
	Total	600	100

Source: Primary Data

The table designates that, 72.20per cent of the total constables have their residences in rural area, and 27.80 per cent of the total constables lived in urban region.

TABLE: 5.7

MARITAL STATUS OF THE RESPONDENTS

Sl. No	Marital status	No. of Respondents	Percentage
1.	Married	276	46.00
2.	Unmarried	284	47.30
3.	Divorced	18	3.00
4.	Separated	22	3.70
	Total	600	100

Source: Primary Data

The above table specifies that 47.30 per cent of the total constables were unmarried, 46per cent of the total constables were married. Followed by, 3.70 per cent of the total constables got divorced from their life partners, and 3per cent of the total constables were separated.

TABLE: 5.8

NUMBER OF DEPENDENTS OF THE RESPONDENTS

Sl. No	Number of dependents	No. of Respondents	Percentage
1.	One member	73	12.20
2.	Two members	359	59.80
3.	Three members	148	24.70
4.	Four members	17	2.80
5.	Five members	2	0.30
6.	Six members	1	0.20
	Total	600	100

Source: Primary Data

It is clearly inferred that, 59.80 per cent of the total constables have two members in their family, 24.70 per cent of the total constables have three dependents in their family, and 12.20 per cent of the respondents' have one member with them. Followed by, 2.80 per cent of the total constables have four members in their family, 0.30per cent of the total constables has five members in their family and the remaining 0.20 per cent of the total constables is have six dependents in their family.

5.3 Job Profile

The job profile outlines the details of an employee's job. These are the key components that you hired the employee to accomplish. In a straight-forward, actionable format, the job profile presents a picture of an employee's key job duties. Job profile of the sample police personnel surveyed is discussed in this section of the study.

The table below shows the classification of police constables based on their designation. The designations given to police constables were Grade I, II and III.

TABLE: 5.9

DESIGNATION OF THE RESPONDENTS

Sl. No	Designation	No. of Respondents	Percentage
1.	Grade III (HC)	194	32.33
2.	Grade II	294	49.00
3.	Grade I	112	18.67
	Total	600	100

Source: Primary Data

The above table depicts that out of the total 600 police constables of the study,49per cent of sample subjects are Grade II police constables, 32.33per cent of them are in the designation of Grade III i.e., head constables, and the rest of 18.67per cent are in Grade I i.e., entry level police personnel.

TABLE: 5.10

YEARS OF EXPERIENCES OF THE RESPONDENTS

Sl. No	Experiences	No. of Respondents	Percentage
1.	Less than 5 years	169	28.20
2.	6-10 years	184	30.70
3.	11-15 years	141	23.50
4.	16-20 years	73	12.10
5.	More than 20 years	33	5.50
	Total	600	100

Source: Primary Data

The table depicts that, 30.70 per cent of the total constables have a service experience of 6 to 10 years, 28.20per cent of the constables are in the service for less than 5 years. Followed by, 23.50per cent of the constables have been working for the past11 to 15 years, 12.10per cent of the total constables are in service for 16 years to 20 years, and the rest of 5.50 per cent of them are have more than 20 years of experience.

TABLE: 5.11

MONTHLY INCOMEOF THE RESPONDENTS

Sl. No	Monthly income	No. of Respondents	Percentage
1.	`.5200-20200 plus grade pay `.2400	200	33.30
2.	`.5000-20000 plus grade pay `.1900	250	41.70
3.	`.5200-20200 plus grade pay `.2800	150	25.00
	Total	600	100

Source: Primary Data

Out of the total 600 police constables of the study, 41.70 per cent have a monthly income of Rs.5000-20000 plus grade pay Rs.1900, 33.30 per cent have a salary slab of Rs.5200-20200 plus grade pay Rs.2400, and the rest 25per cent have a monthly income of Rs.5200-20200 plus grade pay Rs.2800.

5.4 Police Personnel's Perception about Causes for Occupational Stress

The police force faces demands and risks in the field of combat, over the course of their daily working lives. To cope with these risks, such as violent offenders and a hostile environment, police organizations have evolved into tightly organized hierarchies of authoritarian leadership. Police bureaucracies pride themselves upon loyalty to organizational rules and authority; much like a military organization obeys a strict chain of command when it is engaged in decision-making. The climate of the organization is perceived either favorably or unfavorably and has its impact upon organizational effectiveness, stress and other variables. Various factors like organizational context (goals and objectives), organizational structure (size, degree of centralization), organizational processes (leadership style, decision making etc.), nature of work (shifts etc.) and physical environment (employee safety, rewards etc.) constitute the dimensions of the climate.

Police personnel in general and Tamilnadu in particular are exposed to various duty-related stressors that are significantly different, in terms of quality and quantity to those experienced by the general population. Stress and burnout are usually considered to be by products of police work. In and of itself, the nature of police work is regarded to be highly stressful and can even be described as hazardous. The job profile of a police officer includes witnessing a fellow officer killed in the line of duty, killing someone in the line of duty, recovering bodies from motor vehicle accidents, witnessing domestic or community violence, and responding to cases involving child battery, stress also accrue due to job demand and nature. Based on this concept, this section of the study draws attentions on police personnel's perception towards their occupational stress.

TABLE: 5.12

POLICE PERSONNEL'S PERCEPTION ABOUT CAUSES FOR STRESS (JOB DEMAND)

Variables	High	Moderate	Low	Sum	Mean	Rank
Job demand						
Assignment of disagreeable duties	134(22.33)	287(47.83)	179(29.83)	1155	1.93	18
Assignment of new or unfamiliar duties	119(19.83)	325(54.17)	156(26.00)	1163	1.94	17
Performing tasks not in job description	204(34.00)	273(45.50)	123(20.50)	1281	2.14	10
Periods of inactivity	152(25.33)	323(53.83)	125(20.83)	1227	2.05	15
Assignment of increased responsibility	172(28.67)	252(42.00)	176(29.33)	1196	1.99	16
Competition for advancement	184(30.67)	295(49.17)	121(20.17)	1263	2.11	12
Frequent changes from boring to demanding activities	163(27.17)	308(51.33)	129(21.50)	1234	2.06	14
Shift work	255(42.50)	228(38.00)	117(19.50)	1338	2.23	6
Delivering a death message or bad news to someone	248(41.33)	235(39.17)	117(19.50)	1331	2.22	7
Attending to incidences of domestic violence	170(28.33)	319(53.17)	111(18.50)	1259	2.10	13
Reorganization and transformation within the organization	204(34.00)	281(46.83)	115(19.17)	1289	2.15	9
Killing someone in the line of duty	281(46.83)	233(38.83)	86(14.33)	1395	2.33	2
Handling nob/riot etc	250(41.67)	259(43.17)	91(15.17)	1359	2.27	3
Having to handle a large crowd/mass demonstration	261(43.50)	235(39.17)	104(17.33)	1357	2.26	4
A forced arrest or being physically attacked	200(33.33)	285(47.50)	115(19.17)	1285	2.14	10
Having to go to court	222(37.00)	251(41.83)	127(21.17)	1295	2.16	8
Having to deal with the media	259(43.17)	234(39.00)	107(17.83)	1352	2.25	5
Seeing criminals go free (for example because of lack of evidence, court leniency)	278(46.33)	248(41.33)	74(12.33)	1404	2.34	1

Source: Primary Data

Law enforcement personnel are exposed to high levels of stress in their professional life. Personnel belonging to uniformed services, who are allotted field duties are even more prone to stress and its adverse effects. The table clearly depicts that, out of the total constables of the study, majority of the respondents' have said that they become very tensed, when they see the criminals go free because of lack of evidence, court leniency and it is ranked in first place by them. Secondly, they have a guilty conscious in their mind when they kill someone in the line of the duty. The police constables have stress when they handle the criminals and also feel difficulties at time of handling large crowd/mass demonstration; these subjects are ranked in third and fourth place respectively. Followed by, is the very pressure to deal with the media and also the shift work gives pressure to them; they are ranked in fifth and sixth place respectively. Delivering the death message or bad news to someone in the prison is a hard thing to them and having to go the court is also very strainful activity duty for them, these variables are ranked in seventh and eighth place respectively. Reorganization and transformation within the organization gives stress to the constables, it is ranked in ninth place.

The results clearly reveal that the maximum police personnel have exhibited the job demand stress because of a forced arrest or being physically attackedor periods of inactivity, both the subjects are ranked in tenth place respectively. It is clear that, competition for advancement and attending to incidences of domestic violence were giving stress to the constables, these subjects are ranked in twelfth and thirteenth place respectively. It gives pressure when the work frequently changes from boring to demanding activities, periods of inactivity and these matters are ranked in fourteenth and fifteenth place respectively. The police constables get tensed when their responsibilities are increased, assignment of unfamiliar duties, assignment of disagreeable duties, these variables are ranked in sixteenth seventeenth and eighteenth respectively.

EXHIBIT: 5.1
POLICE PERSONNEL'S PERCEPTION ABOUT CAUSES FOR STRESS
(JOB DEMAND)

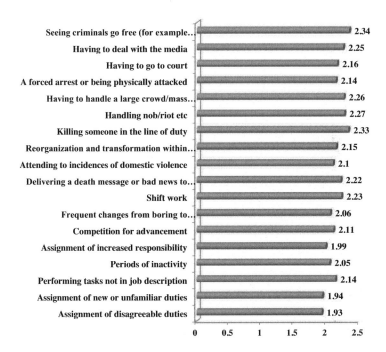

TABLE: 5.13
POLICE PERSONNEL'S PERCEPTION ABOUT CAUSES FOR STRESS(LACK OF RESOURCES)

Variables	High	Moderate	Low	Sum	Mean	Rank
Lack of resources						
Lack of opportunity for advancement	256(42.67)	262(43.67)	82(13.67)	1374	2.29	1
Fellow workers not doing their job	166(27.67)	311(51.83)	123(20.50)	1243	2.07	13
Inadequate support by supervisor	165(27.50)	329(54.83)	106(17.67)	1259	2.10	10
Lack of recognition for good work	246(41.00)	266(44.33)	88(14.67)	1358	2.26	4
Inadequate or poor quality equipment	191(31.83)	276(46.00)	133(22.17)	1258	2.10	10
Inadequate salary	190(31.67)	296(49.33)	114(19.00)	1276	2.13	8
Difficulty getting along with supervisor	210(35.00)	273(45.50)	117(19.50)	1293	2.16	6
Insufficient personnel to handle an assignment	184(30.67)	314(52.33)	102(17.00)	1282	2.14	7
Lack of participation in policy-making decisions	245(40.83)	274(45.67)	81(13.50)	1364	2.27	3
Poor or inadequate supervision	159(26.50)	318(53.00)	123(20.50)	1236	2.06	14
Noisy work area	180 (30.00)	298 (49.67)	122 (20.33)	1258	2.10	10
Insufficient personal time (e.g., coffee breaks, lunch)	205 (34.17)	295 (49.17)	100 (16.67)	1305	2.18	5
Poorly motivated co-workers	182(30.33)	305(50.83)	113(18.83)	1269	2.12	9
Staff shortages	258(43.00)	249(41.50)	93(15.50)	1365	2.28	2

Source: Primary Data

From the above table it is clearly inferred that, majority of the police constables get stress, when they do not get the opportunity for career advancement and it is ranked in first place. Staff shortages and lack of participation in policy making decisions give stress to the constables; these subjects are ranked in second and third place respectively. Followed by, it gives pressure, when they lack the recognition for good work and also they get stress when they don't get personal timings in between their duties for e.g., coffee breaks, lunch, they are ranked in fourth and fifth place respectively. The respondents' get tensed because of their supervisors give difficult situation to them and insufficiency personnel to handle an assignment, these factors are ranked in sixth and seventh place respectively.

The results clearly reveal that the maximum police personnel have exhibited that they get stress because of an inadequate salary and poorly motivated co- workers; they are ranked in eighth and ninth place respectively. It is clear that, inadequate support by supervisor, poor quality equipment and noisy work area gives pressure to the constables; each of the subjects is ranked in tenth place. The police constables get tensed because of, the fellow workers not doing their job correctly and inadequate supervisions, these variables are ranked in thirteenth and fourteenth place respectively.

EXHIBIT: 5.2
POLICE PERSONNEL'S PERCEPTION ABOUT CAUSES FOR STRESS
(LACK OF RESOURCES)

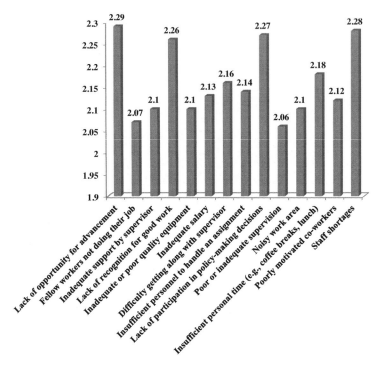

TABLE: 5.14

POLICE PERSONNEL'S PERCEPTION ABOUT CAUSES FOR STRESS (POLICE STRESSES/OCCUPATIONAL STRESS)

Variables	High	Moderate	Low	Sum	Mean	Rank
Police stresses/occupational stress						
Working overtime	184(30.67)	309(51.50)	107 (17.83)	1277	2.13	7
Dealing with crisis situations	231(38.50)	264(44.00)	105(17.50)	1326	2.21	4
Experiencing negative attitudes toward the organization	203(33.83)	297(49.50)	100(16.67)	1303	2.17	6
Making critical on-the-spot decisions	175(29.17)	309(51.50)	116(19.33)	1259	2.10	9
Personal insult from customer/Senior/colleague	253(42.17)	253 (42.17)	94(15.67)	1359	2.27	2
Frequent interruptions	147(24.50)	264(44.00)	189(31.50)	1158	1.93	12
Excessive paperwork	149(24.83)	322(53.67)	129(21.50)	1220	2.03	11
Meeting deadlines	180(30.00)	299(49.83)	121(20.17)	1259	2.10	9
Covering work for another employee	180(30.00)	315(52.50)	105(17.50)	1275	2.13	7
Conflicts with other departments	230(38.33)	249(41.50)	121(20.17)	1309	2.18	5
Too much supervision Stressful Job-Related Events	247(41.17)	253(42.17)	100(16.67)	1347	2.25	3
A fellow officer killed in the line of duty	269(44.83)	240(40.00)	91(15.17)	1378	2.30	1

Source: Primary Data

The above table clearly reveals that, the maximum police personnel have exhibited their occupational stress because of the fellow officer were killed in the line of duty and it gives pressure when they get personal insult from anyone in their service, these factors are ranked in first and second place respectively. Too much of supervisions for stressful job related events and dealing with the crisis situations give strain to the respondents', they are ranked in third, fourth respectively. Followed by, the respondents' have said that they get stress because of the clashes with other departments; experience of the negative attitudes towards the organization gives pressure to them and they are ranked in fifth, sixth place respectively.

It has been clearly inferred that, the police constables get tensed because of the overtime work and covering another employees' work also gives pressure to them, both are ranked in seventh place. Deadline meetings and spot decisions in the critical situations gives pressure to them, both the variables are ranked in ninth the place. It is clear that, excessive paperwork and frequent interruptions give pressure to the police constables; they are ranked in the eleventh and twelfth place respectively.

EXHIBIT: 5.3
POLICE PERSONNEL'S PERCEPTION ABOUT CAUSES FOR STRESS
(POLICE STRESSES/OCCUPATIONAL STRESS)

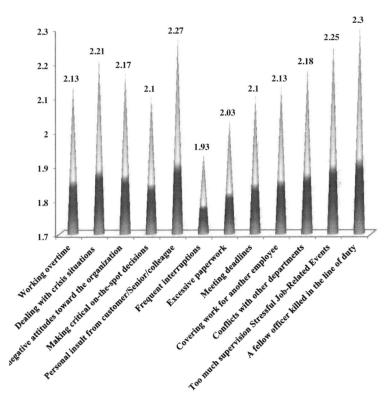

5.5 Occurrence of stress/burnout

Stress is a perceptual phenomenon arising from a comparison between the demand on the person and his ability to cope. More than any other service or job, the police service has the highest level of stress and maximum consequences because of the nature and demand of the service. Of all occupations police work could be considered highly stressful. Burnout thrives in the workplace and is most likely to occur when there has been a mismatch between the nature of the job and the nature of the person doing the job. Different studies that have been conducted reveal that occupational stress that consists of job demands and a lack of resources lead to burnout. Sources of stress that lead to burnout may originate within the organization, although individual characteristics may play a role in an individual's inability to cope with high stress work environments. In this section of the study researcher draws an analytical discussion on the frequency of stress occurrence and the sample police personnel's perception towards it.

128

TABLE: 5.15

POLICE PERSONNEL'S PERCEPTION ON FREQUENCY OF STRESSOCCURRENCE (JOB DEMAND)

Variables	Very frequently	Frequently	Rarely	Sum	Mean	Rank
Job demand						
Assignment of disagreeable duties	180(30.00)	259(43.17)	161(26.83)	1219	2.03	2
Assignment of new or unfamiliar duties	160(26.67)	227(37.83)	213(35.50)	1147	1.91	14
Performing tasks not in job description	160(26.67)	230(38.33)	210(35.00)	1150	1.92	13
Periods of inactivity	163(27.17)	220(36.67)	217(36.17)	1146	1.91	14
Assignment of increased responsibility	184(30.67)	231(38.50)	185(30.83)	1199	2.00	4
Competition for advancement	165(27.50)	208(34.67)	227(37.83)	1138	1.90	16
Frequent changes from boring to demanding activities	175(29.17)	214(35.67)	211(35.17)	1164	1.94	10
Shift work	186(31.00)	215(35.83)	199(33.17)	1187	1.98	6
Delivering a death message or bad news to someone	177(29.50)	221(36.83)	202(33.67)	1175	1.96	7
Attending to incidences of domestic violence	156(26.00)	227(37.83)	217(36.17)	1139	1.90	16
Reorganization and transformation within the organization	153(25.50)	253(42.17)	194(32.33)	1159	1.93	11
Killing someone in the line of duty	202(33.67)	191(31.83)	207(34.50)	1195	1.99	5
Handling nob/riot etc	257(42.83)	175(29.17)	168(28.00)	1289	2.15	1
Having to handle a large crowd/mass demonstration	191(31.83)	190(31.67)	219(36.50)	1172	1.95	8
A forced arrest or being physically attacked	186(31.00)	183(30.50)	231(38.50)	1155	1.93	11
Having to go to court	179(29.83)	210(35.00)	211(35.17)	1168	1.95	8
Having to deal with the media	174(29.00)	194(32.33)	232(38.67)	1142	1.90	16
Seeing criminals go free (for example because of lack of evidence, court leniency)	201(33.50)	214(35.67)	185(30.83)	1216	2.03	2

Source: Primary Data

The above table clearly depicts that, during past six months the police officers have very frequently fell that stress levels were more when they face the problem of handling the criminals, as it gives too much of pressure to them and it is ranked in first place. The respondents become much tensed frequently, when they seeing the criminals go free because of lack of evidence, court leniency and assignment of disagreeable duties, they ranked both of these variables in second place. Followed by, the police constables often get tensed when they have the assignment of increased responsibility and they not often have guilty conscious in their mind when they kill someone in the line of the duty, it is ranked in fourth and fifth place respectively. Shifting the work timings and delivering the death message or bad news to someone in the prison is a hard thing to them, these problems are the common problems for them and they ranked these subjects are ranked in sixth, seventh place respectively.

The police constables have stress when they handle the large crowd/mass demonstration and having to go the court is also very strainful for them; both the factors are ranked in eighth place and they face these problems rarely. It gives pressure when the work frequently changes from boring to demanding activities, this problem is the normal one for them and it is ranked in tenth place. The results clearly reveal that, police personnel have exhibited that they rarely get job demand stress because of a forced arrest or being physically attacked, reorganization and transformation within the organization gives recurrent stress to the constables, both are ranked in eleventh place.

Performing their tasks not in job description gives pressure to the police officers, they face this problem frequently and it is ranked in thirteenth place. Followed by, the periods of inactivity and assignment of unfamiliar duties gives pressure often to them and they both are ranked in fourteenth place. It is clear that, competition for advancement is not often problem for them and attending to incidences of domestic violence is a frequent problem for them and having to deal with media were give stress to the constables very rarely, each of this subject is ranked as sixteenth place.

EXHIBIT: 5.4
POLICE PERSONNEL'S PERCEPTION ON FREQUENCY OF
STRESSOCCURRENCE (JOB DEMAND)

POLICE PERSONNEL'S PERCEPTION ON FREQUENCY OF STRESSOCCURRENCE (LACK OF RESOURCES)

Variables	Very frequently	Frequently	Rarely	Sum	Mean	Rank
Lack of resources						
Lack of opportunity for advancement	163(27.17)	208(34.67)	229(38.17)	1134	1.89	11
Fellow workers not doing their job	161(26.83)	210(35.00)	229(38.17)	1132	1.89	11
Inadequate support by supervisor	163(27.17)	224(37.33)	213(35.50)	1150	1.92	6
Lack of recognition for good work	188(31.33)	192(32.00)	220(36.67)	1168	1.95	5
Inadequate or poor quality equipment	161(26.83)	206(34.33)	233(38.83)	1128	1.88	13
Inadequate salary	181(30.17)	217(36.17)	202(33.67)	1179	1.97	3
Difficulty in getting along with supervisor	150(25.00)	238(39.67)	212(35.33)	1138	1.90	8
Insufficient personnel to handle an assignment	180(30.00)	186(31.00)	234(39.00)	1146	1.91	7
Lack of participation in policy-making decisions	190(31.67)	207(34.50)	203(33.83)	1187	1.98	2
Poor or inadequate supervision	166(27.67)	209(34.83)	225(37.50)	1141	1.90	8
Noisy work area	169(28.17)	202(33.67)	229(38.17)	1140	1.90	8
Insufficient personal time (e.g., coffee breaks, lunch)	199(33.17)	186(31.00)	215(35.83)	1184	1.97	3
Poorly motivated co-workers	145(24.17)	206(34.33)	249(41.50)	1096	1.83	14
Staff shortages	214(35.67)	204(34.00)	182(30.33)	1232	2.05	1

Source: Primary Data

From the above table it is clearly inferred that, during past 6 months the police constables very frequently face the problem of staff shortages and lack of participation in policy making decisions is a frequent problem for them, they ranked these subjects in first and second place respectively. Followed by, rarely does it give pressure, when they don't get personal timings in between their duties for e.g., coffee breaks, lunch and inadequate salary; both are ranked in third place. The police constables not often get depressed when they don't get recognition for good work and inadequate support by supervisor is a frequent problem for them, these variables are ranked in fifth, sixth place respectively. The respondents' rarely get tensed because of the insufficiency personnel to handle an assignment; it is ranked in seventh pace.

The respondents' usually get difficulties, when they try to get along with their supervisors and rarely the poor supervision and noisy work area gives pressure to them, each is ranked in eighth place. Followed by, the police constables get tensed because of, the fellow workers not doing their job correctly, lack of opportunity for advancement, very rarely they face these problems and both are ranked in eleventh place. The results clearly reveal that the maximum police personnel have exhibited that they get stress because of the inadequate quality equipment and poorly motivated co- workers, they rarely face this type of problems and they ranked these variables in thirteenth, fourteenth place respectively.

EXHIBIT: 5.5
POLICE PERSONNEL'S PERCEPTION ON FREQUENCY OF
STRESSOCCURRENCE (LACK OF RESOURCES)

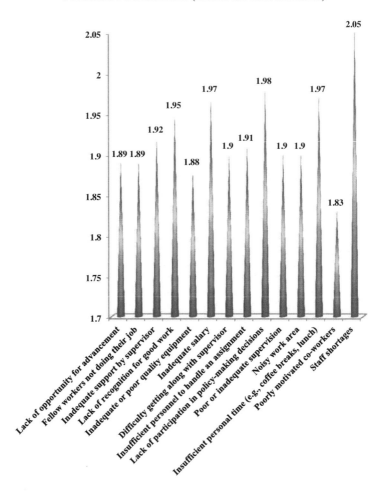

TABLE: 5.17
POLICE PERSONNEL'S PERCEPTION ON FREQUENCY OF STRESSOCCURRENCE (POLICE STRESS/OCCUPATIONAL STRESS)

Variables	Very frequently	Frequently	Rarely	Sum	Mean	Rank
Police stresses/occupational stress						
Working overtime	151(25.17)	236(39.33)	213(35.50)	1138	1.90	9
Dealing with crisis situations	169(28.17)	205(34.17)	226(37.67)	1143	1.91	7
Experiencing negative attitudes toward the organization	168(28.00)	218(36.33)	214(35.67)	1154	1.92	6
Making critical on-the-spot decisions	162(27.00)	220(36.67)	218(36.33)	1144	1.91	7
Personal insult from customer/consumer/colleague	179(29.83)	238(39.67)	183(30.50)	1196	1.99	3
Frequent interruptions	153(25.50)	218(36.33)	229(38.17)	1124	1.87	12
Excessive paperwork	190(31.67)	193(32.17)	217(36.17)	1173	1.96	4
Meeting deadlines	158(26.33)	217(36.17)	225(37.50)	1133	1.89	10
Covering work for another employee	167(27.83)	226(37.67)	207(34.50)	1160	1.93	5
Conflicts with other departments	167(27.83)	201(33.50)	232(38.67)	1135	1.89	10
Too much supervision Stressful Job-Related Events	208(34.67)	218(36.33)	174(29.00)	1234	2.06	2
A fellow officer killed in the line of duty	242(40.33)	186(31.00)	172(28.67)	1270	2.12	1

Source: Primary Data

The above table clearly reveals that, during past six months the maximum police personnel have exhibited their occupational stress because of their fellow officers were killed in the line of duty, very often they face this problem and it is ranked in first place. Often they get tensed when they have too much of supervisions for stressful job related events and also it gives pressure when they get personal insult from anyone in their service, these factors are ranked in second and third place respectively. Excessive paper works gives pressure rarely to them and it is ranked in fourth place. Covering the works for another employee and experience of the negative attitudes towards the organization gives pressure regularly to them; they ranked these stresses in fifth and sixth place respectively.

It has been clearly inferred that, dealing with crisis situations and taking spot decisions is very critical for them, and they frequently face these types of problems and both are ranked in seventh place. The police constables get tensed because of the overtime work, this is often a problem for them and it is ranked in ninth place. Deadline meetings are a recurrent problem for them and conflicts and with other departments rarely give pressure to the police constables both are ranked in tenth place. Frequent interruptions area unusual problem for the police constables and it is ranked in twelfth place.

EXHIBIT: 5.6
POLICE PERSONNEL'S PERCEPTION ON FREQUENCY OF
STRESSOCCURRENCE(POLICE STRESSES/OCCUPATIONAL STRESS)

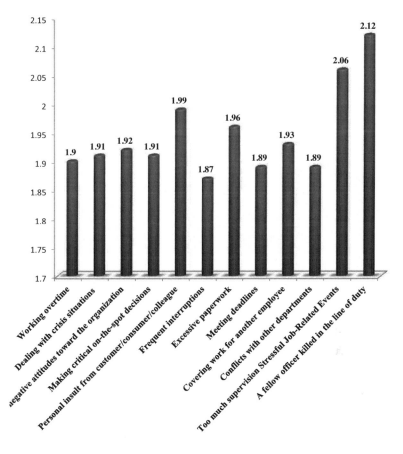

5.6Outcome of Stress

High levels of stress can lead to serious physiological (headaches, stomachaches, backaches, ulcers, heart attacks) and psychological (anxiety, depression, flashbacks, and panic attacks) symptoms. Stress among police officers has also been connected to police misconduct and can also have a negative effect on the law enforcement organization due to lawsuits resulting from officers' performance. Police stress has serious ramifications for the organization, the family and peers. The following table depicts the primary outcome of stress.

TABLE: 5.18

POLICE PERSONNEL'S PERCEPTION ON OUTCOME OF STRESS /SYMPTOMS

Variables	Not at all	Sometimes	Never	Sum	Mean	Rank
Loss of sexual interest or pleasure	347(57.83)	142(23.67)	111(18.50)	1436	2.39	1
Thoughts of ending your life	204(34.00)	271(45.17)	125(20.83)	1279	2.13	3
Poor appetite	188(31.33)	254(42.33)	158(26.33)	1230	2.05	8
Crying easily	239(39.83)	227(37.83)	134(22.33)	1305	2.18	2
A feeling of being trapped or caught	157(26.17)	288(48.00)	155(25.83)	1202	2.00	13
Blaming yourself for things	186(31.00)	251(41.83)	163(27.17)	1223	2.04	11
Feeling lonely	175(29.17)	288(48.00)	137(22.83)	1238	2.06	6
Feeling lovable	162(27.00)	346(57.67)	92(15.33)	1270	2.12	4
Feeling blue	181(30.17)	238(39.67)	181(30.17)	1200	2.00	13
Worrying or stewing about things	191(31.83)	245(40.83)	164(27.33)	1227	2.05	8
Feelings no interest in things	168(28.00)	291(48.50)	141(23.50)	1227	2.05	8
Feeling hopeless about the future	191(31.83)	233(38.83)	176(29.33)	1215	2.03	12
Disbelief in Others	202(33.67)	242(40.33)	156(26.00)	1246	2.08	5
Quarreling with family members	166(27.67)	305(50.83)	129(21.50)	1237	2.06	6
Feeling of insecurity	184(30.67)	223(37.17)	193(32.17)	1191	1.99	15

Source: Primary Data

Policing features among the top three occupations most commonly associated with workplace stress by both occupational physicians and psychiatrists. In this empirical study it has been observed that primary disorder of stress and its symptoms are loss of sexual interest (79.67 per cent), feel of easy crying (72.67 per cent) and thought of committing suicide (71 per cent). Followed by it has also observed that police personnel longing for being treated as lovable by others (70.67 per cent), growing a tendency of distrust (69.33 per cent) and quarreling with family members or feeling lonely (68.67 per cent). Similarly poor appetite, worrying or stewing about things and feelings, no interest in things are found among 68.33 per cent police personnel's surveyed in Thoothukudi district. Occupational stress related harsh working environment leads to psychological symptoms or emotional signs like blaming one-self responsible for any misshapes happened (68 per cent), feel of hopeless about the future (67.67 per cent), a feel of being trapped or caught(66.67 per cent),a feel of depression (66.67 per cent) and insecurity (66.33 per cent).

EXHIBIT: 5.7
POLICE PERSONNEL'S PERCEPTION ON
OUTCOME OF STRESS /SYMPTOMS

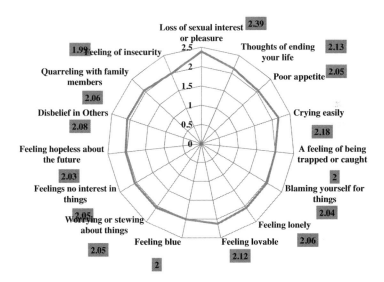

5.7 Coping strategies

Lazarus and Folkman (1984) define coping as "constantly changing cognitive and behavioural efforts to manage specific external and/or internal demands that are appraised as taxing or exceeding the resources of the person" (p. 141). In this definition, coping becomes limited to conditions of psychological stress in which the individual attempts to minimize the stressful conditions in his/her management styles.

Coping can be grouped into two categories, i.e. problem focused and emotion-focused (Amirkhan, 1994; Callan, 1993; Folkman& Lazarus, 1984). Problem-focused types of coping are directed at the problem and in looking for ways to manage and solve the problem. Emotion-focused coping involves reducing the effects of stressful feelings caused by unpleasant experiences through relaxation, the use of substances (alcohol and drugs), social activities and/or defence mechanisms, including avoidance. Based on the theoretical discussion made stress coping styles among police personnel in Tamilnadu is grouped into two sections emotional and problem focused. There are three sub-headings in problem-focused styles: positive reinterpretation and growth, acceptance of fact and focusing on and ventilating. Emotions-focused coping style included five sub-heads: seeking social support for emotional reasons, denial behaviour, turning religious, behavioural disagreement and mental disagreement. The following table depicts the emotional and problem focused coping styles adopted by the sample police personnel.

TABLE: 5.19
POLICE PERSONNEL'S PERCEPTION ON
PROBLEM-FOCUSED STRESS COPING STRATEGIES

Variables	Usually don't do this at all	Usually do this a little bit	Usually do this a medium amount	Usually do this a lot	Sum	Mean	Rank
Positive Reinterpretation and Growth							
I force myself to wait for the right time to do something	64(10.67)	160(26.67)	191(31.83)	185(30.83)	1136	1.89	6
I put aside other activities in order to concentrate on this	90(15.00)	170(28.33)	159(26.50)	181(30.17)	1110	1.85	11
I think about how I might best handle the problem	146(24.33)	191(31.83)	179(29.83)	84(14.00)	1116	1.86	10
I admit to myself that I can't deal with it, and quit instead of trying	238(39.67)	143(23.83)	135(22.50)	84(14.00)	1354	2.26	3
I try to see it on a different light to make it seem more positive	208(34.67)	165(27.50)	143(23.83)	84(14.00)	1408	2.35	2
I try hard to prevent other things from interfering with my efforts at dealing with this	71(11.83)	208(34.67)	200(33.33)	121(20.17)	1129	1.88	8
I do what has to be done one step at a time	91(15.17)	171(28.50)	171(28.50)	167(27.83)	1109	1.85	11
I give up the attempt to get what I want	79(13.17)	249(41.50)	174(29.00)	98(16.33)	1449	2.42	1
I try to come up with the strategy what to do	71(11.83)	165(27.50)	204(34.00)	160(26.67)	1129	1.88	8
I focus on dealing with the problems and it necessary let other things slide a little	52(8.67)	174(29.00)	189(31.50)	185(30.83)	1148	1.91	4
I concentrate on efforts on doing something about it	68(11.33)	174(29.00)	192(32.00)	166(27.67)	1132	1.89	6
I just give up trying to reach my goal	62(10.33)	182(30.33)	160(26.67)	196(32.67)	1138	1.9	5
Acceptance of Fact							
I try to grow as a person as a result of the experience	81(13.50)	188(31.33)	168(28.00)	163(27.17)	1200	2	4
I get used to the idea that it happened	84(14.00)	200(33.33)	205(34.17)	111(18.50)	1116	1.86	7

I say to myself this is't real	91(15.17)	202(33.67)	181(30.17)	126(21.00)	1311	2.19	3
I make sure not to make matters worse by acting too soon	100(16.67)	232(38.67)	166(27.67)	102(17.00)	1432	2.39	1
I make a plan of action	104(17.33)	208(34.67)	181(30.17)	107(17.83)	1408	2.35	2
I learn to live with it	128(21.33)	182(30.33)	183(30.50)	107(17.83)	1093	1.82	9
I take direct action around the problem	75(12.50)	180(30.00)	194(32.33)	151(25.17)	1125	1.88	6
I accept that this has happened and that can't be changed	84(14.00)	156(26.00)	183(30.50)	177(29.50)	1116	1.86	7
I accept the reality of the fact that it/had/ happened	65(10.83)	154(25.67)	191(31.83)	190(31.67)	1135	1.89	5
Focusing on and ventilating emotions							
I sleep more than usual	95(15.83)	198(33.00)	167(27.83)	140(23.33)	1303	2.17	4
I let my feelings out	106(17.67)	198(33.00)	178(29.67)	118(19.67)	1398	2.33	1
I turn to work or other substitute activities to take my mind	143(23.83)	179(29.83)	185(30.83)	93(15.50)	1107	1.85	7
I took for something good that is happening	126(21.00)	200(33.33)	157(26.17)	117(19.50)	1400	2.33	1
I talk to someone to find out more about the situation	87(14.50)	180(30.00)	194(32.33)	139(23.17)	1113	1.86	6
I learn shooting from experience	89(14.83)	208(34.67)	177(29.50)	126(21.00)	1319	2.2	3
I think hard about what step to take	73(12.17)	185(30.83)	211(35.17)	131(21.83)	1127	1.88	5

Source: Primary Data

The table also depicts that, the positive reinterpretation and growth of the police officers. Majority of the respondents' have said that they try to get what they want and face their problems by seeing it on a different manner to make it seem more positive, it is ranked in first, second place respectively. The police officers have said that they admit themselves that they can't deal with it and also they quit trying to solve, it is ranked in third place. The respondents' have tried to focus on dealing with the problems and also they thought that it is necessary to do other things a little side by side; just give up trying to reach their goal and these variables are ranked in fourth, fifth place respectively.

Moreover, the police officers have forced themselves to wait for the right moment for doing something and they concentrate only on their efforts and both the factors are ranked in sixth place. The respondents are trying hard to prevent other things from their efforts and they try to come up with the strategy of what they are going to do in future, both the variables are ranked in eighth place. It is clear that, the sample subjects have sought the best way to handle their problem at the time of their difficulties and it is ranked in tenth place. The respondents try to handle their problem within a step and put aside other activities in order to concentrate only to seek solution to their problems both the subjects are ranked in eleventh place.

It is clear that, the police constables make sure not to make matters worse by taking action too soon and it is ranked in first place. Followed by, the respondents have accepted their situation and try to make a plan of action; it is ranked in second place, sometimes they couldn't believe the position, at that time they itself say it is real to themselves; it is ranked in third place. The respondents' should try to grow as a person as a result of the experience and also they accept the reality of the fact that it happened, these factors are ranked in fourth and fifth place respectively. The respondents' have taken direct action around their problem; it is ranked in sixth place. Usually the constables' used to get the idea of the recent position of the problem and they accepted that this has happened that we can't change; both the subjects are ranked in seventh place. The respondents' have said that they learn to withstand the problem; it is ranked in ninth place.

From the above table it has been clearly inferred that, the respondents' have thought about some good things that make them happy, they let their feelings out of their mind, both the subjects are ranked in first place. The respondents have learned shooting from experience, they slept more than usual in their problematic situation, these subjects are ranked in third and fourth place respectively. The sample subjects think deeply about what step to take in future for the problem and it is ranked in fifth place. The police constables have talked to someone to find out more about the situation, they keep away their mind from stress by focusing on other substitute activities and it is ranked in sixth and seventh place respectively.

EXHIBIT: 5.8
POLICE PERSONNEL'S PERCEPTION ON PROBLEM-FOCUSED STRESS COPING STRATEGIES (POSITIVE REINTERPRETATION AND GROWTH)

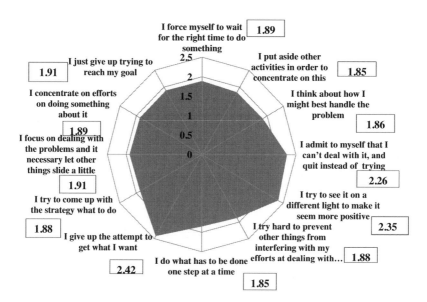

EXHIBIT: 5.9
POLICE PERSONNEL'S PERCEPTION ON PROBLEM-FOCUSED
STRESS COPING STRATEGIES (ACCEPTANCE OF FACT)

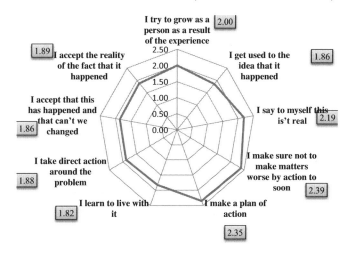

EXHIBIT: 5.10
POLICE PERSONNEL'S PERCEPTION ON PROBLEM-FOCUSED
STRESS COPING STRATEGIES(FOCUSING ON AND VENTILATING
EMOTIONS)

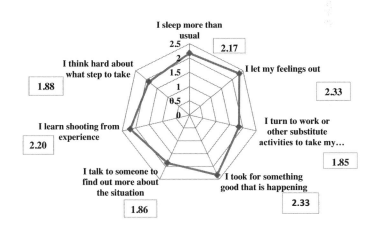

TABLE: 5.20
POLICE PERSONNEL'S PERCEPTION ON
EMOTION-FOCUSED STRESS COPING STRATEGIES

Variables	Usually don't do this at all	Usually do this a little bit	Usually do this a medium amount	Usually do this a lot	Sum	Mean	Rank
Seeking Social Support for Emotional Reasons							
I ask people who have had similar experience what they did	97(16.17)	271(45.17)	138(23.00)	94(15.67)	1471	2.45	1
I talk to someone but how I feel	95(15.83)	225(37.50)	206(34.33)	74(12.33)	1256	2.09	3
I try to get emotional support from friends or relatives	99(16.50)	185(30.83)	188(31.33)	128(21.33)	1101	1.84	8
I try to get advice some- one about what do to	70(11.67)	152(25.33)	198(33.00)	180(30.00)	1130	1.88	7
I get sympathy and understanding from someone	116(19.33)	174(29.00)	191(31.83)	119(19.83)	1200	2	4
I talk to someone who could do some think. About the problem	55(9.17)	158(26.33)	184(30.67)	203(33.83)	1145	1.91	6
I reduce the amount of effort I putting to solving the problem	61(10.17)	154(25.67)	202(33.67)	183(30.50)	1341	2.24	2
I discuss my feelings someone	80(13.33)	174(29.00)	194(32.33)	152(25.33)	1200	2	4
Denial behaviour							
I refuse to believe it has happened	65(10.83)	211(35.17)	176(29.33)	148(24.67)	1135	1.89	2
I take additional action to try to get rid of the problem	66(11.00)	201(33.50)	187(31.17)	146(24.33)	1134	1.89	2
I hold of doing anything about it until the situation permits	55(9.17)	173(28.83)	210(35.00)	162(27.00)	1145	1.91	1
Turing Religious							
I put in my trust in god	77(12.83)	192(32.00)	200(33.33)	131(21.83)	1133	1.89	3
I pray more than usual	65(10.83)	194(32.33)	214(35.67)	127(21.17)	1135	1.89	3
I try to find comfort in my religion	85(14.17)	169(28.17)	199(33.17)	147(24.50)	1314	2.19	2
I seek god's help	61(10.17)	224(37.33)	167(27.83)	148(24.67)	1363	2.27	1
Behavioral Disengagement							
I upset and let my emotion out	82(13.67)	209(34.83)	186(31.00)	123(20.50)	963	1.61	5
I restrain myself form doing anything do quickly	83(13.83)	221(36.83)	194(32.33)	102(17.00)	1421	2.37	1
I go to movies or watch TV to think it	83(13.83)	210(35.00)	197(32.83)	110(18.33)	1117	1.86	4
I act as though it hasn't even happened	78(13.00)	165(27.50)	201(33.50)	156(26.00)	1122	1.87	3
I get upset and am really aware of it	64(10.67)	155(25.83)	218(36.33)	163(27.17)	1354	2.26	2
Mental Disengagement							
I drink alcohol or drink drugs, in order to think about it less	87(14.50)	179(29.83)	164(27.33)	170(28.33)	1113	1.86	4
I pretended that it has not really happened	75(12.50)	154(25.67)	186(31.00)	185(30.83)	1125	1.88	2

I feel a lot of emotional distress and I find myself expressing those feeling a lot	72(12.00)	188(31.33)	176(29.33)	164(27.33)	1128	1.88	2
I keep myself from getting districted by other thought or activates	89(14.83)	186(31.00)	194(32.33)	131(21.83)	1111	1.85	5
I daydream about things other than this	55(9.17)	163(27.17)	198(33.00)	184(30.67)	1145	1.91	1

Source: Primary Data

The above table depicts that, the constables handle their situation of problems by asking the people who have had similar experience, because they believe that the experienced persons give some suggestions for their problems and it is ranked in first place. Followed by, the constables are tried to reduce the amount of effort and they start to seek solution for their problems, this subject is ranked in second place. The respondents' have said that they get little relax in their mind, after talk to someone about what they feel and they ranked it in third place. In the time of difficult situation, the police constables first get sympathy but then they understand from someone in their line and they discuss their problems with someone, both the variables are ranked in fourth place.

Followed by, the respondents' talk about their problems to the one who could do something for them and also they try to get advice from someone about what to do in the time of their problem these variables are ranked in sixth, seventh place respectively. The constables tried to get emotional support from friends or relatives and it is ranked in eighth place.

The above table clearly depicts that, majority of the respondents have said that they cope with their stress by hold nothing until the situation permits and it is ranked in first place. Moreover, they refuse to believe it has happened, they take additional action to try to get rid of the problem and both the factors are ranked in second place.

The table clearly depicts that, the police constables have turned to seek god's help rather than worrying about their problem and it is ranked in first place. The constables have tried to get comfort in their religion when they are in more pressure and it ranked as second. Moreover, the respondents' have put their trusts in god when they are in helpless, they spent more time with prayer than usual and both are ranked in third place.

The police constables have restrained themselves from doing something quickly, get upset and they are really aware of it each of the subject is ranked in first, second place respectively. Followed by, the respondents act as though it hasn't even happened and it is ranked in third place. The respondents have gone to movies or watch television to think about that problem, they get upset and let allow them to come out of their emotions, these factors are ranked in fourth, fifth place respectively.

The respondents' could handle their situation by, having day dreams other than this problem and it is ranked in first place. Moreover, they encourage themselves by pretending that it has not really happened and the constables get feel of emotional distress then they find themselves as a better person to express their feelings a lot, both the variables are ranked in second place. Followed by, the respondents' have drunk alcohol or drugs, in order to think about the problem less, they keep themselves from getting distracted by other thought or activities, these subjects are ranked in fourth and fifth place respectively.

EXHIBIT: 5.11
POLICE PERSONNEL'S PERCEPTION ON EMOTION-FOCUSED
STRESS COPING STRATEGIES (SEEKING SOCIAL SUPPORT FOR
EMOTIONAL REASONS)

EXHIBIT: 5.12
POLICE PERSONNEL'S PERCEPTION ON EMOTION-
FOCUSEDSTRESS COPING STRATEGIES (DENIAL BEHAVIOUR)

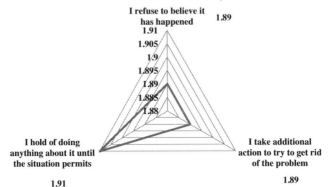

EXHIBIT: 5.13
POLICE PERSONNEL'S PERCEPTION ON EMOTION-FOCUSED
STRESS COPING STRATEGIES (TURING RELIGIOUS)

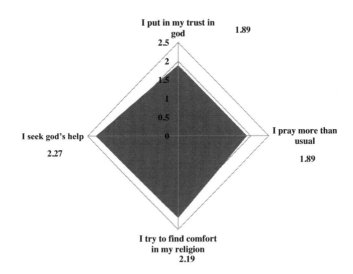

EXHIBIT: 5.14
POLICE PERSONNEL'S PERCEPTION ON EMOTION-FOCUSED
STRESS COPING STRATEGIES (BEHAVIORAL DISENGAGEMENT)

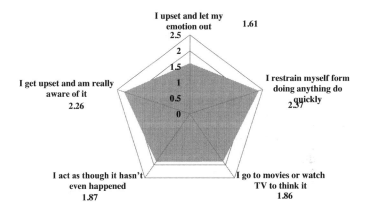

EXHIBIT: 5.15
POLICE PERSONNEL'S PERCEPTION ON EMOTION-FOCUSED
STRESS COPING STRATEGIES (MENTAL DISENGAGEMENT)

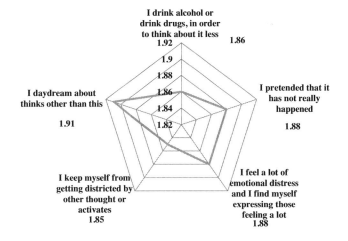

5.8Results of Statistical Analysis and Hypotheses Testing

In recent years India police administrators have stated realizing the impact of stress on police personnel. In the process of literature review and analysis of previous research work it has been understood that Srivatsava et.al (1994) compares organizational role stress and job anxiety among threes group of employee in a private sector organization. Results show that middle level manager faced greater stress and anxiety when compared with top level manager and workers.Alapprendren (2003) indicated that stress appeared to arise when there was a departure from what is considered as the optimum condition that the individual is unable to control. Stress is the result of an imbalance between a demand placed on an organism and the organism's capacity to make the necessary adjustment, or to cope with the demand. Priyanka Sharma (2013) found that there exists significant relationship between perceived organisational climate and stress level of the group of police personnel but insignificant relationship exists between perceived organisational climate and stress for the police personnel at different hierarchical levels. The author found no significant relationship between perceived organisational climate and stress for both the sexes.

From the review of elaborate literature survey it has been inferred that stress among the police personnel varies according to their cadre, working environment and individual emotion & problem solving ability. Based on this literature understanding the researcher framed five hypothetical statements and tested these with appropriate statistical tools.

H1: There exist no association between job profile of the police officers' and their perception about causes for occupational stress.

TABLE: 5.21
RESULT OF ANOVA RELATION BETWEEN JOB PROFILE AND POLICE PERSONNEL'S PERCEPTION ABOUT CAUSES FOR STRESS (JOB DEMAND)

Variables	Age		Educational Qualification		Designation Grade		Years of Experiences		Monthly Income	
	F value	Sig	F value	Sig	F value	Sig	F value	Sig	F value	Sig
Job demand										
Assignment of disagreeable duties	62.38	.000	1.43	.234	917.59	.000	42.39	.000	1024.55	.000
Assignment of new or unfamiliar duties	78.31	.000	1.90	.129	1084.58	.000	45.87	.000	1207.60	.000
Performing tasks not in job description	104.19	.000	3.15	.025	2359.32	.000	71.38	.000	3319.59	.000
Periods of inactivity	85.91	.000	1.71	.163	969.21	.000	55.27	.000	1137.85	.000
Assignment of increased responsibility	78.03	.000	1.20	.310	702.93	.000	53.09	.000	829.31	.000
Competition for advancement	98.91	.000	2.57	.054	1598.02	.000	68.12	.000	2038.42	.000
Frequent changes from boring to demanding activities	81.96	.000	1.84	.138	1238.57	.000	56.64	.000	1497.35	.000
Shift work	126.31	.000	1.94	.122	1024.73	.000	68.71	.000	1181.22	.000
Delivering a death message or bad news to someone	121.03	.000	1.73	.159	1080.65	.000	70.30	.000	1257.74	.000
Attending to incidences of domestic violence	96.96	.000	2.76	.042	1015.48	.000	67.06	.000	1212.66	.000
Reorganization and transformation within the organization	106.56	.000	3.77	.011	1978.74	.000	75.25	.000	2668.12	.000
Killing someone in the line of duty	117.77	.000	1.54	.202	621.35	.000	62.42	.000	692.56	.000
Handling	117.35	.000	1.95	.120	767.55	.000	67.09	.000	878.53	.000
Having to handle a large crowd/mass demonstration	141.79	.000	2.19	.088	828.30	.000	73.84	.000	940.96	.000
A forced arrest or being physically attacked	104.08	.000	3.65	.013	2196.62	.000	76.69	.000	3071.68	.000
Having to go to court	114.03	.000	1.61	.187	1753.51	.000	67.78	.000	2222.83	.000
Having to deal with the media	140.20	.000	2.25	.081	870.32	.000	73.70	.000	992.03	.000
Seeing criminals go free (for example because of lack of evidence, court leniency)	119.13	.000	0.50	.681	561.09	.000	63.57	.000	627.02	.000

Level of Significance: 5 per cent

RESULT OF ANOVA RELATION BETWEEN JOB PROFILE AND POLICE PERSONNEL'S PERCEPTION ABOUT CAUSES FOR STRESS (LACK OF RESOURCES)

Variables	Age		Educational Qualification		Designation Grade		Years of Experiences		Monthly Income	
	F value	Sig	F value	Sig	F value	Sig	F value	Sig	F value	Sig
Lack of resources										
Lack of opportunity for advancement	117.49	.000	1.22	.302	674.02	.000	59.29	.000	766.01	.000
Fellow workers not doing their job	90.02	.000	1.86	.136	1159.98	.000	59.72	.000	1396.23	.000
Inadequate support by supervisor	99.81	.000	2.52	.057	868.06	.000	68.81	.000	1021.56	.000
Lack of recognition for good work	111.18	.000	1.55	.201	767.76	.000	63.31	.000	882.40	.000
Inadequate or poor quality equipment	89.43	.000	2.85	.037	2585.10	.000	64.61	.000	3717.01	.000
Inadequate salary	100.76	.000	3.39	.018	1617.67	.000	74.13	.000	2085.40	.000
Difficulty getting along with supervisor	109.64	.000	2.55	.055	1796.52	.000	75.26	.000	2341.76	.000
Insufficient personnel to handle an assignment	102.92	.000	3.30	.020	1167.36	.000	77.90	.000	1433.46	.000
Lack of participation in policy-making decisions	112.29	.000	1.09	.354	724.57	.000	61.88	.000	833.25	.000
Poor or inadequate supervision	88.96	.000	1.67	.172	1035.62	.000	59.16	.000	1227.62	.000
Noisy work area	99.55	.000	2.41	.066	1489.66	.000	65.63	.000	1871.38	.000
Insufficient personal time (e.g., coffee breaks, lunch)	108.86	.000	4.43	.004	1509.41	.000	77.05	.000	1939.27	.000
Poorly motivated co-workers	99.636	.000	3.14	.025	1320.80	.000	71.37	.000	1637.83	.000
Staff shortages	127.63	.000	2.09	.101	742.82	.000	67.42	.000	843.52	.000

Level of Significance: 5 per cent

TABLE: 5.23
RESULT OF ANOVARELATION BETWEEN JOB PROFILE AND POLICE PERSONNEL'S PERCEPTION ABOUT CAUSES FOR STRESS (POLICE STRESS/OCCUPATIONAL STRESS)

Variables	Age		Educational Qualification		Designation Grade		Years of Experiences		Monthly Income	
	F value	Sig	F value	Sig	F value	Sig	F value	Sig	F value	Sig
Police stresses/occupational stress										
Working overtime	106.27	.000	3.25	.022	1253.81	.000	75.81	.000	1550.09	.000
Dealing with crisis situations	131.97	.000	2.10	.099	1076.68	.000	81.36	.000	1276.75	.000
Experiencing negative attitudes toward the organization	106.88	.000	4.29	.005	1575.95	.000	78.30	.000	2047.89	.000
Making critical on-the-spot decisions	96.49	.000	2.66	.048	1205.80	.000	67.21	.000	1468.88	.000
Personal insult from customer/consumer/colleague	125.92	.000	2.20	.087	775.70	.000	68.76	.000	885.54	.000
Frequent interruptions	63.62	.000	1.22	.300	962.28	.000	38.46	.000	1084.79	.000
Excessive paperwork	80.48	.000	1.67	.173	989.49	.000	51.82	.000	1160.73	.000
Meeting deadlines	100.28	.000	2.47	.061	1460.88	.000	66.30	.000	1830.27	.000
Covering work for another employee	109.78	.000	3.32	.020	1120.57	.000	75.18	.000	1363.60	.000
Conflicts with other departments	121.33	.000	1.44	.230	1389.61	.000	73.55	.000	1686.96	.000
Too much supervision Stressful Job-Related Events	124.37	.000	2.28	.078	867.99	.000	74.31	.000	999.86	.000
A fellow officer killed in the line of duty	126.26	.000	2.01	.112	685.55	.000	66.25	.000	770.86	.000

Level of Significance: 5 per cent

The data indicate in the above table shows that probability value of ANOVA at 5 per cent level establishes good relationship between the variables tested. Therefore, the null hypothesis framed stands accepted and it concluded that there exists no association between job profile of the police officers' and their perception about their occupational stress.

H2: There exist no similarities in the police officers' perception about their occupation stress.

Factor analysis technique has been applied to find the underlying dimension (factors) that exists in the 44 variables relating to the perception about occupation.

TABLE: 5.24
KMO AND BARTLETT'S TEST FOR POLICE PERSONNEL'S PERCEPTION ABOUT CAUSES FOR STRESS

Kaiser-Meyer-Olkin Measure of Sampling Adequacy	.974
Bartlett's Test of Sphericity Approx. Chi-Square	99614.901
DF	946
Sig	.000

Level of Significance: 5 per cent

In the present study, Kaiser-Meyer-Oklin (KMO) Measure of Sampling Adequacy (MSA) and Bartlett's test of Sphericity were applied to verify the adequacy or appropriateness of data for factor analysis. In this study, the value of KMO for overall matrix was found to be excellent (0.974) and Bartlett's test of Sphericity was highly significant ($p<0.05$). Bartlett's Sphericity test was effective, as the chi-square value draws significance at five per cent level. The results thus indicated that the sample taken was appropriate to proceed with a factor analysis procedure. Besides the Bartlett's Test of Sphericity and the KMO Measure of sampling Adequacy, Communality values of all variables were also observed. Therefore the hypotheses framed are accepted and it concluded that there exist no similarities in the police officers' perception about their occupation stress.

TABLE: 5.25
CUMULATIVE
FACTORS INFLUENCE OFPOLICE PERSONNEL'S PERCEPTION ABOUT
CAUSES FOR STRESS

Variables	Initial	Extraction
Job demand		
Assignment of disagreeable duties	1.000	.946
Assignment of new or unfamiliar duties	1.000	.919
Performing tasks not in job description	1.000	.955
Periods of inactivity	1.000	.961
Assignment of increased responsibility	1.000	.859
Competition for advancement	1.000	.978
Frequent changes from boring to demanding activities	1.000	.966
Shift work	1.000	.955
Delivering a death message or bad news to someone	1.000	.955
Attending to incidences of domestic violence	1.000	.963
Reorganization and transformation within the organization	1.000	.966
Killing someone in the line of duty	1.000	.938
Handling	1.000	.978
Having to handle a large crowd/mass demonstration	1.000	.967
A forced arrest or being physically attacked	1.000	.969
Having to go to court	1.000	.928
Having to deal with the media	1.000	.966
Seeing criminals go free (for example because of lack of evidence, court leniency)	1.000	.921
Lack of resources		
Lack of opportunity for advancement	1.000	.969
Fellow workers not doing their job	1.000	.971
Inadequate support by supervisor	1.000	.944
Lack of recognition for good work	1.000	.970
Inadequate or poor quality equipment	1.000	.945
Inadequate salary	1.000	.976
Difficulty getting along with supervisor	1.000	.956
Insufficient personnel to handle an assignment	1.000	.962
Lack of participation in policy-making decisions	1.000	.954
Poor or inadequate supervision	1.000	.965
Noisy work area	1.000	.978
Insufficient personal time (e.g., coffee breaks, lunch)	1.000	.956
Poorly motivated co-workers	1.000	.980
Staff shortages	1.000	.980
Police stresses/occupational stress		
Working overtime	1.000	.973
Dealing with crisis situations	1.000	.955
Experiencing negative attitudes toward the organization	1.000	.957
Making critical on-the-spot decisions	1.000	.975
Personal insult from customer/consumer/colleague	1.000	.980
Frequent interruptions	1.000	.936
Excessive paperwork	1.000	.960
Meeting deadlines	1.000	.979
Covering work for another employee	1.000	.966
Conflicts with other departments	1.000	.939
Too much supervision Stressful Job-Related Events	1.000	.973
A fellow officer killed in the line of duty	1.000	.965

In order to provide a more parsimonious interpretation of the results, 44-item scale was then Factor analyzed using the Principal Component method with Varimax rotation.

Factor analysis attempts to identify underlying variables, or factors, that explain the pattern of correlations within a set of observed variables. Factor analysis is often used in data reduction to identify a small number of factors that explain most of the variance observed in a much larger number of manifest variables. In the current study Rotation Factor analysis is performed to measure the perception about occupation of the study of the respondents. The significance of variables is depicted in the following table.

EXHIBIT: 5.16
SCREE PLOT: POLICE PERSONNEL'S PERCEPTION ABOUT CAUSES FOR STRESS

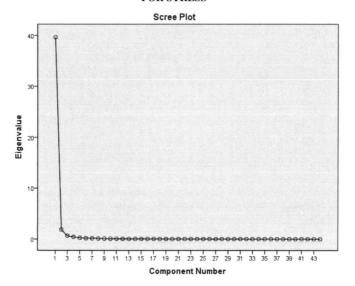

TABLE: 5.26
FACTOR ANALYSIS OF ASSOCIATION OF POLICE PERSONNEL'S
PERCEPTION ABOUT CAUSES FOR STRESS

Variables	Factors		
	Grade II (Junior)	Grade I (Promotion)	Grade III (Head Constable)
Job demand			
X_1-Assignment of disagreeable duties	0.524	-	0.703
X_2-Assignment of new or unfamiliar duties	0.544	-	0.676
X_3-Performing tasks not in job description	0.727	0.581	-
X_4-Periods of inactivity	0.712	-	0.525
X_5-Assignment of increased responsibility	0.704	0.503	-
X_6-Competition for advancement	0.785	0.501	-
X_7-Frequent changes from boring to demanding activities	0.734	-	-
X_8-Shift work	0.505	0.774	-
X_9-Delivering a death message or bad news to someone	0.529	0.763	-
X_{10}-Attending to incidences of domestic violence	0.777	-	-
X_{11}-Reorganization and transformation within the organization	0.737	0.598	-
X_{12}-Killing someone in the line of duty	-	0.829	-
X_{13}-Handling	-	0.834	-
X_{14}-Having to handle a large crowd/mass demonstration	-	0.813	-
X_{15}-A forced arrest or being physically attacked	0.751	0.581	-
X_{16}-Having to go to court	0.631	0.649	-
X_{17}-Having to deal with the media	-	0.804	-
X_{18}-Seeing criminals go free (for example because of lack of evidence, court leniency)	-	0.827	-
Lack of resources			
X_{19}-Lack of opportunity for advancement	-	0.846	-
X_{20}-Fellow workers not doing their job	0.76	-	-
X_{21}-Inadequate support by supervisor	0.758	-	-
X_{22}-Lack of recognition for good work	-	0.826	-
X_{23}-Inadequate or poor quality equipment	0.736	0.519	-
X_{24}-Inadequate salary	0.779	0.54	-
X_{25}-Difficulty getting along with supervisor	0.708	0.62	-
X_{26}-Insufficient personnel to handle an assignment	0.773	0.544	-
X_{27}-Lack of participation in policy-making decisions	-	0.822	-
X_{28}-Poor or inadequate supervision	0.74	-	-
X_{29}-Noisy work area	0.785	-	-
X_{30}-Insufficient personal time (e.g., coffee breaks, lunch)	0.707	0.64	-
X_{31}-Poorly motivated co-workers	0.793	0.51	-
X_{32}-Staff shortages	-	0.841	-

Police stresses/occupational stress			
X_{33}-Working overtime	0.784	0.532	-
X_{34}-Dealing with crisis situations	0.594	0.736	-
X_{35}-Experiencing negative attitudes toward the organization	0.715	0.631	-
X_{36}-Making critical on-the-spot decisions	0.788	-	-
X_{37}-Personal insult from customer/consumer/colleague	-	0.834	-
X_{38}-Frequent interruptions	0.543	-	0.674
X_{39}-Excessive paperwork	0.688	-	0.561
X_{40}-Meeting deadlines	0.787	-	-
X_{41}-Covering work for another employee	0.782	0.522	-
X_{42}-Conflicts with other departments	0.608	0.69	-
X_{43}-Too much supervision Stressful Job-Related Events	0.504	0.807	-
X_{44}-A fellow officer killed in the line of duty	-	0.839	-
Eigen value	**39.645**	**1.856**	**0.651**
% of Variance	**90.102**	**4.218**	**1.48**
Cumulative	**90.102**	**94.32**	**95.8**

Level of Significance: 5 per cent

Three factors were identified as being maximum percentage variance accounted. The variable X_1, X_2, X_3, X_4, X_5, X_6, X_7, X_8, X_9, X_{10}, X_{11}, X_{15}, X_{16}, X_{19}, X_{20}, X_{21}, X_{22}, X_{23}, X_{24}, X_{25}, X_{26}, X_{28}, X_{29}, X_{30}, X_{31}, X_{32}, X_{33}, X_{34}, X_{35}, X_{36}, X_{38}, X_{39}, X_{40}, X_{41}, X_{42} and X_{43} are grouped as factor I and it accounts for 90.102per cent of the total variance. The variable X_3, X_5, X_6, X_8, X_9, X_{11}, X_{12}, X_{13}, X_{14}, X_{15}, X_{16}, X_{17}, X_{18}, X_{19}, X_{22}, X_{23}, X_{24}, X_{25}, X_{26}, X_{27}, X_{30}, X_{31}, X_{32}, X_{33}, X_{34}, X_{35}, X_{37}, X_{41}, X_{42} and X_{44} constitute the factor II and it accounts for 4.218per cent of the total variance. The variable X_1, x_2, X_4, X_{38} and X_{39} are grouped as factor III and it accounts for 1.480 per cent of the total variance.

TABLE: 5.26.1
FACTOR ANALYSIS OF ASSOCIATION OFPOLICE PERSONNEL'S
PERCEPTION ABOUT CAUSES FOR STRESS

Factors	Factor interpretation	Variables included in the factors	Cronbach's Alpha
F_1	Grade II (Junior)	Assignment of disagreeable duties, Assignment of new or unfamiliar duties, Performing tasks not in job description, Periods of inactivity, Assignment of increased responsibility, Competition for advancement, Frequent changes from boring to demanding activities, Shift work, Delivering a death message or bad news to someone, Attending to incidences of domestic violence, Reorganization and transformation within the organization, A forced arrest or being physically attacked, Having to go to court, Fellow workers not doing their job, Inadequate support by supervisor, Inadequate or poor quality equipment, Inadequate salary, Difficulty getting along with supervisor, Insufficient personnel to handle an assignment, Poor or inadequate supervision, Noisy work area, Insufficient personal time (e.g., coffee breaks, lunch), Poorly motivated co-workers, Staff shortages, Working overtime, Dealing with crisis situations, Experiencing negative attitudes toward the organization, Making critical on-the-spot decisions, Frequent interruptions, Excessive paperwork, Meeting deadlines, Covering work for another employee, Conflicts with other departments and Too much supervision of Stressful Job-Related Events	.998
F_2	Grade I (Promotion)	Performing tasks not in job description, Assignment of increased responsibility, Competition for advancement, Shift work, Delivering a death message or bad news to someone, Reorganization and transformation within the organization, Killing someone in the line of duty, Handling, Having to handle a large crowd/mass demonstration, A forced arrest or being physically attacked, Having to go to court, Having to deal with the media, Seeing criminals go free (for example because of lack of evidence, court leniency), Lack of opportunity for advancement, Lack of recognition for good work, Inadequate or poor quality equipment, Inadequate salary, Difficulty getting along with supervisor, Insufficient personnel to handle an assignment, Lack of participation in policy-making decisions Insufficient personal time (e.g., coffee breaks, lunch), Poorly motivated co-workers, Staff shortages, Working overtime, Dealing with crisis situations, Experiencing negative attitudes toward the organization, Personal insult from customer/consumer/colleague, Covering work for another employee, Conflicts with other departments, Too much supervision Stressful Job-Related Events and A fellow officer killed in the line of duty	.994
F_3	Grade III (Head Constable)	Assignment of disagreeable duties, Assignment of new or unfamiliar duties, Periods of inactivity, Frequent interruptions and Excessive paperwork	.816

Source: Computed From Primary Data

The result of reliability analysis declares that the Cronbach's Alpha value .998, .994 and .816establish significant and positive association between the variables tested. It establishes the existence of internal constancy with data collected at time of filed survey. The results of the test establish consistency in the opinion of respondents, expressed by the sample population on perception about occupation.

H3: There exist no similarities in the police officers' perception about occupation stress and its occurrence frequency.

Factor analysis technique has been applied to find the underlying dimension (factors) that exists in the 44 variables relating to the occurrence of stress.

TABLE: 5.27
KMO AND BARTLETT'S TESTPOLICE PERSONNEL'S PERCEPTION ON FREQUENCY OF STRESS OCCURRENCE

Kaiser-Meyer-Olkin Measure of Sampling Adequacy	.772
Bartlett's Test of Sphericity Approx. Chi-Square	1816.414
DF	946
Sig	.000

Level of Significance: 5 per cent

In the present study, Kaiser-Meyer-Oklin (KMO) Measure of Sampling Adequacy (MSA) and Bartlett's test of Sphericity were applied to verify the adequacy or appropriateness of data for factor analysis. In this study, the value of KMO for overall matrix was found to be excellent (0.772) and Bartlett's test of Sphericity was highly significant ($p<0.05$). Bartlett's Sphericity test was effective, as the chi-square value draws significance at five per cent level. The results thus indicated that the sample taken was appropriate to proceed with a factor analysis procedure. Besides the Bartlett's Test of Sphericity and the KMO Measure of sampling Adequacy, Communality values of all variables were also observed. Therefore the hypothesis was framed accepted and it concluded that there exist no similarities in the police officers' perception about occupation stress and its occurrence frequency.

TABLE: 5.28
CUMULATIVE
FACTORS INFLUENCE OF POLICE PERSONNEL'S
PERCEPTION ON FREQUENCY OF STRESS OCCURRENCE

Variables	Initial	Extraction
Job demand		
Assignment of disagreeable duties	1.000	.024
Assignment of new or unfamiliar duties	1.000	.166
Performing tasks not in job description	1.000	.174
Periods of inactivity	1.000	.101
Assignment of increased responsibility	1.000	.173
Competition for advancement	1.000	.179
Frequent changes from boring to demanding activities	1.000	.045
Shift work	1.000	.093
Delivering a death message or bad news to someone	1.000	.222
Attending to incidences of domestic violence	1.000	.058
Reorganization and transformation within the organization	1.000	.142
Killing someone in the line of duty	1.000	.186
Handling	1.000	.143
Having to handle a large crowd/mass demonstration	1.000	.282
A forced arrest or being physically attacked	1.000	.079
Having to go to court	1.000	.108
Having to deal with the media	1.000	.295
Seeing criminals go free (for example because of lack of evidence, court leniency)	1.000	.170
Lack of resources		
Lack of opportunity for advancement	1.000	.187
Fellow workers not doing their job	1.000	.108
Inadequate support by supervisor	1.000	.080
Lack of recognition for good work	1.000	.047
Inadequate or poor quality equipment	1.000	.073
Inadequate salary	1.000	.137
Difficulty getting along with supervisor	1.000	.070
Insufficient personnel to handle an assignment	1.000	.025
Lack of participation in policy-making decisions	1.000	.160
Poor or inadequate supervision	1.000	.111
Noisy work area	1.000	.220
Insufficient personal time (e.g., coffee breaks, lunch)	1.000	.197
Poorly motivated co-workers	1.000	.286
Staff shortages	1.000	.156
Police stresses/occupational stress		
Working overtime	1.000	.084
Dealing with crisis situations	1.000	.048
Experiencing negative attitudes toward the organization	1.000	.130
Making critical on-the-spot decisions	1.000	.058
Personal insult from customer/consumer/colleague	1.000	.117
Frequent interruptions	1.000	.178
Excessive paperwork	1.000	.146
Meeting deadlines	1.000	.127
Covering work for another employee	1.000	.088
Conflicts with other departments	1.000	.078
Too much supervision Stressful Job-Related Events	1.000	.069
A fellow officer killed in the line of duty	1.000	.310

In order to provide a more parsimonious interpretation of the results, 44-item scale was then Factor analyzed using the Principal Component method with Varimax rotation.

Factor analysis attempts to identify underlying variables, or factors, that explain the pattern of correlations within a set of observed variables. Factor analysis is often used in data reduction to identify a small number of factors that explain most of the variance observed in a much larger number of manifest variables. In the current study Rotation Factor analysis is performed to measure the occurrence of stress of the study of the respondents. The significance of variables is depicted in the following table.

EXHIBIT: 5.17
POLICE PERSONNEL'S PERCEPTION ON
FREQUENCY OF STRESS OCCURRENCE

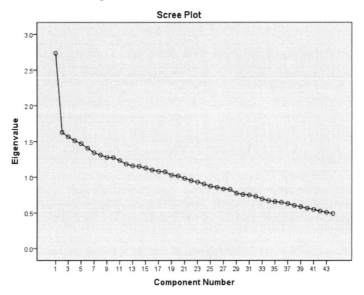

TABLE: 5.29
FACTOR ANALYSIS OF ASSOCIATION OF POLICE PERSONNEL'S
PERCEPTION ON FREQUENCY OF STRESS OCCURRENCE

Variables	Factors		
	Grade II (Junior)	Grade I (Promotion)	Grade III (Head Constable)
Job demand			
X_1-Assignment of disagreeable duties	-	-	-
X_2-Assignment of new or unfamiliar duties	-	-	-
X_3-Performing tasks not in job description	-	-	-
X_4-Periods of inactivity	-	-	-
X_5-Assignment of increased responsibility	-	-	-
X_6-Competition for advancement	-	-	-
X_7-Frequent changes from boring to demanding activities	-	-	-
X_8-Shift work	-	-	-
X_9-Delivering a death message or bad news to someone	-	-	-
X_{10}-Attending to incidences of domestic violence	-	0.517	-
X_{11}-Reorganization and transformation within the organization	-	-	-
X_{12}-Killing someone in the line of duty	-	-	-
X_{13}-Handling	-	-	-
X_{14}-Having to handle a large crowd/mass demonstration	-	-	0.534
X_{15}-A forced arrest or being physically attacked	-	-	-
X_{16}-Having to go to court	-	-	-
X_{17}-Having to deal with the media	-	-	-
X_{18}-Seeing criminals go free (for example because of lack of evidence, court leniency)	-	-	-
Lack of Resources			
X_{19}-Lack of opportunity for advancement	-	-	-
X_{20}-Fellow workers not doing their job	-	-	-
X_{21}-Inadequate support by supervisor	-	-	-
X_{22}-Lack of recognition for good work	-	-	0.553
X_{23}-Inadequate or poor quality equipment	-	-	-
X_{24}-Inadequate salary	-	-	-
X_{25}-Difficulty getting along with supervisor	-	-	-
X_{26}-Insufficient personnel to handle an assignment	-	-	-
X_{27}-Lack of participation in policy-making decisions	0.527	-	-
X_{28}-Poor or inadequate supervision	-	-	-
X_{29}-Noisy work area	-	-	-

X_{30}-Insufficient personal time (e.g., coffee breaks, lunch)	-	-	-
X_{31}-Poorly motivated co-workers	-	-	-
X_{32}-Staff shortages	-	-	-
Police stresses/occupational stress			
X_{33}-Working overtime	-	-	-
X_{34}-Dealing with crisis situations	-	-	-
X_{35}-Experiencing negative attitudes toward the organization	-	0.514	-
X_{36}-Making critical on-the-spot decisions	-	-	0.525
X_{37}-Personal insult from customer/consumer/colleague	-	-	-
X_{38}-Frequent interruptions	-	-	-
X_{39}-Excessive paperwork	-	-	-
X_{40}-Meeting deadlines	-	-	-
X_{41}-Covering work for another employee	-	-	-
X_{42}-Conflicts with other departments	-	-	-
X_{43}-Too much supervision Stressful Job-Related Events	-	-	-
X_{44}-A fellow officer killed in the line of duty	-	-	-
Eigen value	**2.734**	**1.628**	**1.567**
% of Variance	**6.215**	**3.7**	**3.561**
Cumulative	**6.215**	**9.915**	**13.476**

Level of Significance: 5 per cent

Three factors were identified as being maximum percentage variance accounted. The variable $X_{27}$is grouped as factor I and it accounts for 6.215per cent of the total variance. The variable X_{10} and X_{35}constitute the factor II and it accounts for 3.700per cent of the total variance. The variable $X_{14,}$ $X_{22}$and X_{36} are grouped as factor III and it accounts for 3.561 per cent of the total variance.

TABLE: 5.29.1
FACTOR ANALYSIS OF ASSOCIATION OF POLICE PERSONNEL'S
PERCEPTION ON FREQUENCY OF STRESS OCCURRENCE

Factors	Factor interpretation	Variables included in the factors	Cronbach's Alpha
F_1	Grade II (Junior)	Lack of participation in policy-making decisions	.731
F_2	Grade I (Promotion)	Attending to incidences of domestic violence and Experiencing negative attitudes toward the organization	.604
F_3	Grade III (Head Constable)	Having to handle a large crowd/mass demonstration, Lack of recognition for good work and Making critical on-the-spot decisions	.688

Source: Computed From Primary Data

The result of reliability analysis declares that the Cronbach's Alpha value .731, .604 and .668establishes significant and positive association between the variables tested. It establishes the existence of internal constancy with data collected at time of field survey. The results of the test establish consistency in the opinion of respondents by the sample population on occurrence of stress.

H4: There exists wide gap between the police officers' perception about their occupation stress and its occurrence frequencies.

TABLE: 5.30
PAIRED SAMPLES TESTASSOCIATION BETWEENPOLICE
PERSONNEL'S PERCEPTION ON CAUSES FOR STRESS &FREQUENCY
OF STRESS OCCURRENCE

Variables	Perception about occupation		Occurrence of stress/burnout		Mean Difference	t value	Sig
	Mean	SD	Mean	SD			
Job Demand							
Assignment of disagreeable duties	2.08	0.72	1.97	0.75	0.11	2.599	.010
Assignment of new or unfamiliar duties	2.06	0.67	2.09	0.78	0.03	-.645	.519
Performing tasks not in job description	1.87	0.73	2.08	0.78	0.21	-5.033	.000
Periods of inactivity	1.96	0.68	2.09	0.79	0.13	-3.033	.003
Assignment of increased responsibility	1.84	0.62	2.00	0.78	0.16	-4.084	.000
Competition for advancement	1.90	0.71	2.10	0.70	0.20	-4.632	.000
Frequent changes from boring to demanding activities	1.94	0.80	2.06	0.75	0.12	-2.791	.005
Shift work	1.77	0.80	2.02	0.75	0.25	-5.580	.000
Delivering a death message or bad news to someone	1.78	0.80	2.04	0.68	0.26	-5.612	.000
Attending to incidences of domestic violence	1.90	0.79	2.10	0.78	0.20	-4.717	.000
Reorganization and transformation within the organization	1.85	0.71	2.07	0.76	0.22	-5.088	.000
Killing someone in the line of duty	1.68	0.71	2.01	0.83	0.33	-7.633	.000
Handling	1.74	0.71	1.85	0.83	0.11	-2.644	.008
Having to handle a large crowd/mass demonstration	1.74	0.74	2.05	0.83	0.31	-6.832	.000
A forced arrest or being physically attacked	1.86	0.71	2.08	0.83	0.22	-4.938	.000
Having to go to court	1.84	0.75	2.05	0.81	0.21	-4.716	.000
Having to deal with the media	1.75	0.74	2.10	0.82	0.35	-7.530	.000
Seeing criminals go free (for example because of lack of evidence, court leniency)	1.66	0.69	1.97	0.80	0.31	-7.198	.000

Level of significance: 5 per cent

TABLE: 5.31
PAIRED SAMPLES TESTASSOCIATION BETWEENPOLICE
PERSONNEL'S PERCEPTION ON CAUSES FOR STRESS &FREQUENCY
OF STRESS OCCURRENCE

Variables	Perception about occupation		Occurrence of stress/burnout		Mean Difference	t value	Sig
	Mean	SD	Mean	SD			
Lack of resources							
Lack of opportunity for advancement	1.71	0.69	2.11	0.80	0.40	-9.334	.000
Fellow workers not doing their job	1.93	0.69	2.11	0.80	0.18	-4.309	.000
Inadequate support by supervisor	1.90	0.67	2.08	0.79	0.18	-4.363	.000
Lack of recognition for good work	1.74	0.70	2.05	0.82	0.31	-7.218	.000
Inadequate or poor quality equipment	1.90	0.73	2.12	0.80	0.22	-4.868	.000
Inadequate salary	1.87	0.70	2.04	0.80	0.17	-3.681	.000
Difficulty getting along with supervisor	1.85	0.72	2.10	0.77	0.25	-5.883	.000
Insufficient personnel to handle an assignment	1.86	0.68	2.09	0.83	0.23	-5.253	.000
Lack of participation in policy-making decisions	1.73	0.69	2.02	0.81	0.29	-6.818	.000
Poor or inadequate supervision	1.94	0.68	2.10	0.80	0.16	-3.718	.000
Noisy work area	1.90	0.70	2.10	0.81	0.20	-4.344	.000
Insufficient personal time (e.g., coffee breaks, lunch)	1.83	0.69	2.03	0.83	0.20	-4.568	.000
Poorly motivated co-workers	1.89	0.69	2.17	0.79	0.28	-6.795	.000
Staff shortages	1.73	0.71	1.95	0.81	0.22	-5.090	.000

Level of significance: 5 per cent

TABLE: 5.32
PAIRED SAMPLES TESTASSOCIATION BETWEENPOLICE
PERSONNEL'S PERCEPTION ON CAUSES FOR STRESS &FREQUENCY
OF STRESS OCCURRENCE

Variables	Perception about occupation		Occurrence of stress/burnout		Mean Difference	t value	Sig
	Mean	SD	Mean	SD			
Police stresses/occupational stress							
Working overtime	1.87	0.69	2.10	0.77	0.23	-5.530	.000
Dealing with crisis situations	1.79	0.72	2.10	0.81	0.31	-6.985	.000
Experiencing negative attitude toward the organization	1.83	0.69	2.08	0.79	0.25	-5.778	.000
Making critical on-the-spot decisions	1.90	0.69	2.09	0.79	0.19	-4.390	.000
Personal insult from customer/consumer/colleague	1.74	0.71	2.01	0.78	0.27	-6.188	.000
Frequent interruptions	2.07	0.75	2.13	0.79	0.06	-1.239	.216
Excessive paperwork	1.97	0.68	2.05	0.82	0.08	-1.734	.083
Meeting deadlines	1.90	0.70	2.11	0.79	0.21	-4.801	.000
Covering work for another employee	1.88	0.68	2.07	0.79	0.19	-4.469	.000
Conflicts with other departments	1.82	0.74	2.11	0.81	0.29	-6.292	.000
Too much supervision Stressful Job-Related Events	1.76	0.72	1.94	0.80	0.18	-4.238	.000
A fellow officer killed in the line of duty	1.70	0.72	1.88	0.82	0.18	-4.065	.000

Level of significance: 5 per cent

From the above table it has been inferred that probability value of 't' value is observed to be significant at five per cent. Therefore the hypothesis framed stands accepted and it is concluded that there exists wide gap between the police officers' perception about their occupation stress and its occurrence frequencies.

TABLE: 5.33
KMO AND BARTLETT'S TESTPOLICE PERSONNEL'S PERCEPTION ON OUTCOME OF STRESS

Kaiser-Meyer-Olkin Measure of Sampling Adequacy	.894
Bartlett's Test of Sphericity Approx. Chi-Square	1198.802
DF	105
Sig	.000

Level of Significance: 5 per cent

In the present study, Kaiser-Meyer-Oklin (KMO) Measure of Sampling Adequacy (MSA) and Bartlett's test of Sphericity were applied to verify the adequacy or appropriateness of data for factor analysis. In this study, the value of KMO for overall matrix was found to be excellent (0.894) and Bartlett's test of Sphericity was highly significant (p<0.05). Bartlett's Sphericity test was effective, as the chi-square value draws significance at five per cent level. The results thus indicated that the sample taken was appropriate to proceed with a factor analysis procedure. Besides the Bartlett's Test of Sphericity and the KMO Measure of sampling Adequacy, Communality values of all variables were also observed.

TABLE: 5.34
CUMULATIVE OUTCOME OF STRESS

Variables	Initial	Extraction
Loss of sexual interest or pleasure	1.000	.661
Thoughts of ending one's life	1.000	.709
Poor appetite	1.000	.477
Crying easily	1.000	.561
A feeling of being trapped or caught	1.000	.436
Blaming yourself for things	1.000	.685
Feeling lonely	1.000	.637
Feeling lovable	1.000	.524
Feeling blue	1.000	.606
Worrying or stewing about things	1.000	.531
Feeling no interest in things	1.000	.605
Feeling hopeless about the future	1.000	.484
Disbelief in Others	1.000	.623
Quarreling with family members	1.000	.460

Feeling of insecurity	1.000	.622

In order to provide a more parsimonious interpretation of the results, 15-item scale was then Factor analyzed using the Principal Component method with Varimax rotation.

Factor analysis attempts to identify underlying variables, or factors, that explain the pattern of correlations within a set of observed variables. Factor analysis is often used in data reduction to identify a small number of factors that explain most of the variance observed in a much larger number of manifest variables. In the current study Rotation Factor analysis is performed to measure the outcome of stress of the study of the respondents. The significance of variables is depicted in the following table.

TABLE: 5.35
FACTOR ANALYSIS OF ASSOCIATION OF OUTCOME OF STRESS

Variables	Factors		
	GradeI	Grade II	Grade III
X_1-Loss of sexual interest or pleasure	-	-	.784
X_2-Thoughts of ending one's life	-	.629	.555
X_3-Poor appetite	-	.605	-
X_4-Crying easily	-	-	.603
X_5-A feeling of being trapped or caught	.507	-	-
X_6-Blaming yourself for things	-	.765	-
X_7-Feeling lonely	-	-	.647
X_8-Feeling lovable	-	.710	-
X_9-Feeling blue	.718	-	-
X_{10}-Worrying or stewing about things	.534	-	-
X_{11}-Feeling no interest in things	.639	-	-
X_{12}-Feeling hopeless about the future	-	.516	-
X_{13}-Disbelief in Others	-	-	.661
X_{14}-Quarreling with family members	-	-	-
X_{15}-Feeling of insecurity	.679	-	-
Eigen value	**6.234**	**1.432**	**0.954**
% of Variance	**41.561**	**9.546**	**6.360**
Cumulative	**41.561**	**51.107**	**57.467**

Level of Significance: 5 per cent

Five factors were identified as being maximum percentage variance accounted. The variables X_5, X_9, X_{10}, X_{11} and X_{15} are grouped as factor I and it accounts for 41.561 per cent of the total variance. The variables X_2, X_3, X_6, X_9 and X_{12} constitute the factor II and it accounts for 9.546 per cent of the total variance. The variable X_1, X_2, X_4, X_7 and X_{13} are grouped as factor III and it accounts for 6.360 per cent of the total variance.

EXHIBIT: 5.8
SCREE PLOT: OUTCOME OF STRESS

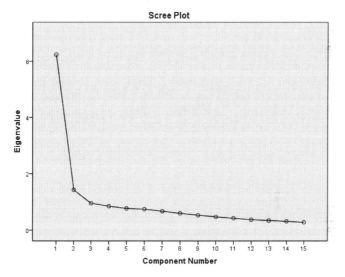

TABLE: 5.35.1
FACTOR ANALYSIS OF ASSOCIATION OF OUTCOME OF STRESS

Factors	Factor interpretation	Variables included in the factors	Cronbanch's Alpha
F_1	Grade I	A feeling of being trapped or caught, Feeling blue, Worrying or stewing about things, Feeling no interest in things and Feeling of insecurity	.909
F_2	Grade II	Thoughts of ending your life, Poor appetite, Blaming yourself for things, Feeling lovable and Feeling hopeless about the future	.752
F_3	Grade III	Loss of sexual interest or pleasure, Thoughts of ending one's life, Crying easily, Feeling	.629

		lonely and Disbelief in Others	

Source: Computed From Primary Data

The result of reliability analysis declares that the Cronbanch's Alpha value .909, .752 and .629establishes significant and positive association between the variables tested. It establishes the existence of internal constancy with data collected at time of field survey. The results of the test establish consistency in the opinion of respondents as expressed by the sample population on outcome of stress.

TABLE: 5.36
THE RESULT OF RELIABILITY STATISTICS FOR POLICE PERSONNEL'S PERCEPTION ON PROBLEM-FOCUSED STRESS COPING STRATEGIES

Variables	Mean	SD	t value	Correlation	Cronbach's Alpha
Positive Reinterpretation and Growth					
I force myself to wait for the right time to do something	2.83	.99	70.205	.297	.776
I put aside other activities in order to concentrate on this	2.72	1.05	63.271	.327	.774
I think about how I might best handle the problem	2.34	1.00	57.452	.040	.784
I admit to myself that I can't deal with it, and quit trying	2.11	1.08	47.706	-.099	.789
I try to see it on a different light to make it seem more positive	2.17	1.06	50.323	-.053	.787
I try hard to prevent other things from interfering with my efforts at dealing with this	2.62	.94	68.468	.081	.782
I do what has to be done one step at a time	2.69	1.04	63.531	.259	.777
I give up the attempt to get what I want	2.49	.92	66.368	.198	.779
I try to come up with the strategy as to what to do	2.76	.98	68.998	.205	.779
I focus on dealing with the problems and if necessary let other things slide a little	2.85	.96	72.556	.229	.778
I concentrate on efforts on doing something about it	2.76	.98	68.856	.212	.778
I just give up trying to reach my goal	2.82	1.01	68.604	.272	.776
Acceptance of Fact					
I try to grow as a person as a result of the experience	2.69	1.01	64.898	.273	.776
I get used to the idea that it happened	2.57	.95	66.535	.209	.778
I say to myself this is not real	2.57	.98	63.916	.205	.779
I make sure not to make matters worse by acting to soon	2.45	.96	62.487	.170	.780
I make a plan of action	2.49	.98	62.297	.144	.780
I learn to live with it	2.45	1.02	59.024	.096	.782
I take direct action around the problem	2.70	.98	67.392	.253	.777
I accept that this has happened and that can't be changed	2.76	1.03	65.647	.291	.776
I accept the reality of the fact that it happened	2.84	.99	70.220	.292	.776
Focusing on and ventilating emotions					
I sleep more than usual	2.59	1.01	62.505	.323	.775

I let my feelings out	2.51	1.00	61.621	.263	.777
I turn to work or other substitute activities to take my mind	2.38	1.01	57.611	.171	.780
I look for some thing good that is happening	2.44	1.03	58.136	.196	.779
I talk to someone to find out more about the situation	2.64	.99	65.201	.273	.776
I learn shooting from experience	2.57	.98	64.039	.250	.777
I think hard about what step to take	2.67	.95	68.711	.226	.778
Seeking Social Support for Emotional Reasons					
I ask people, who have had similar experience, what they did	2.38	.93	62.398	.337	.774
I talk to someone how the feels	2.43	.90	66.181	.064	.783
I try to get emotional support from friends or relatives	2.58	1.00	62.989	.115	.782
I try to get advice from some- one about what do to	2.81	.99	69.372	.262	.777
I get sympathy and understanding from someone	2.52	1.02	60.727	.152	.780
I talk to someone who could do some thing. About the problem	2.89	.98	72.360	.225	.778
I reduce the amount of effort I am putting to solve the problem	2.85	.97	71.654	.302	.775
I discuss my feelings someone	2.70	.99	66.512	.238	.778
Denial behaviour					
I refuse to believe it has happened	2.68	.96	68.039	.349	.774
I take additional action to try to get rid of the problem	2.69	.96	68.552	.325	.775
I hold of doing anything about it until the situation permits	2.80	.94	72.829	.268	.777
Turing Religious					
I put trust in god	2.64	.96	67.287	.349	.774
I pray more than usual	2.67	.93	70.488	.242	.777
I try to find comfort in my religion	2.68	1.00	65.891	.259	.777
I seek god's help	2.67	.96	68.212	.230	.778
Behavioral Disengagement					
I upset and let my emotion out	2.58	.96	65.690	.303	.775
I restrain myself from doing anything quickly	2.53	.93	66.406	.251	.777
I go to movies or watch TV to think it	2.56	.94	66.323	.195	.779
I act as though it hasn't even happened	2.73	.99	67.392	.228	.778
I get upset and am really aware of it	2.80	.96	71.576	.248	.777
Mental Disengagement					
I drink alcohol or drink drugs, in order to think about it less	2.70	1.03	63.805	.308	.775
I pretended that it has not really happened	2.80	1.01	67.706	.304	.775
I feel a lot of emotional distress and I find myself expressing those feeling a lot	2.72	.99	66.965	.270	.776

I keep myself from getting districted by other thought or activates	2.61	.99	64.871	.154	.780
I daydream about thinks other than this	2.85	.96	72.646	.240	.777
Cronbach's Alpha: .781					

The above table displays the means, standard deviations and inter-correlations among the variables tested. It is clear that employees are agreeing that criterion norms considered for opinion on stress coping strategies. This result can be considered as a good sign that the opinion on police personnel's perception on problem-focused stress coping strategies.

Cronbach's alpha is the most common form of internal consistency reliability coefficient. An examination had been made from the reliability of the data to check whether random error causing inconsistency and in turn lower reliability is at a manageable level or not, by running reliability test. From table it is clear that values of Coefficient alpha (Cronbach's Alpha) have been obtained, the minimum value of Coefficient alpha obtained was .781 in total. This shows data has satisfactory internal consistency reliability. The result of Cronbach's alpha draws a significant amount of correlation between the variables tested.

TABLE: 5.37
RESULT OF ANOVA TESTPOLICE PERSONNEL'S PERCEPTION ON PROBLEM-FOCUSED STRESS COPING STRATEGIES

Source		Sum of Squares	DF	Mean Square	F	Sig	Grand Mean
Between people		2488.098	599	4.154			
Within people	Between items	895.771	52	17.226			
	Residual	28293.172	31148	.908	18.965	.000	2.628
	Total	29188.943	31200	.936			
Total		31677.041	31799	.996			

Level of significance: 5 percent

The result of the Cronbach's Reliability Analysis (0.781 i.e., 78.10 percent) and F-test value 18.965 significant at five percent establishes a significant reliability between the variables tested.

H5: Stress coping styles adhered by the police officers does not differ from one to another, based on their designation, grade and work experiences.

TABLE: 5.38
RESULT OF ANOVA POLICE PERSONNEL'S PERCEPTION ON
PROBLEM-FOCUSED STRESS COPING STRATEGIES

Variables	Designation Grade		Years of Experience	
	F value	Sig	F value	Sig
Positive reinterpretation and growth				
I force myself to wait for the right time to do something	.993	.371	**2.807**	.025
I put aside other activities in order to concentrate on this	1.111	.330	.489	.744
I think about how I might best handle the problem	.552	.576	.970	.423
I admit to myself that I can't deal with it, and quit trying	.862	.423	1.608	.171
I try to see it on a different light to make it seem more positive	1.173	.310	2.973	.019
I try hard to prevent other things from interfering with my efforts at dealing with this	3.429	.033	1.621	.167
I do what has to be done one step at a time	1.617	.199	2.439	.046
I give up the attempt to get what I want	3.108	.045	1.133	.340
I try to come up with the strategy about what to do	1.361	.257	.587	.672
I focus on dealing with the problems and if necessary let other things slide a little	.329	.720	1.186	.316
I concentrate on efforts on doing something about it	.042	.959	.600	.663
I just give up trying to reach my goal	.424	.655	3.847	.004
Acceptance of Fact				
I try to grow as a person as a result of the experience	.117	.889	.317	.866
I get used to the idea that it happened	2.167	.115	.483	.748
I say to myself this is not real	1.525	.219	1.511	.198
I make sure not to make matters worse by action to soon	5.627	.004	1.025	.393
I make a plan of action	2.342	.097	1.701	.148
I learn to live with it	.313	.731	.254	.907
I take direct action around the problem	2.227	.109	.769	.546
I accept that this has happened and that we can't change it	.700	.497	1.281	.276
I accept the reality of the fact that it happened	2.811	.061	.824	.510
	F value	Sig	F value	Sig

Focusing on and ventilating emotions				
I sleep more than usual	.571	.565	.434	.784
I let my feelings out	.880	.415	1.801	.127
I turn to work or other substitute activities to take my mind	.186	.830	.568	.686
I look for some thing good that will happen	.010	.990	1.003	.405
I talk to someone to find out more about the situation	2.161	.116	.710	.586
I learn shooting from experience	1.426	.241	1.670	.155
I think hard about what step to take	.040	.961	.751	.557
Seeking Social Support for Emotional Reasons				
I ask people who have had similar experience what they did	1.636	.196	1.714	.145
I talk to someone but how I feel	3.839	.022	.177	.950
I try to get emotional support from friends or relatives	2.247	.107	.693	.597
I try to get advice some- one about what do to	.253	.777	1.428	.223
I get sympathy and understanding from someone	.630	.533	1.191	.314
I talk to someone who could do some think. About the problem	1.046	.352	1.512	.197
I reduce the amount of effort I putting to solving the problem	.853	.427	2.571	.037
I discuss my feelings someone	.578	.562	.504	.733
Denial behaviour				
I refuse to believe it has happened	.648	.524	1.328	.258
I take additional action to try to get rid of the problem	.051	.950	1.943	.102
I hold of doing anything about it until the situation permits	.635	.530	1.197	.311
Turing Religious				
I put in my trust in god	.177	.837	2.172	.071
I pray more than usual	.742	.476	.426	.790
I try to find comfort in my religion	.766	.466	2.126	.076
I seek god's help	.373	.689	1.508	.198
	F value	**Sig**	**F value**	**Sig**
Behavioral Disengagement				
I upset and let my emotion out	.040	.961	.751	.557
I restrain myself form doing anything do quickly	.738	.479	.567	.687
I go to movies or watch TV to think it	1.121	.327	1.711	.146
I act as though it hasn't even happened	1.109	.330	1.948	.101
I get upset and am really aware of it	1.616	.200	1.186	.316
Mental Disengagement				
I drink alcohol or drink drugs, in order to think about it less	.567	.568	.191	.943
I pretended that it has not really happened	.009	.991	.132	.971

I feel a lot of emotional distress and I find myself expressing those feeling a lot	3.660	.026	2.254	.062
I keep myself from getting districted by other thought or activates	1.718	.180	2.462	.044
I daydream about thinks other than this	.379	.685	.625	.645

Level of Significance: 5 per cent

The data in the above table shows that probability value of ANOVA at 5 per cent level does not establish good relationship between the variables tested. Therefore, the null hypothesis framed stands rejected.Therefore, it is concluded that stress coping styles adhered to by the police officers difference from one to another, based on their designation grade and work experiences.

Factor analysis technique has been applied to find the underlying dimension (factors) that exists in the 53 variables relating to the stress coping strategies.

TABLE: 5.39
KMO AND BARTLETT'S TEST POLICE PERSONNEL'S PERCEPTION ONSTRESS COPING STRATEGIES (DESIGNATION GRADE)

Kaiser-Meyer-Olkin Measure of Sampling Adequacy	.679
Bartlett's Test of Sphericity Approx. Chi-Square	2534.109
DF	1378
Sig	.000

Level of Significance: 5 per cent

In the present study, Kaiser-Meyer-Oklin (KMO) Measure of Sampling Adequacy (MSA) and Bartlett's test of Sphericity were applied to verify the adequacy or appropriateness of data for factor analysis. In this study, the value of KMO for overall matrix was found to be excellent (0.679) and Bartlett's test of Sphericity was highly significant ($p<0.05$). Bartlett's Sphericity test was effective, as the chi-square value draws significance at five per cent level. The results thus indicated that the sample taken was appropriate to proceed with a factor analysis procedure. Besides the Bartlett's Test of Sphericity and the KMO Measure of sampling Adequacy, Communality values of all variables were also observed.

TABLE: 5.40
CUMULATIVE POLICE PERSONNEL'S PERCEPTION ONSTRESS COPING STRATEGIES (DESIGNATION GRADE)

Variables	Initial	Extraction
Positive reinterpretation and growth		
I force myself to wait for the right time to do something	1.000	.345
I put aside other activities in order to concentrate on this	1.000	.265
I think about how I might best handle the problem	1.000	.235
I admit to myself that I can't deal with it, and quit trying	1.000	.379
I try to see it on a different light to make it seem more positive	1.000	.295
I try hard to prevent other things from interfering with my efforts at dealing with this	1.000	.029
I do what has to be done one step at a time	1.000	.176
I give up the attempt to get what I want	1.000	.177
I try to come up with the strategy what to do	1.000	.245
I focus on dealing with the problems and it is necessary let other thinks slide a little	1.000	.199
I concentrate on efforts doing something about it	1.000	.222
I just give up trying to reach my goal	1.000	.370
Acceptance of Fact		
I try to grow as a person as a result of the experience	1.000	.299
I get used to the idea that it happened	1.000	.177
I say to myself this is not real	1.000	.194
I make sure not to make matters worse by action too soon	1.000	.296
I make a plan of action	1.000	.254
I learn to live with it	1.000	.272
I take direct action around the problem	1.000	.271
I accept that this has happened and that we can't change it	1.000	.187
I accept the reality of the fact that it happened	1.000	.247
Focusing on and ventilating emotions		
I sleep more than usual	1.000	.333
I let my feelings out	1.000	.190
I turn to work or other substitute activities to take my mind	1.000	.132
I took for some think good what is happing	1.000	.383
A talk to someone to find out more about the situation	1.000	.224
I learn shooting from experience	1.000	.103
I think hard about what step to take	1.000	.177
Seeking Social Support for Emotional Reasons		
I ask people who have had similar experience what they did	1.000	.324
I talk to someone and express how I feel	1.000	.338
I try to get emotional support from friends or relatives	1.000	.090
I try to get advice some- one about what do to	1.000	.227
I get sympathy and understanding from someone	1.000	.135
I talk to someone who could do some think. About the problem	1.000	.273
I reduce the amount of effort I putting to solving the problem	1.000	.391

I discuss my feelings someone	1.000	.104
Denial behaviour		
I refuse to believe it has happened	1.000	.363
I take additional action to try to get rid of the problem	1.000	.258
I don't do anything about it until the situation permits	1.000	.382
Turing Religious		
I put in my trust in God	1.000	.254
I pray more than usual	1.000	.274
I try to find comfort in my religion	1.000	.206
I seek god's help	1.000	.077
Behavioral Disengagement		
I upset and let my emotion out	1.000	.279
I restrain myself form doing anything do quickly	1.000	.217
I go to movies or watch TV to think it	1.000	.241
I act as though it hasn't even happened	1.000	.242
I get upset and am really aware of it	1.000	.141
Mental Disengagement		
I drink alcohol or drink drugs, in order to think about it less	1.000	.222
I pretended that it had not really happened	1.000	.284
I feel a lot of emotional distress and I find myself expressing those feeling a lot	1.000	.110
I keep myself from getting districted by other thought or activates	1.000	.088
I daydream about thinks other than this	1.000	.122

In order to provide a more parsimonious interpretation of the results, 53-item scale was then Factor analyzed using the Principal Component method with Varimax rotation.

Factor analysis attempts to identify underlying variables, or factors, that explain the pattern of correlations within a set of observed variables. Factor analysis is often used in data reduction to identify a small number of factors that explain most of the variance observed in a much larger number of manifest variables. In the current study Rotation Factor analysis is performed to measure the stress coping strategies of the study of the respondents. The significance of variables is depicted in the following table.

EXHIBIT: 5.19
**SCREE PLOT: POLICE PERSONNEL'S PERCEPTION ONSTRESS COPING
STRATEGIES(DESIGNATION GRADE)**

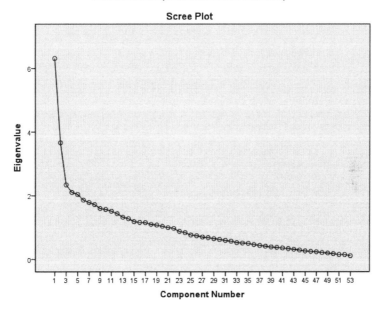

TABLE: 5.41
FACTOR ANALYSIS OF ASSOCIATION OFPOLICE PERSONNEL'S
PERCEPTION ONSTRESS COPING STRATEGIES (DESIGNATION
GRADE)

Variables	Factors		
	Grade II (Junior)	Grade I (Promotion)	Grade III (Head Constable)
Positive reinterpretation and growth			
X_1-I force myself to wait for the right time to do something	-	-	-
X_2-I put aside other activities in order to concentrate on this	-	-	-
X_3-I think about how I might best handle the problem	-	-	-
X_4-I admit to myself that I can't deal with it, and quit trying	-	0.519	-
X_5-I try to see it on a different light to make it seem more positive	-	-	-
X_6-I try hard to prevent other things from interfering with my efforts at dealing with this	-	-	-
X_7-I do what has to be done one step at a time	-	-	-
X_8-I give up the attempt to get what I want	-	-	-
X_9-I try to come up with the strategy about what to do	-	-	-
X_{10}-I focus on dealing with the problems and it necessary let other thinks slide a little	-	-	-
X_{11}-I concentrate on efforts on doing something about it	-	-	-
X_{12}-I just give up trying to reach my goal	-	-	-
Acceptance of Fact			
X_{13}-I try to grow as a person as a result of the experience	-	-	-
X_{14}-I get used to the idea that it happened	-	-	-
X_{15}-I say to myself this is not real	-	-	-
X_{16}-I make sure not to make matters worse by action too soon	-	0.531	-
X_{17}-I make a plan of action	-	-	-
X_{18}-I learn to live with it	-	-	-
X_{19}-I take direct action around the problem	-	-	-
X_{20}-I accept that this has happened and that can't be changed	-	-	-
X_{21}-I accept the reality of the fact that it happened	-	-	0.576
Focusing on and ventilating emotions			
X_{22}-I sleep more than usual	-	-	-
X_{23}-I let my feelings out	-	-	-
X_{24}-I turn to work or other substitute activities to take my mind	-	-	-
X_{25}-I took for some think good what is happing	-	0.542	-

X_{26}-A talk to someone to find out more about the situation	-	-	-
X_{27}-I learn shooting from experience	-	-	-
X_{28}-I think hard about what step to take	-	-	-
Seeking Social Support for Emotional Reasons			
X_{29}-I ask people, who have had similar experience what they did	0.539	-	-
X_{30}-I talk to someone and explain and how I feel	-	0.51	-
X_{31}-I try to get emotional support from friends or relatives	-	-	-
X_{32}-I try to get advice from some- one about what do to	-	-	-
X_{33}-I get sympathy and understanding from someone	-	-	-
X_{34}-I talk to someone who could do some thing about the problem	-	-	-
X_{35}-I reduce the amount of effort put to solve the problem	0.6	-	-
X_{36}-I discuss my feelings someone	-	-	-
Denial behaviour			
X_{37}-I refuse to believe it has happened	0.573	-	-
X_{38}-I take additional action to try to get rid of the problem	-	-	-
X_{39}-I hold of doing anything about it until the situation permits	0.527	-	-
Turning Religious			
X_{40}-I put my trust in god	0.502	-	-
X_{41}-I pray more than usual	-	-	-
X_{42}-I try to find comfort in my religion	-	-	-
X_{43}-I seek god's help	-	-	-
Behavioral Disengagement			
X_{44}-I upset and let my emotion out	-	-	-
X_{45}-I restrain myself from doing anything do quickly	-	-	-
X_{46}-I go to movies or watch TV to forget it	-	-	-
X_{47}-I act as though it hasn't even happened	-	-	-
X_{48}-I get upset and am really aware of it	-	-	-
Mental Disengagement			
X_{49}-I drink alcohol or drink drugs, in order to think about it less	-	-	-
X_{50}-I pretended that it has not really happened	-	-	-
X_{51}-I feel a lot of emotional distress and I find myself expressing those feeling a lot	-	-	-
X_{52}-I keep myself from getting distracted by other thought or activates	-	-	-
X_{53}-I daydream about thinks other than this	-	-	-
Eigen value	**6.311**	**3.665**	**2.341**
% of Variance	**11.908**	**6.915**	**4.416**
Cumulative	**11.908**	**18.823**	**23.239**

Level of Significance: 5 per cent

Three factors were identified as being maximum percentage variance accounted. The variables $X_{29,}$ $X_{35,}$ $X_{37,}$ X_{39} and X_{40} are grouped as factor I and it accounts for 11.908 per cent of the total variance. The variables $X_{4,}$ $X_{16,}$ $X_{25,}$ and X_{30} constitute the factor II and it accounts for 6.915 per cent of the total variance. The variable X_{21} is grouped as factor III and it accounts for 4.416 per cent of the total variance.

TABLE: 5.41.1
FACTOR ANALYSIS OF ASSOCIATION OFPOLICE PERSONNEL'S PERCEPTION ONSTRESS COPING STRATEGIES(DESIGNATION GRADE)

Factors	Factor interpretation	Variables included in the factors	Cronbanch's Alpha
F_1	Grade II (Junior)	I ask people who have had similar experience what they did, I reduce the amount of effort I put to solve the problem, I refuse to believe it has happened, I hold of doing anything about it until the situation permits and I put my trust in god	.852
F_2	Grade I (Promotion)	I talk to someone but how I feel, I admit to myself that I can't deal with it, and quit trying, I make sure not too make matters worse by action to soon and I took for some thing good that is happening	.777
F_3	Grade III (Head Constable)	I accept the reality of the fact that it happened	.643

Source: Computed From Primary Data

The result of reliability analysis declares that the Cronbach's Alpha value .852, .777 and .643 establishes significant and positive association between the variables tested. It establishes the existence of internal constancy with data collected at time of field survey. The results of the test establish consistency in the opinion of respondents expressed by the sample population on stress coping strategies.

TABLE: 5.42
KMO AND BARTLETT'S TESTPOLICE PERSONNEL'S PERCEPTION
ONSTRESS COPING STRATEGIES (YEARS OF EXPERIENCES)

Kaiser-Meyer-Olkin Measure of Sampling Adequacy	.620
Bartlett's Test of Sphericity Approx. Chi-Square	2498.384
DF	1378
Sig	.000

Level of Significance: 5 per cent

In the present study, Kaiser-Meyer-Oklin (KMO) Measure of Sampling Adequacy (MSA) and Bartlett's test of Sphericity were applied to verify the adequacy or appropriateness of data for factor analysis. In this study, the value of KMO for overall matrix was found to be excellent (0.620) and Bartlett's test of Sphericity was highly significant ($p<0.05$). Bartlett's Sphericity test was effective, as the chi-square value draws significance at five per cent level. The results thus indicated that the sample taken was appropriate to proceed with a factor analysis procedure. Besides the Bartlett's Test of Sphericity and the KMO Measure of sampling Adequacy, Communality values of all variables were also observed.

TABLE: 5.43
CUMULATIVE POLICE PERSONNEL'S PERCEPTION ONSTRESS
COPING STRATEGIES (YEARS OF EXPERIENCES)

Variables	Initial	Extraction
Positive reinterpretation and growth		
I force myself to wait for the right time to do something	1.000	.272
I put aside other activities in order to concentrate on this	1.000	.328
I think about how I might best handle the problem	1.000	.298
I admit to myself that I can't deal with it, and quit trying	1.000	.497
I try to see it on a different light to make it seem more positive	1.000	.195
I try hard to prevent other things from interfering with my efforts at dealing with this	1.000	.103
I do what has to be done one step at a time	1.000	.211
I give up the attempt to get what I want	1.000	.259
I try to come up with the strategy what to do	1.000	.287
I focus on dealing with the problems and if necessary let other things slide a little	1.000	.247
I concentrate on efforts on doing something about it	1.000	.294
I just give up trying to reach my goal	1.000	.444
Acceptance of Fact		
I try to grow as a person as a result of the experience	1.000	.266
I get used to the idea that it happened	1.000	.253
I say to myself this is not real	1.000	.294
I make sure not to make matters worse by acting too soon	1.000	.381
I make a plan of action	1.000	.371
I learn to live with it	1.000	.326
I take direct action around the problem	1.000	.211
I accept that this has happened and that can't be changed	1.000	.308
I accept the reality of the fact that it happened	1.000	.325
Focusing on and ventilating emotions		
I sleep more than usual	1.000	.335
I let my feelings out	1.000	.468
I turn to work or other substitute activities to take my mind	1.000	.494
I look for some thing good what is happing	1.000	.392
I talk to someone to find out more about the situation	1.000	.243
I learn shooting from experience	1.000	.313
Seeking Social Support for Emotional Reasons		
I ask people, who have had similar experience, what they did	1.000	.323
I talk to someone how I feel	1.000	.405
I try to get emotional support from friends or relatives	1.000	.249
I try to get advice from some- one about what do to	1.000	.134
I get sympathy and understanding from someone	1.000	.293

I talk to someone who could do some thing. About the problem	1.000	.325
I reduce the amount of effort I putting to solving the problem	1.000	.304
I discuss my feelings someone	1.000	.417
Denial behaviour		
I refuse to believe it has happened	1.000	.335
I take additional action to try to get rid of the problem	1.000	.362
I don't anything about it until the situation permits	1.000	.396
Turning Religious		
I put in my trust in God	1.000	.282
I pray more than usual	1.000	.386
I try to find comfort in my religion	1.000	.253
I seek god's help	1.000	.113
Behavioral Disengagement		
I upset and let my emotion out	1.000	.370
I restrain myself form doing anything do quickly	1.000	.174
I go to movies or watch TV to think it	1.000	.291
I act as though it hasn't even happened	1.000	.178
I get upset and am really aware of it	1.000	.355
Mental Disengagement		
I drink alcohol or drink drugs, in order to think about it less	1.000	.398
I pretended that it had not really happened	1.000	.426
I feel a lot of emotional distress and I find myself expressing those feeling a lot	1.000	.384
I keep myself from getting districted by other thought or activates	1.000	.240
I daydream about thinks other than this	1.000	.184

In order to provide a more parsimonious interpretation of the results, 53-item scale was then Factor analyzed using the Principal Component method with Varimax rotation. Factor analysis attempts to identify underlying variables, or factors, that explain the pattern of correlations within a set of observed variables. Factor analysis is often used in data reduction to identify a small number of factors that explain most of the variance observed in a much larger number of manifest variables. In the current study Rotation Factor analysis is performed to measure the stress coping strategies of the study of the respondents. The significance of variables is depicted in the following table.

TABLE: 5.44

FACTOR ANALYSIS OF ASSOCIATION OF POLICE PERSONNEL'S PERCEPTION ONSTRESS COPING STRATEGIES (YEARS OF EXPERIENCES)

Variables	Factors				
	Less than 5 years	6-10 years	11-15 years	16-20 years	More than 20 years
Positive reinterpretation and growth					
X_1-I force myself to wait for the right time to do something	-	-	-	-	-
X_2-I put aside other activities in order to concentrate on this	-	-	-	-	-
X_3-I think about how I might best handle the problem	-	-	-	-	-
X_4-I admit to myself that I can't deal with it, and quit trying	0.561	-	-	-	-
X_5-I try to see it on a different light to make it seem more positive	-	-	-	-	-
X_6-I try hard to prevent other things from interfering with my efforts at dealing with this	-	-	-	-	-
X_7-I do what has to be done one step at a time	-	-	-	-	-
X_8-I give up the attempt to get what I want	-	-	-	-	-
X_9-I try to come up with the strategy as to what to do	-	-	-	-	-
X_{10}-I focus on dealing with the problems and if necessary let other things slide a little	-	-	-	-	-
X_{11}-I concentrate on efforts on doing something about it	-	-	-	-	-
X_{12}-I just give up trying to reach my goal	0.549	-	-	-	-
Acceptance of Fact					
X_{13}-I try to grow as a person as a result of the experience	-	-	-	-	-
X_{14}-I get used to the idea that it happened	-	-	-	-	-
X_{15}-I say to myself this is not real	-	-	-	-	-
X_{16}-I make sure not to make matters worse by acting too	-	-	-	-	-
X_{17}-I make a plan of action	-	0.573	-	-	-
X_{18}-I learn to live with it	-	-	-	-	-
X_{19}-I take direct action around the problem	-	-	-	-	-
X_{20}-I accept that this has happened and that can't be changed	-	-	-	0.519	-
X_{21}-I accept the reality of the fact that it happened	-	-	-	-	-
Focusing on and ventilating emotions					
X_{22}-I sleep more than usual	-	-	0.565	-	-
X_{23}-I let my feelings out	-	-	-	-	0.621

X_{24}-I turn to work or other substitute activities to take my mind	-	0.672	-	-	-
X_{25}-I look for something good that is happening	-	-	-	-	-
X_{26}-I talk to someone to find out more about the situation	-	-	-	-	-
X_{27}-I learn shooting from experience	-	-	-	-	-
X_{28}-I think hard about what step to take	-	-	-	-	-
Seeking Social Support for Emotional Reasons					
X_{29}-I ask people, who have had similar experience, what they did	-	-	-	-	-
X_{30}-I ask someone how she feels.	-	-	-	-	-
X_{31}-I try to get emotional support from friends or relatives	-	-	-	-	-
X_{32}-I try to get advice from some- one about what do to	-	-	-	-	-
X_{33}-I get sympathy and understanding from someone	-	-	-	-	-
X_{34}-I talk to someone who could do something about the problem	-	-	-	0.538	-
X_{35}-I reduce the amount of effort I am putting to solve the problem	-	-	-	-	-
X_{36}-I discuss my feelings someone	-	-	-	-	-
Denial behaviour					
X_{37}-I refuse to believe it has happened	-	-	-	-	-
X_{38}-I take additional action to try to get rid of the problem	0.534	-	-	-	-
X_{39}-I hold of doing anything about it until the situation permits	-	-	-	-	0.53
Turing Religious					
X_{40}-I put trust in god	-	-	-	-	-
X_{41}-I pray more than usual	0.567	-	-	-	-
X_{42}-I try to find comfort in my religion	-	-	-	-	-
X_{43}-I seek god's help	-	-	-	-	-
Behavioral Disengagement					
X_{44}-I upset and let my emotion out	-	-	-	-	-
X_{45}-I restrain myself from doing anything quickly	-	-	-	-	-
X_{46}-I go to movies or watch TV to think it	-	-	-	-	-
X_{47}-I act as though it hasn't even happened	-	-	-	-	-
X_{48}-I get upset and am really aware of it	-	-	-	-	-
Mental Disengagement					
X_{49}-I drink alcohol or drink drugs, in order to think about it less	-	-	-		-
X_{50}-I pretended that it has not really happened	-	-	-		-
X_{51}-I feel a lot of emotional distress and I find myself expressing those feeling a lot	-	-	0.5		-
X_{52}-I keep myself from getting districted by other thought or activates	-	-	-		-

X_{53}-I daydream about thinks other than this	-	-	-	-	-
Eigen value	**5.686**	**3.484**	**2.509**	**2.229**	**2.264**
% of Variance	**10.728**	**6.573**	**4.734**	**4.338**	**4.272**
Cumulative	**10.728**	**17.301**	**22.035**	**26.373**	**30.645**

Level of Significance: 5 per cent

Five factors were identified as being maximum percentage variance accounted. The variable X_4, X_{12} and X_{41} is grouped as factor I and it accounts for 10.728per cent of the total variance. The variable X_{17} and X_{24} constitute the factor II and it accounts for 6.573per cent of the total variance. The variable X_{22} and X_{51} is grouped as factor III and it accounts for 4.734 per cent of the total variance. The variable X_{20} and X_{34} is grouped as factor IV and it accounts for 4.338 per cent of the total variance. The variable X_{24} and X_{39} is grouped as factor V and it accounts for 4.272 per cent of the total variance.

EXHIBIT: 5.20
SCREE PLOT: POLICE PERSONNEL'S PERCEPTION ON STRESS COPING STRATEGIES (YEARS OF EXPERIENCES)

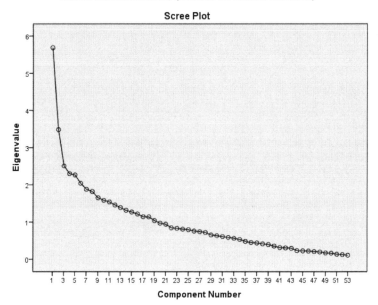

Five factors were identified as being maximum percentage variance accounted. The variables X_{12}, X_{20}, X_{22} and X_{34} aregrouped as factor I and it accounts for 10.728 per cent of the total variance. The variable X_{28} and X_{39} constitute the factor II and it accounts for 6.573 per cent of the total variance. The variable X_{37} andX_{53} are grouped as factor III and it accounts for 4.734 per cent of the total variance. The variable X_6 andX_{31} are grouped as factor IV and it accounts for 4.338 per cent of the total variance. The variable X_{23} andX_{37} are grouped as factor V and it accounts for 4.272 per cent of the total variance.

TABLE: 5.44.1
FACTOR ANALYSIS OF ASSOCIATION OFPOLICE PERSONNEL'S PERCEPTION ONSTRESS COPING STRATEGIES (YEARS OF EXPERIENCES)

Factors	Factor interpretation	Variables included in the factors	Cronbanch's Alpha
F_1	Less than 5 years	I admit to myself that I can't deal with it, and quit trying, I just give up trying to reach my goal, I take additional action to try to get rid of the problem and I pray more than usual	.852
F_2	6-10 years	I make a plan of action and I turn to work or other substitute activities to take my mind	.777
F_3	11-15 years	I sleep more than usual and I feel a lot of emotional distress and I find myself expressing those feeling a lot	.643
F_4	16-20 years	I talk to someone who could do some think. About the problem and I accept that this has happened and that can't we changed	.626
F_5	More than 20 years	I don't' do anything about it until the situation permits and I let my feelings out	.613

Source: Computed From Primary Data

The result of reliability analysis declares that the Cronbanch's Alpha value .852, .777, .643, .626 and .613 establishes significant and positive association between the variables tested. It establishes the existence of internal constancy with data collected at time of field survey. The results of the test establish consistency in the opinion of respondents expressed by the sample population on stress coping strategies.

5.9 Conclusion

From the study the primary causes identified for occurrence of occupational stress among the police personnel are: when the police personnel see the criminals go free because of lack of evidence, court leniency and when a fellow officer killed in line of duty. It has also inferred that majority of the police constables get stress, when they do not get the opportunity for career advancement. Similarly, frequency of burnout and stress symptoms are observed to be more when police constable face the problem of handling the criminals, at the time of staff shortages and lack of participation in policy making decisions and also when their fellow officers were killed in the line of duty. Due to constant stress the police personnel experiences stress outcome symptoms like: loss of sexual interest or pleasure, crying easily and thoughts of ending one's life i.e., committing suicide.   Further the study reveals that at stress situations 61.25 per cent of police constables on average seek solution from the other police personnel, 60.50 per cent of the sample subjects have opined that they positively take an attempt to get out stress, 47.75 per cent of the sample police constables have said that they practice negative coping strategies like denying to accept the problems and they restrict themselves from doing other acts, 58.25 per cent of the sample subjects have said that they search for alternative ventilation, 25 per cent of the police constables under stressful situation restrain themselves from doing anything quickly and 47.75 per cent daydream about things other than stress causes.

Under any circumstance police personnel must be ready to serve the society. This is the first lesson teaching to selected candidates during their training period and passing out stage, they must be prepared to coping with all type of situations. Moreover police person are also human beings and they cannot be treated in unhumanitical manner, also there is a possibilities of rewarding in good and most appreciable manner.

CHAPTER VI

SUMMARY, FINDINGS, SUGGESTIONS AND CONCLUSION

6.1 Summary

Job stress is a universal phenomenon which is part of mankind's work environment. It is widely viewed as a product of mismatch between the individual and his/her physical or social environment. Police work often places officers in situations where reaction, speed, coordination and the capacity to make rapid decisions and accurate judgments under pressure is critical, and inefficient mental and emotional responses to stress can significantly impair these abilities. At the extreme level, stress can cause officers to lose balance and composure to the degree that they employ inappropriate or excessive force in dealing with subjects

At the psychological level, the stress of police work may result in chronic negative emotions such as anger, anxiety or depression. Police officers operating under severe and chronic stress may well be at greater risk of error and over-reaction that can compromise their performance and public safety. The unrealistic expectations imposed by this occupational culture discourage officers from admitting feeling stressed and openly expressing negative emotions. The current study aims to analyze the occupational stress and the coping styles among the police constables in Thoothukudi District of Tamilnadu.

The following objectives were constructed for the effective conduct of the study: to study the socio-economic status and job profile of the police officers in the study area, to evaluate the police officers' perception about the nature of occupational stress faced by them, to measure the frequency of occurrence of occupation stress among the police officers, to analyse the gap between police officers' perception about their occupation stress and its occurrence frequencies and to study the stress coping styles adhered by the police officers and suggest suitable techniques to reduce their stress levels.

The research methodology of the study consists of two stages. First stage of the research is exploratory by nature and the second stage of descriptive in nature. This study is based on the police constables in Tuticorin district. The researcher has adopted Cluster based random Sampling Procedure (Probability) for defining the entire population area i.e., police stations and further researcher has adopted convenience sampling techniques in collection of primary data. The respondents' are approached with the support of the affluent and references groups support and only voluntary respondents' were included in the survey and no monetary benefits were paid as remuneration to the sample subjects.

6.2 Findings of the Study

The major findings of the study are briefly summarized in this sub-section.

6.2.1 Demographic Profile

- It has been observed that80.17 per cent of the total constables are Male and the rest of 19.83 per cent of the total constables are female. Further the data analysis indicates that 49.80 per cent of the police constables are in the age group of 20-29 years that is, they are very young for the job and moreover 47.30 per cent of the sample subjects are unmarried 69.50 per cent of the total constables have done their education at undergraduate level. It has been observed that 77 per cent of the respondents are Hindus, 46.70 per cent of the total constables' belonged to upper caste or other caste and 72.20 per cent of the total constables are from rural area. Further, it has been observed that

47.30 per cent of the total constables were unmarried and 59.80 per cent of the total constables have two dependent members in their family.

6.2.2 Job Profile

- The sample participants of the study constitutes 49 per cent of Grade II police constables, 32.33 per cent of designation of Grade III i.e., head constables, and the rest of 18.67 per cent were in Grade I i.e., entry level police personnel. And 30.70 per cent of the total constables have a service experience of 6 to 10 years. Since most of the police constables have 6-10 years of work experiences, their monthly salary fall in the slab of `.5000-20000 plus grade pay`.1900.

6.2.3 Police Personnel's Perception about Causes for Occupational Stress

- The primary causes identified for occurrence of occupational stress among the police personnel are: when the police personnel see the criminals go free because of lack of evidence, court leniency and when a fellow officer killed in line of duty. It has also been inferred that majority of the police constables get stress, when they do not get the opportunity for career advancement.

- Frequency of burnout and stress symptoms are observed to be more when police constable faces the problem of handling the criminals, at the time of staff shortages and lack of participation in policy making decisions and also when the their fellow officers were killed in the line of duty.

6.2.4 Outcome of Stress

From the elaborate data analysis the following prominent stress outcomes are identified: loss of sexual interest or pleasure, crying easily and thoughts of ending one's life i.e., committing suicide.

6.2.5 Coping Strategies

- It has been observed that 61.25 per cent of police constables on average seek solution from the other police personnel who had experience of similar problems, as they had faced to resolve their stressful situations.

- On the contrary 60.50 per cent of the sample subjects have opined that they positively make an attempt to get what they want under the stressful situations.

- Similarly it has been observed 47.75 per cent of the sample police constables have said that they practice negative coping strategies like denying accepting the problems and they restrict themselves from doing other acts.

- And 58.25 per cent of the sample subjects have said that they search for alternative ventilation to let out their stress and they think pleasant happening that had occurred in the past.

- Similarly the study had identified that 59.25 per cent of the police constables under stressful situation restrain themselves from doing anything quickly and 47.75 per cent daydream about things other than stress causes.

6.2.6 Results of Hypotheses Testing

- The study concluded that there exists no association between job profile of the police officers' and their perception about their occupational stress.

- It has been inferred that there exist no similarities in the police officers' perception about their occupation stress i.e., between Grade III, II and I constables. It differs according to their age, work experience and position held.

- The results of the data analysis reveal the fact that there exist no similarities in the police officers' perception about occupation stress occurrence frequency. It significantly varies among the Grade III, II and I police constables surveyed.

- The results of Paired't' test confines that there exists wide gap between the police officers' perception about their occupation stress and its frequencies of occurrence.

- It has also been inferred that the stress coping styles adhered to by the police officers differs from one another, based on their designation grade and work experiences.

6.3 Implication of the Study

In the current study it has been observed that the police personnel in Thoothukudi district faces stress as they see the criminals go free because of lack of evidence, court leniency, when a fellow officer killed in line of duty and also when they do not get the opportunity for career advancement. More over the tough working conditions, lack of basic amenities, long working hours, physical separation from the family, tight controls and rigidly stratified hierarchies have been considered the reasons for the high level of stress.

6.3.1 Suggestion to the Higher Officials

- The police administration may develop modalities to define career path for lower levels of police personnel.

- Police constables should be encouraged to improve their potentialities so that they can be involved in decision making in their functional areas of work.

- Police personnel should be consulted with immediate boss to find out what are the barriers that are preventing them from making better use of Psychological Services such as yoga, meditation and monetary reward and professional reward and their suggestions should be taken into account.

- Police constables are suggested to develop or reorganize the personal growth habits, plans like yoga, meditation, walking, dieting which together are helpful in dealing with adverse effects of occupational stress.

- Police authorities in the higher post must realize the importance of developing a work culture where all personnel are given more human treatment and opportunities of participation in policy/ decision making. In practicing such HR behaviour may help in promoting the morale of the their sub-ordinate working in police force as it likely to increase more positive response from the police personnel in the process of their career growth.

- Police management should pay immediate attention to stress caused by a lack of resources (e.g. inadequate salary, staff shortages and other officers not doing their job). By reducing the stress caused by these factors, tiredness and distrust prevailing among the police personnel can be reduced to a minimum expectant. In this case the author would like to highlight similarly suggestion proposed by earlier researchers: reduction of job hours is one of the important measures they have suggested followed by recruitment of more staff, participation of constables in policy formulation and/or allocation of duty, increase in salary, proper coordination of interaction of different categories of staff irrespective of political categorizations.

- Police management should conduct regular personnel interactions, training and seminar session to increasing awareness of stress, burnout and coping strategies) should be introduced in order to enhance the capacity of police members to cope with stress in the workplace.

- By means of teaching effective stress coping strategies the police management can increase the feelings of work accomplishment, job satisfaction and a sense of pride among the police constables. At the same time active coping strategies lead to higher feelings of professional efficacy among the police officers engaged at critical work.

- Psychological Services could play a pivotal role in alleviating stress and developing pro-active programs to this effect. Programs should be run encouraging police members to come forward with their problems and to attend psychotherapy. They should be told how psychotherapy can help them and what to expect in therapy. Programs should be developed for the spouses and children so that they can support each other and ultimately understand the member.

- Training should be given to senior police members teaching them how to work with people and how to give instructions minimizing stress for the police member on the receiving end.

6.3.2 Suggestions to the Police Personnel

Police work tends to impose a high degree of stress and a multiplicity of stressful situations which can affect the physical, mental and interpersonal relationships of police personnel. Thus, they are suggested to master effective stress management techniques.

- Police personnel must understand that maintaining healthy interpersonal relationship is a very important motivating factor for the staff in discharging their duties efficiently. Maintaining positive attitude by the police constable will support and help them to resolve personal problems with their colleagues.

- Police personnel will better maintain attitude toward work and his/her family will be much more supportive of his/her career in law enforcement.

6.4 Conclusions and Recommendations

Police work is often regarded as an extremely stressful occupation, and personnel involved in field duties often report variety of psychological, behavioral and health-related problems. In India, there are a sizeable number of police members who are stressed and are coping with ineffectively.

From the study the primary causes identified for occurrence of occupational stress among the police personnel are: when the police personnel see the criminals go free because of lack of evidence, court leniency and when a fellow officer killed in line of duty. It has also been inferred that majority of the police constables get stress, when they do not get the opportunity for career advancement. Similarly, frequency of burnout and stress symptoms are observed to be more when police constable face the problem of handling the criminals, at the time of staff shortages and lack of participation in policy making decisions and also when the their fellow officers were killed in the line of duty. Due to constant stress the police personnel experiences stress outcome symptoms like: loss of sexual interest or pleasure, crying easily and thoughts of ending one's life i.e., committing suicide. Further the study reveals that at stress situations 61.25 per cent of police constables on average seek solution from the other police personnel, 60.50 per cent of the sample subjects have opined that they positively take an attempt to get out of stress, 47.75 per cent of the sample police constables have said that they practice negative coping strategies like denying to accept the problems and they restrict themselves from doing other acts; 58.25 per cent of the sample subjects have said that they search for alternative ventilation; 25 per cent of the police constables under stressful situation restrain themselves from doing anything quickly and 47.75 per cent daydream about thinks other than stress causes.

Other forms of stress can come from management. All of those not in management positions know we can do it better. We have better ideas, better plans and would change as much as we could. We create that stress upon ourselves. We should see our own ideas as helpful suggestions to be brought in work group meetings as a way to promote a better situation for all involved. Management is a difficult position to have in any place of employment. The police have to handle all of the office politics, personal issues and be able to work well with those above and below cadres. It is a delegate balance that put you in the middle everyday he goes to work. Managing requires that not only to take orders; the police have to issue them too. Stress will come from knowing some of the orders the police give will not make him a popular person. Management is not a popularity contest though and the personal feelings again have to put aside in order to achieve the ultimate goal. To be successfully in charge of people that will do the job that is given them to do the best of their ability whether or not they agree with it.

The department had no means at the time for officers need counseling. The cost of the counseling is severely straining police personnel financially, because health insurance does not cover the services. The confidentiality aspect has been lost and everyone in the department knows personal situation. This is not by any loss of confidentiality through the department chief. It is because of getting so emotional at the time of built up the courage to speak to the department chief, that everyone knew something was seriously wrong in their professional as well as personal life. For the most part of the department has been fully supportive but as was stated before, know that things relating to personal life are being talked about behind which again adds to the stress.

The author likes to conclude the study by stating that the stress is affecting them mentally and physically. It is also affecting their interpersonal relationships. Reducing occupational stress from a frequent evaluation by the superiors can help equal distribution of workload and there by the quality of work of subordinate i.e., police constables can be enhanced. This in turn may lead to high satisfaction with regards to the nature of work rendered by the police constables. More rigorous studies are needed in order to evaluate the efficacy of stress management interventions among police officers and recruits.

6.5 Further scope for the study

Primary limitations of the present study are that the data are to be collected from the respondents of Thoothukudi district. Moreover, since this study was based on a cross-sectional research design as it covers three different grades of police constables and it does not cover higher rank police officials like sub-inspector or inspectors or commissioners. Thus, the researcher believes that there is adequate scope for further researcher to extent this study both in term of adding more sample regions, i.e., other districts or prominent districts/ police circles in Tamilnadu and also this study provides a base for comparing the stress levels faced by different cadres of police officers i.e., both low rank and high rank officers.

1. Abdul LatifSalleh, Raida Abu Bakar, Wong KokKeong (2008); How Detrimental is Job Stress?: *A Case Study of Executives in the Malaysian Furniture Industry;*International Review of Business Research Papers Vol. 4 No.5 Pp. 64-73 October-November 2008.

2. Alexander, C. (1999); Police psychological burnout and trauma. In J. M. Violanti and D. Paton (Eds.), *Police trauma: Psychological aftermath of civilian combat.* (pp. 54 – 64). Springfield Ill: Charles C. Thomas.

3. Andrea Kohan and Dwight Mazmanian (2003); A Consideration of Daily Work Experiences, doi: 10.1177/0093854803254432 *Criminal Justice and Behavior* October 2003 vol. 30 no. 5 559-583.

4. Arnsten, A. (1998), The Biology of being Frazzled, Science, 280, 1711-1712

5. Associate Professor Tony LaMontagne from the McCaughey (2008); *Source HRM review*, September, page: 24.

6. B Kirkcaldy (1993); Job stress and satisfaction: *international police officers. ,Psychological Reports,* Volume: 72, Issue: 2, pp: 386.

7. Basson, A. (2005); *Skoksyferswyspolisie is oorbelaai.* Beeld. , August 4.

8. Beehr, T. A., & Newman, J. E. (1978), Job Stress, Employees Health and Organizational Effectiveness: A Facet, Analysis, Model, and Literature Review. Personnel Psychology, 31, 665-699

9. Beehr, T.A. (1995); Psychological Stress in the Workplace, *Routledge, London; Journal of Applied Psychology,* Vol. 261 No. 1, pp. 11-17.

10. Bernie L. Patterson (1992); Job Experience and Perceived Job Stress among Police, Correctional, and Probation/Parole Officers, *Criminal Justice and Behavior,* September 1992 vol. 19 no. 3 260-285.

11. Bhasker,S. (1982); Measuring job stress of the Indian police: An empirical approach. *Abhigyan,* 30-44.

12. Bhuian, S.N., Menguc, B. and Borsboom, R. (2005); "Stressors and job outcomes in sales: a triphasic model versus a linear-quadratic-interactive model", *Journal of Business Research,* Vol. 58, pp. 141-50.

13. Biswas, S.N.; and Tripathi, R.C. (1998); " Organisational Culture and Contexual Culture: A Cross Cultural and Cross Organisational Study," Prajanan: *Journal of Social and Management Science,*Vol. 27(3), Dec., pp. 247-252.

14. Bordia P, Jones E, Gallosis C, Callan VJ, Difonzo N(2006); Rumors and stress during organizational change; *Group & Organization Management;* October, Vol: 31, No: 5.

15. Buker, Hasan and Wiecko, Filip, (2007), "Are causes of police stress global: Testing the effects of common police stressors on the Turkish National Police",

16. Carver, C. S., Scheier, M. F., &Wientraub, J. K. (1989); assess coping strategies: A theoretical based approach. *Journal of Personality and Social Psychology, 56,* pp. 267 – 283.

17. Christine Randall, Nicholas Buys and Elizabeth Kendall (2006); Developing an occupational rehabilitation system for workplace stress, *The International Journal of Disability Management Research,* Print ISSN: 1833-8550, Vol: 1, Issue: 1, pp. 64-73, May.

18. Clarke E (2006); *People Management;* 31 August, Vol: 12, No: 17.

19. Cordes, C. L., & Dougherty, T. W. (1993); A review and integration of resources on job burnout. *Academy of Management Review, 18,* 621 – 656.

20. Davies Rinisstudy (2005); *explain how to manage stress in the work place and Engineering Management:* Feb-March.

21. Dhillan T K Sharma (1992); Role stress among the executives of private organization of India; *Journal of physiology,* Bangladesh, volume 13, 17-26.

22. Donald R. McCreary, Frank Y. Wong, Willie Wiener, Kenneth M. Carpenter, Amy Engle and Pauline Nelson (1996); *The relationship between masculine gender role stress and psychological adjustment: A question of construct validity?;*Sex Roles, Volume 34, Numbers 7-8.

23. Edwards, M. J., & Holden, R. R. (2001); Coping, meaning in life and suicidal manifestations: Examining gender differences. *Journal of Clinical Psychology, 59*(10), pp. 1133 – 1150.

24. Endler, N. S., & Parker, J. D. A. (1990b); Multidimensional assessment of coping: A critical evaluation. *Journal of Personality and Social Psychology, 58*, pp. 884 – 854.

25. Eric G. Lambert, Nancy L. Hogan and Marie L. Griffin (2008); *Being the Good Soldier - Organizational Citizenship Behavior and Commitment Among Correctional Staff,*doi: 10.1177/0093854807308853 *Criminal Justice and Behavior* January 2008 vol. 35 no. 1 pp. 56-68.

26. Folkman, S., & Lazarus, R. S. (1985); if it changes it must be a process: Study of emotional and coping during three stages of a college examination. *Journal of Personality and Social Psychology, 144,* 35 – 40.

27. Gul, SerdarKenan, (2008), "Police Job Stress in the USA", Turkish Journal of Police Studies (Polis BilimleriDergisi), V.10, I.1, pp.1-13.

28. Gulle, G., Tredoux, C., & Foster, D. (1998); Inherent and organisational stress in the SAPS: An empirical survey in the Western Cape. *South African Journal of Psychology, 28*(3), pp. 129 -134.

29. H.L. Kaila (2007); "Women Mangers in Indian Organizations", *Journal of the Indian Academy of Applied Psychology,* January, Vol: 33, No: 1, pp. 93-102.

30. Harigopal K. (1997); *Organizational Stress: A Study of Role Conflict;*Published by Orient Longman; EAN code No:9788173710018; No. of pp: 184.

31. John J. Rodwell, René Kienzle and Mark A. Shadur(1998); The relationship among work-related perceptions, employee attitudes, and employee performance: *The integral role of communications; Human Resource Management, Special Issue: Employee Communications;*Volume 37, Issue 3-4, pp 277–293, Autumn (Fall) - Winter .

32. Journal of Management in Engineering Report (2004); *Gender Differences in Occupational Stress among Professionals in the Construction Industry,* Volume 20, Issue 3, pp. 126-132, July.

33. KalpanaKohli and G.S.Bajpai(2006), A Comparative Study of Frustration, Depression and Deprivation amongst Trainee and Serving Police Officials, Indian Journal of Criminology and Criminalistics,Vol.XXVII, No 3 Sept-December

34. Kamble SV and Phalke DB (2011); Study of occupational stress as a risk factor for various morbidities among policemen.Journal of the Indian Medical Association 2011 Apr; 109 (4):pp. 238-40.

35. Karena J. Burkel and Jane Shakespeare- Finch (2011); Markers of Resilience in New Police Officers Appraisal of Potentially Traumatizing Events, Published online before print December 29, 2011, doi: 10.1177/1534765611430725 *Traumatology* December 2011 vol. 17 no. 4, pp. 52-60.

36. Kop, N., &Euwema, M. C. (2001). Occupational stress and the use of force by Dutch polce officers. *Work & Stress, 13,* pp. 326 – 340.

37. Kroes, H. William, (1985), Society's Victim, The Policeman: An Analysis of Job Stress in Policing,Revised Ed. of 1976c.Illinois: Charles C. Thomas.

38. Lazarus, R. S., &Folkman, S. (1984); *Stress, appraisal and coping.* New York: Springer Publishing Company, Inc.

39. Martin, C. A., McKean, H. E., &Veltkamp, L. J. (1986); Post-traumatic stress disorder in police working with victims: A pilot study. *Journal of Police Science and Administration,* 14,pp.98 – 101.

40. Martocchio, J. J., &O"Leary, A. M. (1989); Sex differences in occupational stress: A meta-analytic view. *Journal of Applied Psychology,* 74, pp. 495 – 501.

41. Maureen F. Dollard and Anthony H. Winefield (1996); Managing occupational stress: A national and international perspective; *International Journal of Stress Management,*Volume 3, Number 2, 69-83, DOI:10.1007/BF01857716

42. McCafferty, F. L. (1992); Stress and suicide in police officers: Paradigm of occupational stress. *Southern Medical Journal,* 85, pp. 233 – 243.

43. Mohan V. Chauhan D (1999); A Comparative study of organisational role stress amongst managers of government, public and private sectors; *Journal of the Indian Academy of Applied Psycholog,* 1999 Jan-Jul; 25(1-2): pp. 45-50.

44. Mokowska Z. (1995); psychosocial characteristics of work and family as determinants of stress and well being of women; a preliminary study, *Int J Occup Med Environ Health.* Vol. 8(3), pp. 215-22.

45. Moore, L., & Donohue, J. (1976). The Patrol Officer: Special Problems/ Special Cures, Police Chief,45(Nov.), 42.

46. Nel, J. & Burgers, T. (1996); *The South African Police Service: „Symptom bearer" of the new South Africa? Track Two,* pp. 17 – 20.

47. Ongori Henry and Agolla Joseph Evans (2008); Occupational Stress in Organizations and its effects on organizational performance; *Book- Stress Management for primary health care professionals;* Publisher – Spring US,

DOI- 10.1007/b 108476, ISBN- 978-0-306-47240-4 (print) 978-0-306-47649-5(online), pp- 25-39, date- Tuesday, May 08.

48. Ortega, A., Brenner, S., & Leather, P. (2007); Occupational stress, coping and personality in the police: An SEM study. *International Journal of Police Science and Management, 9*(1), pp. 36 - 50.

49. Pandey, A. (1995); *"Role efficacy and role stress relationship: Some experience with workers"*, Vol. 31, pp. 193-208.

50. Patterson, G. T. (2001); The relationship between demographic variables and exposure to traumatic incidents among police officers. *The Australasian Journal of Disaster and Trauma Studies,* 2, pp. 1 – 9.

51. Pestonjee, D.M. (1999); Stress and Coping: *The Indian Experience,*Newyork: Sage Publishers.

52. Pienaar, J., &Rothmann, S. (2006); Occupational stress in the South African Police Service. *South African Journal of Industrial Psychology, 32*(3), pp. 72 – 78.

53. Policing: An International Journal of Police Strategies and Management, V.30, I.2, pp.291-309.

54. Priyanka Sharma (2013), A Study of Organizational Climate And Stress of Police Personnel, International Journal of Advanced Research in Management and Social Sciences, ISSN: 2278-6236, Vol. 2, No. 2, February.

55. R. Ravichandranand R. Rajendran (2007); Perceived Sources of Stress among the Teachers; Journal of the Indian Academy of Applied Psychology, January 2007, Vol. 33, No.1, pp. 133-136.

56. RashmiShahu and S.V. Gole (2008); Effect of Job Stress and Job Satisfaction on Performance: *An Empirical Study;*Vol: 2, No: 3, September, pp. 237-246.

57. RituLehal (2007); A Study of Organisational Role Stress and Job Satisfaction among Executives in Punjab; Indain management Studies Journal; Issues- 11; pp. 67-80.

58. Rutledge John Edward (2001), "Ph.D. Thesis", *Dissertation Abstract International,* Vol. 62, No.2, August.

59. S E Pandi(1998); Relationship between personality dimension of industry and their perceived organizational role stress (with Special Refernce to BHEL); *"Indian journal of IR,* volume33 – 4).

60. Sahu, Kiran and Misra, Neelam (1995); Life stress and Burn out in female college teachers, *Journal of Indian Academy of Applied Psychology,* Vol: 21, No: 2, pp. 109-113.

61. Sanjav Kumar Singh, Shalilendra Singh (2008); Managing role stress through emotional intelligence: a study of Indian medico professionals: Address: HRM Group, Institute of Management Technology, Ghaziabad HRM Group, Indian Institute of Management, Lucknow. Published in Journal: International Journal of Indian Culture and Business Management 2008 – Vol. 1, No. 4, pp: 377-396.

62. Satyanarayana,K.(1995); "Stressors among Executives and Supervisors: A Comparative Study in Public Sector Undertaking", *Osmania Journal of Psychology,* Vol. 19, pp. 1-9.

63. Sever, Murat and HüseyinCinoglu, (2010), "AmerikanPolisindeİşStre-sindenKaynaklananAileiçiŞiddetOlaylarınınSosyolojikveİstatis-tikselAnalizi", Polis BilimleriDergisi (Turkish Journal of Police Studies), C.12, S.1, ss.125-146.

64. Sexena M.R. (1996); Indian Journal of Psychometry and Education, Vol: 27 (1); pp. 41-46.

65. Sharon Conley and Sherry A. Woosley (2000); Teacher role stress, higher order needs and work outcomes", *Journal of Educational Administration,* Vol. 38 Iss: 2, pp.179 -201

66. Sibnath Deb, TanusreeChakraborty, PoojaChatterjee and NeerajakshiSrivastava (2008); Job-Related Stress, Causal Factors and Coping Strategies of Traffic Constables,*Journal of the Indian Academy of Applied Psychology* ,January 2008, Vol. 34, No.1, 19-28.

67. Spielberger, C. D., Vagg, P. R., &Wasala, C.F. (2003); Occupational stress: Job pressures and lack of support. In J. C. Quick & L. E. Tetrick (Eds.), *Handbook of occupational health psychology* (pp. 185 – 200). Washington, DC: American Psychological Association.

68. Srivatsava S, Hagtvet K A, A K Sen, (1994); "A study on role stress, and job anxiety among three group of employee in a private sector organization", *social science international,* volume 10, 1-2 & 25-30.

69. Stewart Collins (1995); Stress and social work lectures: *Dreaming spires, ivory towers or besieged in concrete blocks?,* "University of Wales, Bangor, DOI: 10.1080/02615479511220251, Vol: 14, Issue: 4, pp. 11-37.

70. Sze-Sze Wong, GerardineDeSanctis and Nancy Staudenmayer (2007); The Relationship Between Task Interdependency and Role Stress: A Revisit of the Job Demands Control Model; Journal of Management Studies, Vol. 44, Issue 2, pp. 284-303, March 2007.

71. Tim Morton (2003), Job-Related Stressors on African American Police Officers, A Dissertation Submitted in Partial Fulfillment of the Requirements for the Degree of Doctor of Philosophy in Applied Management and Decision Science, Walden University, February.

72. TriantoroSafaria and Ahmad bin Othman (2010); The Role of Leadership Practices on Job Stress among Malaysian University Academic Staff: Two Step Analysis; PhD student University Malaysia Pahang & Faculty of

Psychology Ahmad DahlanUniversity,Yogyakarta, Indonesia University Malaysia Pahang,Malaysia; paper presentation, The First International Conference Of Indigenous & Cultural Psychology; Edited by Tim Center for Indigenous & Cultural Psychology, UGM ; Book Of Abstracts; The First International Conference Of Indigenous & Cultural Psychology; ISBN: 978-979-95876-6-4; UniversitasGadjahMada; Yogyakarta, Indonesia.

73. Tripathi, R.C., Naidu, R.K.M. Thapa, K. and Biswas, S.N. (1993); Stress, Health and Performance: A study of Police Organization in Uttar Pradesh. Report submitted to Bureau of police Research & development February, 1993.

74. Vickie A. Lambert and Clinton E. Lambert (2001); Literature review of role stress/strain on nurses: An international perspective; *Nursing & Health Sciences;*Volume 3, Issue 3, pp 161–172, September.

75. Violanti, J. M., &Aron, F. (1994); Ranking police stressors. *Psychological Reports,* 75, pp. 824 – 826.

76. Wendy R. Boswell, Julie B. Olson-Buchanan and Marcie A. LePine(2004); Relations between stress and work outcomes: The role of felt challenge, job control, and psychological strain; *Journal of Vocational behaviour;* Volume 64,issues 1, page 165,18[th]Feburary.

ABOUT TAMIL NADU POLICE

The administrative control of Tamil Nadu Police vests with the Chief Minister of Tamil Nadu who holds the portfolio of Home Minister. The supervision and coordination of Police is done by the Home Department Govt. of Tamil Nadu. **The Tamil Nadu Police Force is over 150 years old.** It is the fifth largest State Police Force in India.

The Force, headed by the Director General of Police, is responsible for maintenance of law and order and prevention and detection of crimes in an area spanning 130058 sq. Kms with a population of over 7.21 crores (provisional) as per the Census 2011. Tamil Nadu has a coastline of 1076 Kms. State is divided into convenient territorial divisions called Zones, ranges with a number of districts constituting a range. District police is further sub-divided into police divisions, circles and police-stations. The State is divided into 4 Police Zones - North, Central, West and South. Each Zone is headed by one Inspector General of Police. In each of the 6 Metropolitan Cities of Tamil Nadu, the City Police force is headed by a Commissioner of Police. These cities are -- Chennai, Madurai, Coimbatore, Tiruchirapalli, Salem and Tirunelveli. There are 33 Police districts including 2 railway districts in Tamil Nadu, each headed by a Superintendent of Police. In each City and District, the Commissioner of Police / Superintendent of Police has, besides the civil police force, an Armed Reserve of Police personnel. One Deputy Inspector General (DIG) of police supervises the work of 2-3 districts, which constitute a Police Range. There are Twelve (including 1 Railway) Ranges in Tamil Nadu.

Besides the civil police, state also maintains its own armed police and have separate intelligence branches, crime branches, etc. Police set-up in big cities like Delhi, Kolkata, Mumbai, Chennai, Bangalore, Hyderabad, Ahmedabad, Nagpur, Pune, etc. is directly under a Commissioner of Police who enjoys magisterial powers. All senior police posts in various states are manned by the Indian Police Services (IPS) cadres, recruitment to which is made on all-India basis.

The police are on guard against any attempts at infiltration and smuggling in of contraband over coast line for which Standard Operating Procedures (SOP) has been prepared and Crisis Management plans are in place for various situations. The Tamil Nadu Commando Force (TNCF) is also being adequately equipped. Quick Reaction Teams (QRT) are also strategically located all over the State. NSG hub has been set up at Vandalur. Apart from being available for deployment at short notice NSG Personnel have also been undertaking joint exercises with other Police Personnel,thereby enhancing the skills and capabilities of these teams and promoting co-ordination in times of need.

In G.O.Ms.No.471, Home (Pol.XIV) Dept., dt. 24.08.2011 Govt. have ordered merger of Chennai Suburban Police with Chennai City Police and form a **Greater Chennai Police Commissionerate**divided into four L & O zones viz. East Zone (27 Police Stations), West Zone (35 Police Stations), North Zone (30 Police Stations), South Zone (37 Police Stations) each zone having jurisdiction of 3 Districts.

Recruitment of police personnel of the rank of Constables and Sub-Inspectors of police is entrusted with the **Tamil Nadu Uniformed Services Recruitment Board (TNUSRB).** The Board also recruits Jail Warders and Firemen. Rank-wise information on „Sanctioned" as well as „Actual" and "vacancy" in police strength in the State are presented in table.

Police manpower alone is not sufficient to curb the crime unless they are motivated and facilitated with basic necessities such as equipment, transport, housing, medical insurance, free education for children, etc. Therefore, an attempt has been made to compile auxiliary information such as availability of housing facility to various categories of police officials, availability of vehicles and sophisticated gadgets with the police, etc.

The **Tamil Nadu Police Housing Corporation** looks after the construction, repairs and maintenance of police buildings and quarters.

Information on the availability of police housing facility districtwise&unitwise against the sanctioned police force for different categories is presented in table.

Motor Vehicle details viz. 2 wheelers, 3 wheelers, 4 wheelers, vans, buses, lorries, ambulances, lockup vans, prisoner escorts, etc. available with police all over Tamilnadu to enable them to perform their duties efficiently is presented in table under **"police fleet strength"**.

The zonewise, rangewise, city/districtwise details on sub-divisions, police stations, outposts & All Women Police Stations all over Tamilnadu are presented in table.

Just as the crime incidence in an area is a deceptive pointer to the crime situation, the absolute strength of police personnel is also not a true indicator of the magnitude of crime and its combating machinery as well as performance of other assigned tasks by police. Number of policemen per 100 sq. kms and per lakh of population are considered to be important indicators in planning for their deployment. With a view to instilling confidence in the minds of the public on the maintenance of law and order by removing the fear created by anti-social elements indulged in unlawful activities causing threat to the life and rights of individuals and to restore peace in the State, it is ordered the law and order machinery to deal with such elements with an iron hand giving no room for their escape and to deal firmly as per law.

In G.O.Ms.No.423, Home (Pol-XI) Dept., dt. 28.07.2011 Govt. have sanctioned the formation of 36 **Anti Land Grabbing Special Cells** in the State with one cell each at the State Police Headquarters, all Commissionerates and all Districts except Karur, Tiruvannamalai and Nagapattinam for a period of one year on temporary basis. In those 3 Dists. Dist. Crime Branch will handle the investigation. The Govt. have also ordered on 01.08.2011 the constitution of 25 **Fast Track Special Courts** in Tamil Nadu for the quick disposal of these cases. During the concluding speech of Hon"ble Chief Minister at the Police Officers Conference on 14.11.2011 new announcement was made that Anti Land Grab Cells will be formed in Karur, Nagapattinam and Thiruvannamalai Districts.

Special Units of Tamil Nadu Police

The following Special Units of Tamil Nadu Police perform specific functions support service

Armed Police or T.N. Spl. Police	Core Cell	Anti-Dacoity Cell CB- CID
Coastal Security Group	Prohibition Enforcement Wing	Narcotic Intelligence Bureau, CID
Crime Branch, CID	Railway police	Special Investigation Team
Cyber Crime Cell	Social Justice And Human Rights	Video Piracy Cell
Economic Offences Wing	Special Branch CID	Intelligence Wing
CCIW	"Q" branch CID	Home Gaurds
Idol wing	Special Division CID	Technical Services
EOW (Financial Institutions)	Security Branch CID	Civil Supplies CID
Anti-Land Grabbing Spl. Cell		TNUSRB

Armed Police: The Battalion was originally formed as Special Armed Police II Battalion and was raised in a short notice on 21.11.1962 in the wake of the Chinese Aggression on India. After this, it was reformed as Reserved Armed Police by replacement of 8 Companies of Malabar Special Police and Special Armed Police with its Headquarters at Manimuthar. On the eve of reorganization of state on linguistic basis, the Malabar Special Police was divided into two, one for Kerala and the other for Madras state. The Headquarters of MSP or (Madras state) Tamilnadu was shifted to Trichy for maintaining the law and orders situation as per GO No. 4112(Home) Deptdt. 07.11.1947. The erstwhile Madras state came to be called as "Tamilnadu " asper GO. Ms .No. 2051 dated 03.08.1972. The MSP and SAP battalions of this state were renamed as Tamilnadu Special Police Battalions. The police personnel are being deputed for duty all over Tamilnadu to assist the local police in Law and Order duty, coastal security duty, Central prison guard duty etc., and the companies are moved to various places, as per the orders of the Director General of Police and Additional Director of Police, Armed Police, Chennai then and there. When the companies are in Head Quarters, they will attend to routine physical training, parade movements and Arms cleaning duties. 16 Tamil Nadu Special Battallions (TSP) including 1 Regimental Centre at Avadi 1 Special Force at Veerapuram constitute the Tamil Nadu Special Police. The TSP VIII Battallion is one special duty at Tihar in New Delhi.

Coastal Security Group, CID The Coastal Security Group, CID., was formed as per G.O.Ms.No.718, Home (Pol. XV) Dept., dated 27.06.1994 with the objectives of (i) Prevention of smuggling of fuel and medicines and other essential commodities from the Tamil Nadu Coast to Sri Lanka (ii) Prevention of intrusion of militants into Tamil Nadu and (iii) Prevention of collusion between fishermen and militants

Crime Branch CID Started in the year 1906, the erstwhile Madras Presidency Crime Branch CID has grown into a strong organization headed by an ADGP. Apart from 34 Detachments, 7 Organised Crime Units and 4 Counterfeit Currency Wings are also functioning in various districts/ commissionarates. Cyber Crime Wing, Anti-Trafficking Cell and Police Research Centre are the other Specialized Units. Main function of this unit is to investigate the cases entrusted by Government, DGP, Tamil Nadu and Hon"ble High Court.

Cyber Crime Cell: In Tamil Nadu, in the year 2002, two Cyber Crime Cells were created; one is exclusively for Chennai Police and another at CB CID, having jurisdiction through out State of Tamil Nadu. The role of this Cell is to detect, prevent and investigate Cyber crimes that come under the ambit of Information Technology Act 2000 and assist the other Law Enforcement in the investigation of crimes in which elements of Computer related crime exists.

The cases under I.T. Act 2000 have to be investigated by not below the rank of Dy. Superintendent of Police.

Economic Offences Wing: The Economic Offences Wing of Tamil Nadu consists of three units i.e. Commercial Crime Investigation Wing, Idol Wing and EOW (Financial Institutions). Chronologically speaking the three units came into existence at different points of time.

CCIW: The CCIW was first to be constituted as per GO.Ms.No.170, dated: 20.01.1971 to investigate the offences relating to defalcation of funds in co-operative societies pertaining to 12 departments. This unit is headed by one SP and assisted by 7 DSPs in 7 CCIW Sub-Divisions. Besides, there are 32 CCIW units all over Tamil Nadu, which are headed by Inspectors of Police at field level.

Idol Wing – CID It was created in the year 1983 as per G.O.Ms.No.2098/Home(POL.IV) Dept. dt:7.10.83 to investigate cases of i)theft of idols declared as Antiques;ii)theft of Idols more than 100 Years old;iii)cases which have state-wise/ inter-state remification, iv)theft of idols whose value is Rs.5 Lakhs and more & v)theft idols which are of sensitive nature and which are ordered to be taken up by the state Govt. Apart from detecting and investigating cases referred to it, is also monitoring cases of Idol thefts reported in the Local Police Stations all over Tamil Nadu. This unit gives clues and useful instructions to the District Police for the detection of offences involving idols. This unit is monitoring the functioning of the temple protection force

EOW (Financial Institutions): Concerned with the alarming rise of large scale cheating and fraud committed by several non-banking financial institutions, the Honourable High Court of Madras ordered to form a Specially Dedicated Police Unit under the Economic Offences Wing. While hearing the Company petitions 479 and 480/1999 in M/s.Anubhav Plantations Ltd., based on the above direction of the Honourable High Court, Chennai, Economic Offences Wing II (Financial Institutions)" came into existence from 01.01.2000 as per the Govt. orders in G.O.Ms.No.1697/Home (Court IIA) Dept. dated 24.12.1999

Core Cell: This unit attached to the SB CID was created during 1997 to look after the proximate security arrangements for the functions, meetings and tours of the Hon"ble Chief Minister of Tamil Nadu. It comprises of Commando Teams, Bomb Detection and Disposal Squad (BDDS), Motor Transport Wing (MT) and Technical Wing.

Prohibition Enforcement Wing: Headed by IGP with effect from 01.06.2009. It is functioning with the objective of eradicating illicit distillation, transportation, possession and sale of illicit liquor and preventing smuggling of arrack / spurious & seconds IMFS from other States. There are 94 units throughout the State, declared as Police Stations to enforce the Tamil Nadu Prohibition Act, 1937.

Railway Police: Railway Police was formed in 1932 with Headquarters at Trichy. In 1981, the Unit was bifurcated and a new Railway Police District was created with Headquarters at Chennai. In 1991, the post of IGP, Railways was created. Railway Police prevents and investigates crimes that take place in trains and platforms, and provides protection to railway property. It maintains close coordination with the Railway Protection Force and the local Police. Railway Police covers a vast railway jurisdiction extending to 5525 Kms.

Social Justice and Human Rights The enforcement of the "Protection of Civil Rights Act 1955 and the scheduled caste and the scheduled tribe (Prevention of Atrocities) Act 1989" are both enforced by this wing headed by an Inspector General of Police. Apart from taking steps to prevent atrocities against members of the Scheduled Castes and Scheduled Tribes, the wing also works for the relief and rehabilitation of the victims of such atrocities. The wing also plays a major role in resolving disputes affecting the members of Scheduled Castes and Scheduled Tribes.

State Intelligence Wing: This wing headed by DGP (Int.) assisted by 2 IGPs, 5 SPs with supporting staff deals with collection, collation and dissemination of information relating to matters affecting security & peace and other matters of public importance. This comprises SB CID, "Q" Branch CID, Spl. Division, Security Branch CID & OCIU.

Special Branch CID It collects Intelligence on political activities; open as well as secret; on subversive activities of individuals and organizations which are likely to cause disturbance to public order, promote disharmony or hatred between people of different religions or castes or community; monitors developments such as labour, students, youth, farmers, trade unions and service associations; watches the circulation of rumours, news, letters, posters, leaflets likely to disturb public peace; monitors the activities of different non-governmental organizations, functioning of essential services and existence of any widespread popular feeling on political, social, economic, religious or other subjects of importance. This Branch collates, processes and disseminates the collected information in advance to take appropriate preventive action at all levels to maintain law and order in the state.

"Q" Branch CID This was created in 1970 to exclusively deal with the Naxalite menace. In 1993, the „Q" Branch detachments functioning in the districts and cities were declared as Police Stations and bestowed with investigating powers under CrPC. This wing collects information on Left Wing Extremists, in specific, CPI (Maoists), and Sri Lankan Tamil militants and takes appropriate action against them. It monitors the influx of Sri Lankan refugees and the activities of the Sri Lankan refugees in the camps and settlements. It also takes action against smuggling activities in the coastal belt, where LTTE is involved.

Special Division CID This was created in the aftermath of Coimbatore serial bomb blasts (1998) and it collects information on all fundamental and terrorist organisations, religious machineries, and inflow of foreign funds and passes information on actionable intelligence to the local police for taking action. It also closely monitors the proscribed fundamentalist organisations, such as, Al-umma, All India Jihad Committee, SIMI and other radical groups.

Security Branch CID This is looking after the security matters in respect of VVIPs/VIPs including foreign Heads of States and other protected persons visiting Tamil Nadu besides protecting the VIPs/PPs based in Tamil Nadu. Apart from this, it handle matters relating to activities of foreigners, preparation of schemes to protect vital installations, verification of passports and citizenship applications & matters relating to immigration.

Core Cell: A separate unit attached to the Security Branch CID was created during 1997 exclusively to look after the proximate security arrangements of the Hon. C.M. of Tamil Nadu during functions, meetings and tours. This cell comprises Commando Teams, Bomb Detection and Disposal Squad (BDDS), Motor Transport Wing (MT) & Technical Wing.

OCIU: A new separate unit "Organaised Crime Intelligence Unit" was created on 15.07.2010 in State Intelligence Wing which collects useful actionable intelligence on the activities of organized criminal gangs, rowdy elements, smuggling of narcotic drugs, trafficking of arms and explosives, human trafficking, hawala transactions, counterfeit currency, etc.and disseminate the intelligence to the field officers. The OCIU staff are building full fledged profiles on notorious criminals and collect all details.

ANTI-DACOITY CELL CB-CID Anti-Dacoity Cell was formed vide G.O. Ms. 805 Home (Pol.XII) dated 30.05.1995 headed by the SP and functioning under the control of ADGP (Crime), Chennai. The Cell collects information on Dacoity cases from the districts as well as takes up investigation in the cases referred to it by the High Court, Government and DGP.

Narcotic Intelligence Bureau, CID Created initially as per order 14/63 dated 17.12.1963. In G.O. Ms.No. 2934, dated 13.11.1973 P.I.B redesignated as N.I.B. As per G.O. Ms. No. 1730, Home (Pol XIII) dated 4.8.84, the NIB CID unit was declared as police station for the whole state of Tamil Nadu. The G.O. Ms.No.2051, Home Police-IV, dated 27.8.87 first augmented the strength of the NIB, with sanction of three new units at Trichy, Madurai and Salem, which commenced functioning from first half of 1988. Other subsequent units are Chennai, Trichy, Madurai, Salem, Dindigul, Theni, Villupuram, Tuticorin, Vellore, Ramnad, Coimbatore,Nagapattinam, Kancheepuram, Sivagangai, Kanniyakumari.

Special Investigation Team To investigate and prosecute the all fundamentalist cases in successful manner, the **SIT** was constituted in CB CID as per Chief Office Memo in Rc.No.237359/R.A.I (2)/1997 dated 29.09.97 at Chennai, Trichy, Coimbatore, Madurai and Tirunelveli.

Video Piracy Cell To control the menace of Video Piracy and to check violations relating to the Copyright Act, this separate cell was constituted on 17.02.1995 in Chennai –I, Chennai – II, Thomas Mount, Salem, Coimbatore, Vellore, Trichy, Cuddalore, Madurai, Virudunagar, Dindigul, Tirunelveli.

Home Guard: The Tamil Nadu Home Guards organisation came into being in 1963 as per Tamil Nadu Home Guards rules 1963 as a voluntary citizen"s force to assist Police in the maintenance of Law and Order and for meeting emergencies like floods, fires, cyclones etc. The Home Guards organisation renders valuable assistance in regulation of traffic, crowd control, maintenance of internal security, promotion of communal harmony, spread of awareness on health, hygiene and road safety. During the year 2009 there are 105 ½ companies of Home Guards (80.05 men companies and 25 women companies totaling 11,622 Home Guards including 2750 women Home Guards. All the districts and all the Police Commissionerates are having Home Guards units including women Home Guard wing.

Technical Service

Communication setup of the police department is maintained by the Technical Services wing of Tamil Nadu Police. This wing is headed by an officer of the rank of Inspector General of Police. A VHF High band network for police station level communications is provided for all districts and Commissionerates. VHF repeaters, VHF Static / Mobile sets and VHF Handheld sets are functioning for supporting the entire VHF network. UHF static & mobile sets, UHF Handheld sets, UHF repeater sets and HF sets are used in the state for voice communication. Microwave phone facility is also provided upto district level. The state is constantly endeavouring to upgrade the communication facilities of the Police Department. Data transfer among police units including police stations is possible through a fully operational Wide Area Network (WAN) For police units in Chennai City and suburbs Cor-DECT WLL telephone for voice and data transfer is also made fully operational and functioning.

Civil Supplies CID: This unit enforces the Essential Commodities Act and various control orders issued by the GOI and Govt. of Tamil Nadu by receiving administrative support from the Police Dept. but is operationally under the control of the Food Dept. In G.O.Ms.No.196, Co-operation, Food & Consumer Protection Dept., dt. 25.09.1998 this was lastly reorganized to the present stage. 5 flying squad for border States were sanctioned in G.O.Ms.No.125, Co-operation, Food & Consumer Protection Dept., dt.28.11.2011.

Antil Land Grabbing Special Cell: This cell was formed to deal with the land grabbing cases in the State as per G.O.Ms.No.423, Home (Pol-XI) Dept., dt.28.07.2011 with one cell each at the State Police H.Q., 7 Commissionerates and 28 Dists.exceptKarur, Tiruvannamalai&Nagapattinam dist. for a period of one year on temporary basis. During the Police Officers Conference on 14.11.2011, Hon. C.M. have made new announcement that Anti Land Grab Cells will be formed in Karur, Nagapattinam&Tiruvannamalai Dist. Also

TNUSRB

The Government constituted the Tamil Nadu Uniformed Service Recruitment Board with:

Chairman   : A police officer in the rank of DGP either serving or retired

Member   : A serving or retired police officer in the rank of ADGP

Member Secretary   : A Police Officer in the rank of IG of Police

The Board is manned by SP, DSP and a team of ministerial staff. It was constituted to select personnel for: Police Department (Men & Women) : S.I.s of police, Grade II P.C. & S.I.s (Technical)

Fire&RescueService :   Firemen

Prison Department (Men & Women): Jail Warders

- HOD intimate estimated vacancies to Govt.by Sep. every year for which recruitment conducted next year.
- Notification of vacancies calling applications will be released in consultation with the Head of depts.
- Processing of applications prescribed in different format for each category.
- Application fee:SI(Men/Women/Technical)=Rs.250/-   Grade   II P.C./Firemen/Jail Warders = Rs.150/-
- **Tamil Nadu Police Academy (TNPA) (ISO 9002-2001)**

The Police Recruit School was established as early as in 1896 in Vellore and this was upgraded as Police Training College during 1905. The Police Training College was subsequently shifted to Chennai in 1976 and has been upgraded as Tamil Nadu Police Academy located at Vandalur - 35 kms from Chennai.and started functioning with effect from 15.04.2008. There are four permanent Police Recruit Schools at Vellore, Coimbatore, Perurani at Thoothukudi, and Tiruchy meant to train police constables recruited thro" TNUSRB, who are the grassroots of the police service. Besides,formation of 4 more new permanent Police Recruit Schools at Avadi, Salem, Madurai and Villupuram has been ordered in G.O.Ms.No.735, Home (Police-XI) Dept., dt. 08.11.2011

RANGE	IN CHARGE	COVERED DISTRICTS
1.Chennai (East)	DSP	Chennai city Police and Railway Police
2.Chennai (West)	DSP	All Special Units of CID & Units not Covered by chennai (E)
3. Chengi Range	DSP	Chengalpattu (East), Kanchipuram and Tiruvalllur Districts
4.Vellore	DSP	Vellore and Dharmapuri Districts
5.Villupuram	DSP	Vilupuram, Cuddalore and Thiruvannamalai Districts
6.Trichy	DSP	Trichy, Trichy City, Perambalur, Karur&PudukkottaiDist
7.Madurai	DSP	Madurai Rural, Madurai City, Dindugal, Theni Districts and Railway Police Units Coming Under SRP,Trichy
8.Tirunelveli	DSP	Tirunelveli, Tirunelveli City, Thoothukudi, and Kanyakumari
9.Coimbatore	DSP	Coimbatore, Coimbatore City, Erode and The Nilgiris
10.Salem	DSP	Salem, Salem City and Namakkal Districts
11.Thanjavur	DSP	Thanjavur, Nagapattinam and Tiruvarur Districts
12. Ramnad	DSP	Ramnad , Sivagangai and Virudhunagar Districts

Grievance Redressal for Police Personnel

The Hon'ble CM has directed all Unit Officers to conduct the grievance day for the Police personnel on the following specified dates earmarked for them.

All the SsP of districts should attend the AR parade and hold orderly rooms to listen to and to redress the grievances of the police personnel	Every Friday
All the SsP of districts should hold Grievance Day for Local Police personnel attached to the various units in the districts	Every Tuesday
Range DIsG should hold Grievance Days at Range Headquarters	Once in a Month
ADGsP/ Zonal IGsP/ IGsP of Special Units should hold Grievance Day	Once in two Month
DGP will conduct the Grievance Day once in three months in State Headquarters	

Grievance Day Meeting for Public in Police Dept.

Govt. have ordered in G.O.Ms.No.677, Home (Police-1) Dept., dt. 17.08.2009 introducing Grievances Day Meetings for the Public in Police Dept. to be held by the Commissioners of Police & Dist. S.P.s for the public on the 1st and 3rd Mondays of every month between 10.00 hrs. and 13.00 hrs. w.e.f. 01.09.2009 for the redressal of public grievances.

Women Helpline

The Government of Tamil Nadu has launched a new scheme to aid women in distress. "Women Helpline" Units have been ordered to be opened throughout the state. Today "WOMEN HELPLINE UNITS" are functioning in most districts of Tamil Nadu. Women Police provide prompt help round the clock to women in distress in these "WOMEN HELPLINE UNITS".

Helpline Ideals

Render help with compassion	Rehabilitate Women Criminals	Provide relief to victims
Provide legal advice to women in distress	Provide self-confidence to insecure women.	Upliftment of Women and Children.

Helpline - Areas of Concern

Dowry Harassment	Alcoholic spouses.	Prostitution
Sexual harassment	Female infanticide	Street fights
Missing Girls/Children	Child Harassment	Domestic violence/Problems by in-laws
Problems related to love affairs	Problems related to promiscuity	Problems arising out of Bigamy

Welfare Activities

Tamil Nadu Police Benevolent Fund

Introduced in the year 1957 with the objective of providing monetary and other reliefs to the Non-gazetted Staff and their Family Members. This fund is being generated by way of collecting subscriptions from the Police Personnel as well as from the Ministerial Staff of the Police Department and also by way of donations from the Officers of the Police Department.

(a)   The family relief provided from the Fund is as follows:-

Rs.15,000/- In case of death of the subscriber

Rs.5,000/- In case of death of family members of the subscriber

(a) Providing scholarships to the children of the Employees of Police Department who pursue higher studies in the Colleges & Polytechnics (i.e.) from Rs.3,500/- to Rs.10,000/-.

Supply of Essential Commodities to the Police Personnel at Subsidised Rates

In G.O.Ms.No.1162, Home (Pol.12) Department, dated 11.09.2008 Government have issued orders for the implementation of the New Food Subsidy Scheme for the supply of some essential commodities to Police Personnel from the rank of Police Constables to Inspectors through the Public Distribution System at 50% rate with effect from 01.10.2008.

Ex-Gratia Payments

Government in G.O.Ms.No.284, Home (Pol.12) Department, dated 6.04.2009 have sanctioned following ex-gratia payable to the next of kin of the Police Personnel working in the Tamil Nadu Police who are killed/disabled/Injured under heroic or tragic circumstances in the course of duty.

1.	Killed	5 lakhs
2.	Totally Disabled	2 lakhs
3.	Single amputee and one eye blind, loss of toes, fingers	1 lakh
4.	Burns Gunshot wounds multiple compound fracture	Rs.50,000/-
5.	Simple injuries for all ranks	Rs.10,000/-

In case of death in harness, the legal heirs of the deceased are paid along with the pay last drawn by the deceased Police Personnel as family pension till the date of superannuation of the deceased.

Tamil Nadu Police Insurance Scheme

The Police Personnel from the rank of Gr II Police Constable to the Director General of Police are covered under the Tamil Nadu Police Insurance Scheme. The legal heirs and the nominees are benefited under this scheme in case of death of Police Officers and Personnel. This scheme includes accidental death or permanent incapacitation or partial disability suffered during the course of their duties. The following are the insurance amount sanctioned for the Police Personnel.

Cadre	For death	For Permanent Disablement	For Permanent Disablement
I. In General Police PCs to Addl.SPs SPs to IGs. ADGPs. DGP.	1 lakh 5 lakhs 7½ lakhs 10 lakhs	1 lakh 5 lakhs 7½ lakhs 10 lakhs	According to the percentage of disablement (decided by the Dean, Government General Hospital Chennai)
II. All Police Officers and Personnel and other staff of Special Task Force, Commando Force, Commando School, Swift Action force and Core Cell	10 lakh	10 lakhs	50% of the Lumpsum

The Tamil Nadu Police Commission had recommended for Uniform payment for sanction of Insurance amount as follows:-

SL. NO.	Rank	Death In Accident While on Duty	Incapacitation While on Duty
1.	DGP AND ADGP	10 LAKHS	In proportion to nature of
2.	DIG AND IGP	7½ LAKHS	impairment,
3.	S.P.	6 LAKHS	incapacitation or
4.	DSP, ADSP	5 LAKHS	disablement, not
5.	S.I. AND INSPECTORS	4 LAKHS	exceeding 50% of the
6.	PC TO HC	3 LAKHS	amount for death.

The Government have issued orders that the Insurance amount for the police personnel from P.C. to Inspector of Police be enhanced from Rs.1 lakh to Rs.2 lakhs.

Prize Scheme

This is mooted with an objective to award prizes to the children of the Employee of the Police Department who secure the first 10 ranks in SSLC and 12th Standard respectively every year in each District / City. Both in 10th and 12th Standard in each Districts and Commisionerates. The Prize amount is awarded at the rate of **Rs.6500/-, Rs.4500/- Rs.2500/-** for first three places and **Rs. 2000/-** for the remaining 4th to 10th ranked students for **10th std.** and **Rs.7500/-, Rs.5500/- Rs.3000/-** for first three places and **Rs. 2500/-** for the remaining 4th to 10th ranked students for **12th std.**

Tamil Nadu Police Centenary Scholarship Fund:

This was introduced in the year 1959 with an objective to motivate the deserving children of the non-gazetted Police Personnel to pursue higher education. The annual donations and Lumpsumcontributions, constitute to this fund. Students who have applied for availing this scholarship will be paid **Rs.3500/- to Rs.10,000/-** as one time measure.

Tamil Nadu Government Special Scholarship Fund

In order to encourage and facilitate the bright and promising young children of the Employee of the Police Department, Government had introduced in G.O.Ms.(D) No.837, Home (Pol. IX) Department, Dated 18.07.2008 to pursue higher education and in which the First 100 wards who secure highest marks in +2 standard will be paid **Rs.20,000** or the amount paid to the institutions whichever is less for 4 years or till the course is completed. The Govt. have also recently announced raising the amount from Rs.20,000/- to Rs.25,000/- including hostel fees.

Tamil Nadu Government Employees New Health Insurance Scheme:

This scheme was inaugurated w.e,f. 11.06.2008 as per G.O.No.174 Finance (salaries) Department dated 28.04.2008 to avail Rs.2 lakhs for every 4 years for medical treatment for Govt. servant and Family members. If the Government servant is unmarried father and mother are eligible. If the Government servant is married wife/Husband and children are eligible, Ifchildren"s age is above 25 years (or) if the children got married (or) if the children of the Government servant serves Government /Private concern they are not eligible. A sum of Rs.25/- is recovered as monthly subscription from the salary of Government servants with effect from June 2008.

MODERNISATION OF POLICE FORCE:

The Government has initiated steps to moderise the police in a planned manner from the year 2001-02 with the main objective of making the Tamil Nadu Police Force modern, efficient and people-friendly, Special emphasis is given to improving the capabilities in certain areas such as counter terrorism, cybercrimes, video piracy, organized crimes, operation against extremists, economic offences, etc. To achieve this objective, the Government is facilitating the department to acquire modern equipment to improve the communication, mobility, computing, weaponry and thereby adequately equipping the police department to meet the present as well as the future challenges.

MPF ALLOTMENT OF FUNDS (IN CRORES)

YEAR	GOVT OF INDIA	STATE GOVT	TOTAL	FUNDS RATIO (%) CENTRAL/STATE
2001-01	76.50	76.50	153.00	50:50
2001-02	68.10	68.10	136.20	50:50
2002-03	68.10	68.10	136.20	50:50
2003-04	52.47	36.67	89.14	60:40
2004-05	56.76	37.84	94.60	60:40
2005-06	65.46	21.82	87.28	75:25
2006-07	59.40	19.80	79.20	75:25
2007-08	75.75	25.25	101.00	75:25
2008-09	51.00	17.00	68.00	75:25
2009-10	60.67	20.22	80.89	75:25

| 2010-11 | 92.07 | 30.69 | 122.76 | 75:25 |
| 2011-2012 # | 57.97 | 19.32 | 77.29 | 75:25 |

#under Part-A Rs.42.27 crores released & Part-B will be considered subject to availability of addl. funds.

HON'BLE CHIEF MINISTER"S SPECIAL CELL PETITIONS

The petitions received from Chief Minister"s Special Cell in the Chief Office "X" section entered in the relevant registers and sent to the Superintendents of Police concerned and requested them to send the action taken to Chief Office in stipulated time. The replies of the same have been sent through online. This systems have been provided by the Chief Minister"s Cell since 4/2009. The replies from other offices such as Range / Zonal and Special Units are received in Chief Office have also been sent through online to Chief Minister"s Cell.

2. The petitions are categorized based on seriousness and source of receipts by the C.M.Cell are as follows:-

1.	Priority (P)	Petitions should be attended immediately and instead of viewing it as a regular petition. Care should be taken to see that the extra mile is traversed and redressal is done to the farthest extent possible within the frame work of rules.
2.	"A" Petitions referring	Srirangam Petitions
3.	"O" Petitions referring	Hon"ble C.M"s Office Petitions
4.	"R" Petitions referring	Hon"ble C.M"s Residence Petitions
5.	"M" Petitions referring	MLA / MP Petitons
6.	"Y" Petitions referring	RTI Petitions
7.	"I" Petitions referring	Government of India
8.	"H" Petitions referring	Speaker

The total no. of petitions received from 14.5.2011 to 31.12.2011 is 1961 out of which 756 replies have been sent. Out of 19 priority petitions, replies have been sent for 4.

TAMIL NADU AT A GLANCE

Population (2001 census): 6,24,05,679

➢ Male = 3,14,00,909 Female = 3,10,04,770

Geographical area of Tamil Nadu	130058 Sq. K.m.
Density of Population per sq.km	480
Percentage of Scheduled Castes to total Population (2001)	19.00
Percentage of Scheduled Tribes to total Population (2001)	1.04

Revenue Administration (2009-10)

1.	Revenue Districts	32
2.	Revenue Divisions	76
3.	Taluks	220
4.	Firkas	1,127
5.	Revenue Villages	(Rev.Dept.16564) (Stat Dept (TRS) 17289)
6.	Coastal Districts (2007-08)	13

Local Bodies (2009-10)

1.	Corporations	10
2.	Municipalities	148
3.	Panchayat Unions.	385
4.	Town Panchayats	561
5.	District Panchayats	29

6.	Village Panchayats	12620
7.	Hamlets (as per TNEB Report)	48117

Legislature

> Members of Legislative Assembly Elected – 234 + 1 (nominated – Anglo-Indian member)
> Members of Parliament (LokSabha) - 39
> Members of RajyaSabha - 18

Length of Roads:

> National Highways (2009-10) **4832.000 kms.**
> State Highways (2009-10) **56767.833 kms.**
> Corporation & Municipality Roads (2008-09) **18262.497 kms.**
> Panchayatunion&VillagePanchayatRoads(2008-09)**102837.918 kms.**
> Town Panchayat Roads (2007-08) **15592.000 kms.**
> Others Roads (Forest Roads) (2009-10) 2547.**511 kms.**
> Length of Coastal Line **1,076 KM**
> Railways: Route Length (2009-10) **3879.80 KM**

Registered Motor Vehicles:

> Commercial Vehicles(2009-10) **833948**
> Non-Commercial Vehicles(2009-10) **11323013**

Source: "Statistical Handbook of Tamil Nadu 2011" by Dept. of Economics & Statistics, Ch-6

POLICE DEPARTMENT AT A GLANCE

Coastal Security Group, CID	=	100 check-posts - 12 Marine Police stations - 12 outposts
Police Hospitals	=	12 (Chennai/Madurai/Trichy/Coimbatore/ Salem/St.thomas Mount/Vellore/Cuddalore/ Virudunagar/Tirunelveli (OP block only)/ TSP-II Bn., Avadi/TSP-IX Bn. Manimuthar.
Crime Branch CID (CB CID)	=	34 detachments - 7 crime units 4 counterfeit currency wings 1 cyber crime wing @ H.Q. 1 Anti-human trafficking cell @ H.Q. 1 police research cell @ H.Q.
Narcotic Intelligence Bureau (NIB)	=	15 units
Video Piracy Cell (VPC)	=	12 units
Economic Offences Wing (EOW)	=	Commercial Crime Investigation Wing (CCIW) (7 HQ & 32 Dist.units) - Idol Wing - Economic Offences Wing-II (EOW-II) (financial institutions)
State Crime Records Bureau (SCRB)	=	Police Computer Wing (PCW) - Single Digit Finger Print Bureau - Statistical Cell Modus Operandi Bureau (MOB)
Prohibition Enforcement	=	94 units
Dog squads	=	85 tracker dogs for crime detection 98 sniffer dogs for explosive detection 12 sniffer dogs for narcotics
Mounted Branch	=	3 (Chennai/Madurai/Coimbatore) = 30 horses

Civil Supply CID	=	20 Units
Civil Supply - Flying Squad	=	5 Teams at border States
Forensic Sciences Dept.	=	Tirunelveli/Krishnagiri/ Vellore/Kanniyakumari/ Coimbatore 15 divisions & 9 Regional Laboratories One mobile forensic science lab. Available in each Dist./Commissionerate
State Traffic Planning Cell	=	122 Highway Patrol Teams through GPS
Mobility	=	13516 vehicles
Housing & Buildings	=	47,520 quarters
VHF/UHF High band network	=	6563 static/mobile sets 11918 handheld sets – 262 repeater sets
Social Justice	=	30 units in Dist& 6 units in Commissionerates
Police Training Wing	=	13 In-service Training Centres
Police communication network	=	1899 broadband connections provided for police Stations and other units out of 2000 sanctioned
	=	12181 cell phones (CUG) for SI of police and above 236 laptops for senior police officers
Technical Services	=	2 Sub units (Technical Wing & Operational wing) 58 field units under Technical wing 53 field units under Operational wing

1.	Total Executive Strength	112363
2.	Zones	4
3.	Police Ranges	12 (Including 1 Railway Range)
4.	Police Districts	33 (including Tiruppur)
5.	Police Sub-Divisions	247
6.	**Police Stations (L & O)**	14 (Including Railway PS) Excluding AWPS & Traffic PSs)
7.	Traffic Police Stations	**213**
	a) Trichy Range Railway Police Stations	18
	b) Chennai Range Railway Police Stations	19
8.	**All Women Police Stations (AWPSs)**	196
9.	**Out-Posts (Law and Order)**	**60** (including 20 Railway OP)
10.	a) Trichy Range Railway Outposts	12
	b) Chennai Range Railway Outposts	8
13.	PS(L&O) housed in Govt. Buildings	1130 (Including Rly.PSs)
	PS(L&O) housed in rented buildings	170
14.	AWPS housed in Govt. Buildings	183
	AWPS housed in Rented Buildings	13
15	**CATEGORY OF POLICE STATIONS** a) Type I Design b) Type II Design c) Type III Design d) Type IV Design e) Type V Design **Note:** *In the G.O.Ms.No.72, Home (Pol.XIV) Dept., dt. 28.01.09 it is ordered to reclassify into HEAVY/ MEDIUM/LIGHT in the ratio of 20:30:50 in a phased manner over 3 years*	1300 156 85 171 358 530 G.Os issued for reclassification of P.S.s for 8 Dist. Viz. Theni, Tiruppur, Ariyalur, Sivagangai, Tiruneveli, Thoothukudi, Villu-puram&Virudhunagar

17	**Communication equipment's**: a) Static & mobile sets b) Walkie/Talkie (handheld) sets c) Repeater sets d) HF SET	VHFUHF 6663 35 12388 150 258 4 266
18.	**Armed Battalions**	16 (one Regimental Centre at Avadi& one Special Force at Veerapuram)
19.	**Police Commissionerates**	1. Greater Chennai 2. Madurai 3. Trichy 4. Coimbatore 5. Salem 6. Tirunelveli
20.	**Training Institutions** a) Police Academy b) Regl. Police Computer Trg. centre. c) Police Recruit School(Permanent) d) Police Trg. College, Ashok Nagar	1 1 4 *(Vellore/Coimbatore/Trichy/Perurani)* 1
21.	**RATIOS: DATA FOR THE YEAR 2010** i) Policemen per 100 Sq.Km. ii)Policemen per Lakh Population iii) Unit cost per Policeman per annum iv) % of civil police to total police *(source: "Crime Review T.N.2010" & "Crime in India 2010")*	**Tamil Nadu(2010) All India 2010** 66.70 49.9 129.0 133.0 285000.0 200899.0 84.0 77.4
22.	Police Personnel killed while on duty: 2010-11 2011-12	19 9
23.	Police Personnel injured while on duty: 2010-11 2011-12	02 4
24.	Total Ex-Gratia amount paid (killed) 2010-11 2011-12	95 lakhs 45 lakhs

25.	Total Ex-Gratia amount paid (Injurled) 2010-11 2011-12	40 thousands 40 thousands		

EXECUTIVE STRENGTH IN TAMILNADU POLICE AS ON 01.01.2012

Sl. No	Name of the Posts	Sanctioned	Actual	Vacancy
1.	Director General of Police	4	2	2
2.	Addl. Director Genl. Of Police	23	21	2
3.	Inspr. Genl. Of Police	37	26	11
4.	Dy. Inspr. Genl. Of Police	34	23	11
5.	Supdt. Of Police (Cat. I)	104	93	11
6.	D.C (A.R, S.P Cat-II)	5	5	0
7.	Commandant (Cat I & III)	17	17	0
8.	Addl. Supdt. Of Police (Cate.I)	94	58	36
9.	Addl. Supdt. Of Police(AR) (Cate.II)	9	5	4
10.	Dy. Commandant cat-III TSP	16	11	5
11.	Dy. Supdt. Of Police (Cate-I)	634	611	23
12.	D.S.P. (Cate-II) (AR)	74	56	18
13.	Asst. Commandant (TSP)	52	34	18
14.	Inspector of Police (Taluk) (men)	2185	2158	27
15.	Inspector of Police (Taluk) (women)	196	191	5
16.	Inspector of Police (TSP)	148	148	0
17.	Inspector of Police (A.R)	214	203	11
18.	Sub-Inspector of Police (Taluk) (men)	6022	3180	2842
19.	Sub-Inspector of Police (Taluk) (women)	1413	1296	117

20.	Sub-Inspector of Police (Taluk) (A.R)	1017	920	97
21.	Sub-Inspector of Police (Taluk) (T.S.P)	468	458	10
22.	Havildar (T.S.P)	1580		
23.	Naik (T.S.P)	1715	13080	1631
24.	Gr. II P.Cs (T.S.P)	11425		
25.	HC (Taluk / AR)	10405		
26.	Gr-I / Gr. II PCs (Taluk / AR)	65943		
27.	Women HCs	589	73140	11737
28.	Women Gr-I PCs	0		
29.	Women Gr-II PCs	7940		
	Total	112363	95745	16618

Source:GB & NGB sections of chief office

STRENGTH OF MINISTERIAL STAFF IN TAMIL NADU POLICE

Sl. No	Category	Sanctioned	Actual	Vacancy
1.	Financial Controller.	1	1	0
2.	Chief Administrative Officer	1	1	0
3.	Dy.Director/PRO	1	1	0
4.	Legal Adviser	1	0	1
5.	Senior Administrative Officer	26	13	13
6.	Personal Assistant.(Admn.)	180	149	31
7.	Asst. Director of Statistics	1	1	0
8.	Asst. Director (Internal Audit)	1	0	1
9.	Statistical Officer	1	1	0
10.	Statistical Inspector	1	1	0
11.	Chief Manager	1	0	1
12.	Senior Manager	4	3	1
13.	Works Manager, PTWCTS, Avadi	1	1	0
14.	Automobile Engr.,PTWCTS, Avadi	1	1	0
15.	Automobile Engr.PTW, Trichy	1	1	0
16.	Superintendent	838	838	0
17.	Assistants	1559	1074	485
18.	Steno-Typist	129	74	55
19.	Junior Assistant	1318	977	341
20.	Typist	313	196	117
21.	Record Clerk.	131	93	38
22.	Office Assistant.	782	644	138
23.	Sweepers	870	662	208
	Total	**6162**	**4732**	**1430**

PTWCTS= Police Transport Workshop-cum-Training School; PTW = Police

Transport Workshop

STRENGTH OF SHORTHAND BUREAU

Sl. No	Category	Sanctioned	Actual	Vacancy
1.	Senior Chief Reporter	1	1	0
2.	Chief Reporters	15	13	2
3.	Senior Reporters	41	39	2
4.	Junior Reporter	68	23	45
	Total	**125**	**76**	**49**

Source: Estt.2(1)/SB of DIG- In

STRENGTH OF POLICE TELECOMMUNICATION BRANCH

Sl. No	Category	Sanctioned	Actual	Vacancy
	Ministerial Staff:			
1.	Personal Assistant	2	1	1
2.	Superintendents	12	12	0
3.	Assistant	19	14	5
4.	SB. Assistant	1	1	0
5.	Junior Assistant	21	6	15
6.	Typist	3	2	2
7.	Steno-Typist	2	2	0
8.	Record Clerk	4	3	1
9.	Office Assistant	8	7	1
10.	BGS(sweeper/gardener/scaveng)	34	19	15
	SUB TOTAL	**106**	**66**	**40**
	Technical Staff:			
11.	SP (Technical)	1	1	0
12.	Addl. Supdt. Of Police (Tech.)	3	2	1

13.	DSP (T)	11	4	7
14.	Inspector (Technical)	135	123	12
15.	Accelerated promotion in the rank of Inspector(Technical)	7	7	0
16.	Upgraded Inspector (technical)	0	26	0
17.	Sub Inspector (Technical)	534	354	154
	SUB TOTAL	**691**	**517**	**174**
	Executive Staff			
18.	DSP(Communication)	1	1	0
19.	DSP (Crypto)	1	1	0
20.	Inspector of Police	57	50	7
21.	Sub Inspector of Police	218	196	22
22.	Head Constables	258	9	249
23.	Grade I PC	165	12	153
24.	Grade II PC	278	10	268
	SUB TOTAL	**978**	**279**	**699**

Source: Technical services

STRENGTH OF STATE CRIME RECORDS BUREAU

Sl. No	Category	Sanctioned	Actual	Vacancy
Executive Staff				
1.	Addl. DSP	1	0	1
2.	D.S.P.	1	1	0
3.	Inspectors	9	9	0
4.	Sub-Inspectors	8	6	2
5.	Headconstables	5	4	1
6.	Gr.I P.C.s	7	7	0
7.	Naik	2	2	0
8.	Gr.II P.C.s	40	40	0
9.	Driver PC	3	3	0
Ministerial Staff:				
1.	P.A. (ADMN.)	**1**	**1**	**0**
2.	Superintendents	5	4	1
3.	Assistants	8	6	2
4.	Junior Assistants	5	4	1
5.	Record Clerk	3	3	0
6.	Office Assistant	6	6	0
7.	Sweepers	4	3	1
8.	Steno-typist	2	0	2
9.	Typist	1	1	0
10.	Domestic Asst.	**2**	**0**	**2**
FINGER PRINT STAFF				
1.	S.P.	1	1	0
2.	A.D.S.P.	15	1	14
3.	DSP	36	32	4
4.	Inspectors	160	36	124
5.	S.I.s	88	33	55
PHOTO CELL				
1.	Technical Officer (Photography)	3	0	3
2.	Sr. Photographers	**12**	**12**	**0**

3.	Photographers	37	36	1
4.	Senior Photo Attendant	6	5	1
5.	Junior Photo Attendant	5	3	2
6.	Statistical Inspector	1	1	0
7.	A/C Plant Operator	3	2	1
MODUS OPERANDI BUREAU (CBCID)				
1.	DSP	1	1	0
2.	Inspectors	4	4	0
3.	Sub-inspectors	3	2	1
4.	Head constables	4	4	0
5.	Constables (Gr.I)	4	4	0
6.	Constables (Gr.II)	10	8	2

Source: SCRB Admn.

STRENGTH OF DIG/CID-INTELLIGENCE

Sl. No	Category	Sanctioned	Actual	Vacancy
	SPECIAL CATEGORIES			
1.	Manager	5	5	0
2.	Asst. Manager	20	20	0
3.	S.B. Assistants	96	89	7
4.	Technical Officer (Photo)	1	0	1
5.	Photographer	7	5	2
6.	Sr. Photo attendant	2	1	1
	Ministerial Staff:			
1.	Personal Assistant	4	3	1
2.	Office Superintendents	18	15	3
3.	Assistants	25	17	8
4.	Junior Assistants	24	16	8
5.	Typist	8	5	3
6.	Record Clerk	3	2	1
7.	Office Assistant	8	7	1
8.	Scavenger	2	0	2
9.	Sweeper	3	1	2
10.	Sanitary worker	1	0	1
11.	Waterman	1	1	0
12.	Pumpset Operator	1	0	1
13.	Chief Manager	1	0	1
14.	Senior Manager	4	3	1
	EXECUTIVE STAFF IN SB CID			
1.	S.P.	1	1	0
2.	A.D.S.P.	3	3	0
3.	DSPs	10	10	0
4.	INSPRs	85	83	2
5.	S.I.s	204	156	48
6.	HCs & Driver HC	256	252	4
7.	P.Cs & Driver PC	361	323	38
	EXECUTIVE STAFF IN SD CID			

1.	S.P.	1	1	0
2.	A.D.S.P.	2	2	0
3.	DSPs	9	6	3
4.	INSPRs	25	25	0
5.	S.I.s	41	23	18
6.	HCs & Driver HC	29	21	8
7.	P.Cs & Driver PC	30	26	4

ORGANIZED CRIME INTELLIGENCE UNIT (OCIU)				
Sl.No	Category	Sanctioned	Actual	Vacancy	Redeployed
1.	S.P	1	0	1	1
2.	ADSP	1	1	0	1
3.	DSPs	12	9	3	12
4.	INSPRs	22	17	5	21
5.	Sis	90	9	81	29
6.	Other Ranks	330	203	127	314

Source: SB-CID sec

DETAILS OF ZONES/RANGE/CITIES/DIST/SUBDIVISION/POLICE STATION/OP/ AWPS

Zone	Range	Cities/ Districts	Sub.Div	P S	OP	AWPS
North @ Chennai	Kancheepuram	Kancheepuram	5	37	2	5
		Thiruvallur	5	29	1	4
	Vellore	Vellore	8	55	2	7
		Thiruvannamalai	7	39	0	6
	Villupuram	Villupuram	7	49	0	6
		Cuddalore	7	46	0	6
Central @ Trichy	Trichy	Trichy City	8	14	0	4
		Trichy	5	29	2	4
		Perambalur	1	8	0	2
		Ariyalur	2	16	0	1
		Karur	3	16	0	2
		Pudukottai	6	36	2	5
	Thanjavur	Thanjavur	8	43	0	6
		Nagapattinam	4	28	0	4
		Thiruvarur	5	26	3	4
Western @ Coimbatore	Coimbatore	Coimbatore City	5	15	0	3
		Coimbatore	4	31	2	3
		Erode	5	35	1	4
		Tiruppur	7	29	1	6
		The Nilgiris	5	26	2	5
	Salem	Salem	6	33	0	5
		Namakkal	4	25	0	4
		Dharmapuri	3	24	0	3
		Krishnagiri	5	30	0	4
		Salem City	6	11	0	4
South @ Madurai	Madurai	Madurai City	5	17	0	3
		Tirunelveli City	4	8	0	2
		Madurai	7	44	0	5
		Virudhunagar	7	48	1	6

	Dindigul	Dindigul	7	36	0	6
		Theni	5	30	3	4
	Ramnad	Ramanathapuram	7	41	1	6
		Sivagangai	5	36	3	5
	Tirunelveli	Tirunelveli	9	60	5	7
		Thoothukudi	8	48	2	7
		Kanniyakumari	4	33	2	4
	Railway	R.P. Trichy	2	18	12	0
		R.P. Chennai	3	19	8	0
		Greater Chennai	43	132	5	35
TOTAL			247	1300	60	196
Source: RA - II						

ZONES IN GREATER CHENNAI	DISTRICT
EAST	Kilpauk, Triplicane, Mylapore
WEST	Ambattur, Anna Nagar, Pulianthope
NORTH	Flower Bazaar, Washermepet, Madhavaram
SOUTH	T.Nagar, Adayar, St. Thomas

TYPE OF POLICE STATIONS IN TAMIL NADU

Sl. No	Name of the Dist. City	Details of Type Design					Total
		I	II	III	IV	V	
1.	Greater Chennai	93	6	14	11	8	132
2.	Coimbatore City	15	0	0	0	0	15
3.	Madurai City	16	0	0	0	1	17
4	Salem City	0	11	0	0	0	11
5.	Trichy City	14	0	0	0	0	14
6.	Tirunelveli City	8	0	0	0	0	8
7.	Kancheepuram	1	4	3	16	13	37
8.	Tiruvallur	1	1	1	9	17	29
9.	Villupuram	0	3	4	11	31	49
10.	Cuddalore	0	3	13	11	19	46
11.	Tiruvannamalai	0	3	6	16	14	39
12.	Vellore	0	7	9	22	17	55
13.	Dharmapuri	0	1	4	3	16	24
14.	Krishnagiri	0	2	1	5	22	30
15.	Salem	0	0	7	10	16	33
16.	Namakkal	0	1	3	5	16	25
17.	Coimbatore	0	0	7	21	3	31
18.	Tiruppur	0	0	4	9	16	29
19.	The Nilgiris	0	2	3	9	12	26
20.	Erode	0	3	5	22	5	35
21.	Pudukottai	0	0	1	10	25	36
22.	Trichy	0	0	2	19	8	29
23.	Karur	0	1	2	9	4	16
24.	Ariyalur	0	0	0	9	7	16
25.	Perambalur	0	0	0	4	4	16
26.	Thanjavur	0	3	8	10	22	43
27.	Nagapattinam	0	2	4	3	19	28

28.	Thiruvarur	0	2	4	3	17	26
29.	Dindigul	0	3	4	7	22	36
30.	Theni	0	0	7	8	15	30
31.	Madurai	0	0	10	9	25	44
32.	Virudhunagar	0	3	10	10	25	48
33.	Ramanathapuram	0	3	6	7	25	41
34.	Sivagangai	0	1	4	7	24	36
35.	Tirunelveli	0	0	7	14	39	60
36.	Thoothukudi	0	6	3	25	14	48
37.	Kanniyakumari	4	5	8	2	0	19
38.	S.R.P. Chennai	4	6	5	3	0	18
39.	S.R.P. Trichy	4	6	5	3	0	18
	Total	**156**	**85**	**171**	**358**	**530**	**1300**

Note: As per G.O.Ms.No.72,Home (Pol-XIV) Dept., dt. 28.01.2009 existing police stations have been classified into 3 types as HEAVY, MEDIUM and LIGHT in the ratio of 20:30:50 in a phased manner over a period of 3 years i.e. 2009-10 to 2011-12.

GO.s have been issued for reclassification of police stations for 8 Dists. Viz. Theni, Tiruppur, Ariyalur, Sivagangai, Tirunelveli, Thoothukudi, Villupuram and Virudhunagar.

RECLASSIFICATION OF 5 TYPES INTO 3 TYPES POLICE STATIONS AS PER G.O. MS. NO.72, HOME (Pol-XIV) DEPARTMENT, DATED: 28.01.2009

Type of ps	Inspectors	Sub inspectors	Head cons.	Other ranks	Total
HEAVY	2	5	8	65	80
MEDIUM	1	3	5	41	50
LIGHT	0	2	2	26	30

DEATH UNDER HEROIC TRAGIC CIRCUMSTANCES

Year	SP	D.S.P	Inspector	S-I	H.C	Naik	P.C	Total
1986	-	-	-	1	-		-	1
1987	-	-	1	1	-		1	3
1988	-	-	-	-	-		1	1
1989	-	-	-	-	-		-	-
1990	-	-	-	1	-		2	3
1991	1	-	2	1	-		6	10
1992	-	-	-	1	1		2	4
1993	-	1	-	1	-		7	9
1994	-	-	-	-	-		1	1
1995	-	-	-	-	-		10	10
1996	-	-	-	-	-		1	1
1997	-	-	-	-	-		4	4
1998	-	-	-	-	-		1	1
1999	-	-	-	-	-		2	2
2000	-	-	-	1	3		3	7
2001	-	-	-	-	-		2	2
2002	-	-	-	-	-		-	-
2003	-	-	-	-	-		-	-
2004	-	-	-	-	-		-	-
2005	-	-	-	1	-		-	1
2006	-	-	-	-	-		-	-
2007	-	-	-	-	-		-	-
2008	-	-	-	1	8		1	10
2009	0		0	0	0		0	0
2010-11	0	0	2	5	4	2	6	19
2011-12				5	3		1	9

Source: Welfare Section

BUDGET AT A GLANCE

YEAR	BUDGET (Rupees in Crore)		PERCENTAGE
	STATE	HOME-POLICE	
2000 - 2001 Actual	64317.23	1007.39	1.57
2001 - 2002 Actual	67732.10	1075.41	1.59
2002 – 2003 Actual	39562.62	1127.46	2.85
2003 – 2004 Actual	35713.72	1177.54	3.30
2004 – 2005 Actual	43329.83	1446.07	3.34
RE 2005 – 2006	42228.05	1352.43	3.20
RE 2006 -2007	54266.95	1890.60	3.48
BE (2007 -2008)	57510.58	2190.99	3.81
BE (2008 – 2009)	66140.94	1922.92	2.91
BE (2009-10)	75,146.91	2604.32	3.47
BE 2010-11	83,079.25	2962.00	3.57
BE 2011-12 (Revised)	**1,06,842.92**	**3294.97**	**3.08**

Source: Budget cell

POLICE FLEET STRENGTH

Sl. No.	Type of vehicles	Total vehicles	Vehicles on road	Vehicles off road
1	Car	459	427	32
2	Jeep	4404	4066	338
3	Van	1110	1038	72
4	Minibus	477	440	37
5	Lorry	548	532	16
6	Bus	196	191	5
7	Motorcycle	6152	5419	733
8	Ambulance	80	77	3
9	Mortuary Van	18	18	0
10	Water cannon	17	17	0
11	Vajra	36	36	0
12	Crane	7	7	0
13	Wrecker	77	70	7
14	Water Lorry	15	15	0
15	BP car	15	15	0
16	Lockup van	18	18	0
17	Prisoner escort	30	30	0
18	Santro car	1	1	0
19	Autorickshaw	2	2	0
20	BP car carrier/ container	1	1	0
	Total	**13663**	**12420**	**1243**

Source- Mt I & II

DETAILS OF BATTALIONS IN TAMIL NADU

Sl. No	Name of the Battalion	Location
1	TSP I Bn	Trichy
2	TSP II Bn	Avadi
3	TSP III Bn	Veerapuram, Avadi
4	TSP IV Bn	Kovaipudur
5	TSP V Bn	Avadi (Women Battalion)
6	TSP VI Bn	Madurai
7	TSP VII Bn	Pochampalli
8	TSP VIII Bn	New Delhi
9	TSP IX Bn	Manimuthar
10	TSP X Bn	Ulundurpet
11	TSP XI Bn	Rajapalayam
12	TSP XIII (Special Force)	Veerapuram, Avadi
13	TSP XII Bn	Mandapam (Manimuthar)
14	TSP XIV Bn	Palani
15	TSP XV Bn	Sundarampalli, Vellore
16	Regimental Centre	Avadi

VEHICULAR POSITION IN TAMIL NADU

AS ON	TRANSPORT	NON- TRANSPORT	TOTAL
01.04.1993	238990	1460650	1699640
01.04.1994	258109	1894835	2152944
01.04.1995	280512	2142936	2423448
01.04.1996	283404	2488442	2771846
01.04.1997	309817	2872002	3181819
01.04.1998	344244	3270004	3614248
01.04.1999	368922	3701812	4070734
01.04.2000	399300	4207928	4607228
01.04.2001	421365	4740717	5162082
01.04.2002	432106	5225991	5658097
01.04.2003	457448	5751589	6209037
01.04.2004	472172	6280301	6752473
01.04.2005	493926	6909818	7403744
01.04.2006	581106	7640624	8221730
01.04.2007	608325	8495295	9103620
01.04.2008	706869	9362141	10069010
01.04.2009	784714	10255655	11040369
01.04.2010	833948	11323013	12156961
01.04.2011	928539	12732178	13660717
01.05.2011	932726	12836739	13769465
01.06.2011	943295	12960660	13903955
01.07.2011	950623	13095561	14046184
01.12.2011			14751330
01.01.2012	984601	13877094	14861695

Source: Transport dept.

RANK WISE POLICE QUARTERS AVAILABLE AS ON
01.01.2012

Sl. No	Units	Gazetted Officers	Inspr.	S.Is	H.Cs/PCs	Total
1	Greater Chennai city	92	168	461	8704	9425
2	Salem city	13	29	45	670	757
3	Madurai city	20	37	104	1405	1566
4	Coimbatore city	15	40	120	988	1163
5	Tirunelveli city	7	10	29	565	611
6	Trichy city	8	37	84	576	705
7	Kancheepuram	8	17	49	808	882
8	Thiruvallur	0	15	40	490	545
9	Cuddalore	6	13	44	830	893
10	Villupuram	5	20	50	736	811
11	Vellore	6	31	64	1349	1450
12	Tiruvannamalai	6	6	38	906	956
13	Dharmapuri	6	25	62	934	1027
14	Salem	10	19	55	925	1009
15	Namakkal	7	15	41	855	918
16	Krishnagiri	0	1	4	180	185
17	Erode	6	20	51	891	968
18	The Nilgiries	2	20	64	596	682
19	Coimbatore	8	24	51	1044	1127
20	Trichy	5	7	36	837	885
21	Perambalur	7	15	40	465	527
22	Karur	4	9	33	512	558
23	Nagapattinam	6	23	54	893	976
24	Thanjavur	5	23	73	1329	1430
25	Tiruvarur	4	18	40	887	949
26	Madurai	1	6	44	1024	1075
27	Pudukottai	5	15	35	642	697
28	Dindigul	6	10	42	1038	1096

		Gazetted Officers	Inspr.	S.Is	H.Cs/PCs	Total
29	Sivagangai	6	21	65	1002	1094
30	Theni	5	7	34	619	665
31	Virudhunagar	7	24	75	1149	1255
32	Ramanathapuram	7	24	66	1042	1139
33	Tirunelveli	0	23	64	1216	1303
34	Kanyakumari	8	15	52	920	995
35	Thoothukudi	6	17	44	740	807
36	Railway Police, Trichy	0	0	10	393	403
37	Railway Police,Chennai	0	11	30	544	585
	BATTALIONS	**Gazetted Officers**	**Inspr.**	**S.Is**	**H.Cs/PCs**	**Total**
38	TSP 1 Bn, Tiruchy	4	14	30	466	514
39	TSP 2 BnAvadi	5	15	39	397	456
40	TSP 3 BnVeerapuram	5	9	0	370	384
41	TSP 4 BnKovaipudur	4	6	35	719	764
42	TSP 5 BnAvadi	5	12	33	640	690
43	TSP 6 Bn Madurai	5	12	18	493	528
44	TSP 7 BnPalani	6	10	35	487	538
45	TSP 9 BnManimuthar	5	8	17	465	495
46	TSP 10 BnUlundurpet	5	11	33	252	301
47	TSP 11 BnRajapalayam	5	12	24	238	279
48	RC, Avadi	1	0	20	60	81
19	SF	1	4	0	0	5
50	Other Units: SBCID	0	25	45	124	194
51	PRO	8	19	29	116	172
	Total	366	972	2651	43531	47520

Source - Build-1

FOOD SUBSIDY SCHEME FOR POLICE PERSONNEL

Year (Apr-Mar)	No. of persons benefitted	Expenditure (Rs. in lakhs)
1996-97	23722	130.81
1997-98	32604	220.28
1998-99	46000	400.18
1999-2000	33250	339.57
2000-01	32018	309.35
2001-02	30650	249.16
2002-03	30050	212.49
2003-04	30050	198.62
2004-05	30050	330.00
2005-06	27500	315.98
2006-07	27470	179.01
2007-08	27966	115.00
2008-09	27966	135.00
2009-10	60870	916.39
2010-11	70973	978.21
2011-12 (up to 31.12.11)	70000	

Source: FSS Section

DETAILS OF POLICE FIRING

Details	2001	2002	2003	2004	2005	2006	2007	2008	2009	2010	2011
Total No. of occasions in which firing was resorted to	**32**	**20**	**13**	**12**	**9**	**17**	**13**	**17**	**8**	**12**	**6**
b) In riot control Operations	18	7	2	4	3	3	5	6	2	5	5
(b) In dacoity operations	0	0	0	0	0	0	0	0	1	0	0
(c) In operations against other criminals	14	13	11	8	5	13	8	9	5	7	
(d) Misc	0	0	0	0	1	1	0	2	0	0	1
Total No. of persons killed	**13**	**9**	**4**	**6**	**3**	**7**	**4**	**10**	**4**	**8**	**6**
1. Police Personnel (in the incident)	0	0	0	0	0	0	0	0	0	0	0
2. Civilians (in police firing)	13	9	4	6	3	7	4	10	4	8	6
Total No. of Persons injured	**207**	**42**	**22**	**24**	**13**	**32**	**37**	**52**	**15**	**47**	**164**
1. Police Personnel (in the incident)	178	37	20	23	12	29	32	48	13	46	123
2. Civilians (in police firing)	29	5	2	1	1	3	5	5	2	1	41

Source :SB CID

DETAILS OF DEATH IN POLICE CUSTODY

Year	2001	2002	2003	2004	2005	2006	2007	2008	2009	2010	2011
No. of cases	6	15	5	7	2	6	4	1	5	3	5

Source: Con III

PAY SCALES OF POLICE DEPARTMENT

Name of the post	Scale of pay + Grade Pay
Director General of Police	80,000
Additional Director General of Police	67000-79000+0
Inspector General of Police	37400-67000+10000
Deputy Inspector General of Police	37400-67000+8900
Commissioners of Police	37400-67000+12000
SPs IPS including Asst. Inspector, Jt. SP, Addl. SP	15600-39100+6600
Asst SP, DSP Cat.I including Asst.	15600-39100+5400
SP State Cadre	15600-39100+7600
Inspector of Police.	9300-34800+4900
Sub Inspector of Police including Women	9300-34800+4800
Head Constable including Women HC	5200-20200+2800
Police Constable Gr-I incl. Women PC	5200-20200+2400
Police Constable Gr-II including women	5200-20200+1900
ARMED RESERVE	
SP, Addl. DSP	15600-39100-6600
Deputy Superintendent of Police [Category-II]	15600-39100+5400
Inspector [AR] including Band Master and Store Keeper	9300-34800+4600
Sub Inspector of Police [AR] including Band	9300-34800+4300
HC incl. Band &Armourer, PC Gr-I/NK incl. Band, Armourer and Women	5200-20200+2400
Police Constable Grade-II/LNK including Band, Armourer and Women	5200-20200+1900
ARMED POLICE BATTALION	
SP, Addl. DSP	15600-39100-6600

Deputy Superintendent of Police [Category-II]	15600-39100+5400
Inspector [AR] including Band Master and Store Keeper	9300-34800+4600
Sub Inspector of Police [AR] including Band	9300-34800+4300
HC incl. Band &Armourer, PC Gr-I/NK incl. Band, Armourer and Women	5200-20200+2400
Police Constable Grade-II/LNK including Band, Armourer and Women	5200-20200+1900
ARMED POLICE BATTALION	
Commandant Non-Grade including Small Arms	15600-39100+7600
Deputy Commandant	15600-39100+6600
Deputy Superintendent of Police Category-III/Assistant	10600+39100+5400
Inspector of Police	9300-34800+4600
Sub Inspector of Police	9300-34800+4400
Havildar/Head Constable	5200-20200+2400
Naik	5200-20200+2000
Lance Naik, PC Gr-II	5200-20200+1900
Follower/Cook, barber	4800-10000+1400
Dhoby	4800-10000+1300
SPECIAL BRANCH CID INCLUDING INTELLIGENCE SECTION, CITY POLICE	
Chief Manager	15600-39100+6600
Senior Manager	15600-39100+6000
Manager	15600-39100+5700
Assistant Manager including Private Secretary to Director	15600-39100+5400
Special Branch Assistant	9300-34800+4800
AC Plant Operator	9300-34800+4200
Librarian in O/o ADGP, CB CID	9300-34800+4500
POLICE TELECOMMUNICATION BRANCH	
Superintendent of Police [Techn.]	15600-39100+7600
Deputy Superintendent of Police [Techn.]	15600-

	39100+5400
Inspector [Techn.] including Women, Inspector of police	9300-34800+4900
SB Asst., SI [Techn.] incl. Women, SI	9300-34800+4300
Head Constable	5200-20200+2400
Police Constable Grade-I	5200-20200+2000
Police Constable Grade-II	5200-20200+1900
SHORTAND BUREAU	
Senior Chief Reporter	15600-39100+6600
Chief Reporter	15600-39100+5700
Shorthand Reporter	9300-34800+4600
Senior Reporter	15600-39100+5400
Junior Reporter	9300-34800+4500
LEGAL BRANCH	
Sr.Legal Advisor to Dy.Ins.Gen.ofPolice,CID/Asst. Public Prosecutor/Senior Law Advisor	15600-39100+7600
Addl. City Public Prosecutor	15600-39100+6600
Legal Advisor to DIG,CID,COP,CSCID & Chief Office, Asst. Public Prosecutor [Metro] Gr-I	15600-39100+5700
Assistant Public Prosecutor Grade-II	15600-39100+5400
POLICE TRANSPORT WORKSHOP-CUM-TRAINING SCHOOL	
Works Manager	15600-39100+6600
Automobile Engineer	15600-39100+5400
Technical Assistant	9300-34800+4500
Foreman (Mechn.)	5200-20200+2800
Fitter Special / Asst. Storekeeper, Mechanic Gr.I, Chargeman	5200-20200+2400
Mechanic Gr.II, Reborer, Works Clerk Time-Keeper, Fitter–II, Grade I of Electrician, Welder, Bench	5200-20200+2200

Fitter,Tinker,Blacksmith,Painter,Carpenter,Liner& Turner	
Batteryman,Fitter,ElectricianGr.II,Tyreman,Gr.II,ToolKeeper,Bench Fitter Gr.II,Scrubber	5200-20200+1900
Hammerman	4800-10000+1400
BOAT CREW	
Syrang	9300-34800+4300
FINGER PRINT BUREAU	
Superintendent of Police [FP]	15600-39100+7600
Additional Superintendent of Police [FP]	15600-39100+6600
Deputy Superintendent of Police [FP]	15600-39100+5400
Inspector of Police [FP]	9300-34800+4600
Sub Inspector of Police [FP]	9300-34800+4300
Photographer	9300-34800+4200
PHOTOGRAPHIC SECTION	
Technical Officer [Photography]	15600-39100+5400
Senior Photographer	9300-34800+4500
Photographer, Photo Assistant	9300-34800+4200
Audio Visual Technician	9300-34800+4200
Senior Photo Attendant, Photo Attendant	4800-10000+1650
Photo Attender	4800-10000+1400
Dark Rook Assistant	5200-20200+1900
PRINTING PRESS	
Imposer / Composer / Machine Minder	5200-20200+1900
Senior Binder, Carpenter	5200-20200+1800
Junior Binder	
POLICE RECRUTIMENT SCHOOL AND TRAINING COLLEGE	
Principal (SP / ADSP)	15600-39100+6600
Vice Principal (DSP)	15600-39100+5400
Law Instructor, Sports Officer, Plan Drawing Instructor	9300-34800+4600

Librarian	5200-20200+2400
Assistant Law Instructor	9300-34800+4200
SI Of Police AR	9300-34800+4300
Assistant Drill Instructor	5200-20200+2000
Plumber	5200-20200+1800
OTHER CATEGORIES	
Director, Aviation	-
Wing Commander	-
Deputy Director	15600-39100+6600
Public Relation Officer / Technical Officer	15600-39100+5400
Scientific Assistant Gr.I	9300-34800+4500
Scientific Assistant Gr.Ii, Hindi PanditGr.I	9300-34800+4200
Dog Handler [Gr.II.PC Scale], Sheroff	5200-20200+1900
Technical Attender CID	4800-10000+1650
Cook In Police Hospital	4800-10000+1400
Syce,Lascar (Stores), Gardener / Water Carrier, Dog Boy, Pumpset Operator, Watchman	4800-10000+1300
MINISTERIAL BRANCH	
Financial Controller	37400-67000-8800
Chief Administrative Officer	15600-39100+6600
Senior Administrative Officer	15600-39100+5700
Personal Assistant (Admn.)	15600-39100+5400
Superintendent	9300-34800+4800
Stenographer Gr.I	9300-34800+4400
Stenographer Gr.Ii	9300-34800+4200
Assistant, Stenographer Gr.Iii	5200-20200+2400
Junior Asst. / Record Asst.,Typist, Telephone Operator	5200-20200+2000
Date Entry Operator	5200-20200+1900
Record Clerk	4800-10000+1400
Office Assistant including Sweeper, Sanitary Worker,	4800-10000+1300

Scavenger and Water Carrier Officer Asst. including Masalchi, Sanitary Worker, Menials And Sweepers	
DEPUTATION POST / PROTECTION OF CIVIL RIGHTS	
Economist, Sociologist	15600-39100+5400

POLICE HOSPITAL	
Medical Officer	15600-39100+7600
Civil Surgeon	15600-39100+5700
Assistant Surgeon / Doctor	15600-39100+5400
Head Nurse	9300-34800+4600
Staff Nurse	9300-34800+4200
Radiographer	5200-20200+2800
Pharmacist	9300-34800+4300
Laboratory Technician Gr.II, Auxiliary Nurse Midwife	5200-20200+2400
Maternity Asst.	5200-20200+2000
ECG Technician	5200-20200+1900
Male Nursing Asst.	5200-20200+1800
Dhoby, Sanitary Worker	4800-10000+1650
Male Hospital Worker	4800-10000+1400
Gardener /Hospital Worker, Nursing Orderly, Gr.II, Female Nursing Assistant, Cook	4800-10000+1300
OTHER CATEGORY – II	
Deputy Registrar of Co-Operative Societies	15600-39100-5400
Internal Audit	15600-39100+5700
Assistant Director Of Statistics	15600-39100+5400
Statistical Officer	9300-34800+4600
Statistical Assistant	9300-34800+4400
Statistical Inspector	9300-34800+4400

As per VI pay commission G.O.Ms.No.234, Finance (Pay cell) Dept., dt. 01.06.09

One man commission-2009 orders by finance (pay cell) dept.,dt.26.08.2010 - G.O.Ms.No.254, G.O.Ms.No.308 & G.O.Ms.No.309, etc.

As per report of the one man commission – March 2010 - by Thiru Rajeev Ranjan, I.A.S., Principal Secretary to Government, Industries Department

Source: PBA Section

Hon"ble Chief Minister"s Announcements 2011-12

Demand No.22   **Announcement made on 24.08.11**

1.	Sanction of 1125 additional posts for Chennai City Traffic Police
2.	Formation of new Traffic Police Stations at Valasarawakkam and Semmenchery for which 32 new posts shall be created.
3.	Formation of 5 new Traffic P.S. in important cities for which 80 police posts shall be created.
4.	Formation of new Law & Order Police Stations of Metro-I Type at Koyambedu with 125 posts, Metro-II Type at Taramani and Kanathur with 100 posts each shall be created.
5.	Formation of permanent Police Training School at Avadi, Villupuram, Salem and Madurai for which 75 new posts shall be created
6.	Procurement of All Terrain Vehicles for 12 Coastal Security Group police stations
7.	Achieving 100% satisfaction in housing facilities. Action shall be taken to construct 5,440 quarters at the cost of 446.84 crores.
8.	Enhancement of Insuranmce amount from Rs.1 lakh to Rs.2 lakhs for Police personnel upto Inspectors of Police
9.	Procurement of additional 87 patrol vehicles for Modern Control Room in Chennai City for which 838 new posts shall be created
10.	Enhancement of Special Allowance for night duty from Rs.20 to Rs.50 to Railway Police
11.	Upgradation of 12 Outpost into Light Type Police Stations for which 500 new posts shall be created.
12.	Sanction of 927 additional Police posts for Virudhunagar District for Heavy, Medium & Light Type Police Stations
13.	Enhancement of risk allowance from Rs.270 to Rs.300 to Police Constables to Inspectors of police and Rs.315 to Rs.350 to DSPs & Addl. Superintendent of Police
14.	Sanction of additional 10 ministerial staff viz. 1 P.A., 2 Superintendents, 3 Assistants, 2 Typists & 2 Junior Assistant for each four police zones
15.	Reclassification of Railway Police Stations into Metro Type-1, Metro Type-2, Heavy, Medium & Light and for which new posts shall be created.
16.	Construction of Prison and Fire & Rescue Services Offices and Buildings by the Tamil Nadu Police Housing Corporation Ltd. henceforth.
17.	Enhancement of feeding charges from Grade II Police Constables to Inspector of Police @ Rs.100/ per day for all worked days without any ceiling limit
18.	Enhancing the cadre strength of Home Guards from 11,622 to 16,000
19.	Enhancement of Daily Allowance to Home Guards from Rs.65/- to Rs.150/-

20.	Enhancement of Night Duty Allowance to Home Guards in Chennai from Rs.75/- to Rs.200/-
21.	Formation of Out-patient unit with Dispensary at 26 Armed Reserve Headquarters and 10 Tamil Nadu Special Batallion Headquarters
22.	Creation of 50 Boys Clubs so as to make good citizens and to prevent any other crimes
23.	Enhancement of Feeding charges for Sniffer & Tracker Dogs from Rs.54/- to Rs.85/- per day
24.	Enhancement of Grooming charges for Sniffer & Tracker Dogs from Rs.250 to Rs.300 p.m.
25.	Creation of a new Asst. Commissioner of Police range at Neelankarai at Chennai and for which one ACP, necessary staff and infrastructure shall be created.
26.	Modernisation of Police Force at an estimated cost of Rs.134.26 crores
27.	Construction of own buildings for 22 police stations functioning in rented buildings and 82 police stations in dilapidated building
28.	Setting up of Cyber Cells at Salem and Tirunelveli and Laboratories at Salem, Tirunelveli, Coimbatore, Madurai, Trichy cities.
29.	Filling up of vacancies of 896 SIs, 121 Technical SIs & 5,588 Gr.II PCs in the Police Force
30.	Formation of Greater Chennai Police Commissionerate by merging Chennai Suburban Police Commissionerate with the Chennai City Police Commissionerate for which 4 posts of JC (Crimes), Traffic - (South), (West), (H.Q.) shall be created.

PARLIAMENTARY CONSTITUENCIES IN TAMIL NADU

1.	Arakkonam	14.	Madurai	27.	Sivaganga
2.	Chengalpattu	15.	Mayiladuthurai	28.	Sivakasi
3.	Chennai Central	16.	Nagapattinam (SC)	29.	Sriperumbudur (SC)
4.	Chennai North	17.	Nagercoil	30.	Tenkasi (SC)
5.	Chennai South	18.	Nilgiris	31.	Thanjavur
6.	Chidambaram (SC)	19.	Palani	32.	Tindivanam
7.	Coimbatore	20.	Perambalur (SC)	33.	Tiruchendur
8.	Cuddalore	21.	Periyakulam	34.	Tiruchengode
9.	Dharmapuri	22.	Pollachi (SC)	35.	Tiruchirappalli
10.	Dindigul	23.	Pudukottai	36.	Tirunelveli
11.	Gobichettipalayam	24.	Ramanathapuram	37.	Tiruppattur
12.	Karur	25.	Rasipuram (SC)	38.	Vandavasi
13.	Krishnagiri	26.	Salem	39.	Vellore

275

TAMIL NADU POPULATION CENSUS 2011 (PROVISIONAL)

SL. NO.	DISTRICTS	Total	Male	Female	CENSUS-WISE POPULATION	
1.	Ariyalur	752481	373319	379162	YEAR	IN LAKHS
2.	Chennai	4681087	2357633	2323454	1901	193
3.	Coimbatore	3472578	1735362	1737216	1911	209
4.	Cuddalore	2600880	1311151	1289729	1921	216
5.	Dharmapuri	1502900	772490	730410	1931	235
6.	Dindigul	2161367	1081934	1079433	1941	263
7.	Erode	2259608	1134191	1125417	1951	301
8.	Kancheepuram	3990897	2010309	1980588	1961	337
9.	Kanniyakumari	1863174	926800	936374	1971	412
10.	Karur	1076588	534392	542196	1981	484
11.	Krishnagiri	1883731	963152	920579	1991	559
12.	Madurai	3041038	1528308	1512730	2001	624
13.	Nagapattinam	1614069	797214	816855	2011	721
14.	Namakkal	1721179	866740	854439		
15.	Perambalur	564511	281436	283075		
16.	Pudukkottai	1618725	803337	815388		
17.	Ramanathapuram	1337560	676574	660986		
18.	Salem	3480008	1780569	1699439		
19.	Sivaganga	1341250	670597	670653		
20.	Thanjavur	2402781	1183112	1219669		
21.	The Nilgiris	735071	360170	374901		
22.	Theni	1243684	624922	618762		
23.	Thiruvallur	3725697	1878559	1847138		
24.	Thiruvarur	1268094	627616	640478		
25.	Thoothukkudi	1738376	858919	879457		
26.	Tiruchirappalli	2713858	1347863	1365995		

27.	Tirunelveli	3072880	1518595	1554285		
28.	Tiruppur	2471222	1242974	1228248		
29.	Tiruvannamalai	2468965	1238688	1230277		
30.	Vellore	3928106	1959676	1968430		
31.	Viluppuram	3463284	1744832	1718452		
32.	Virudhunagar	1943309	967437	975872		
	TAMIL NADU	**72138958**	**36158871**	**35980087**		

Source: Directorate of Census Operations

CONSTITUTION OF WARDS COMMITTEE FOR THE EXPANDED
CHENNAI CORPORATION

Wards Committee	Wards Number	Wards Committee	Wards Number
I Thiruvottiyur	1 TO 14	IX Teynampet	109 TO 126
II Manali	15 TO 21	X Kodambakkam	127 TO 142
III Madhavaram	22 TO 33	XI Valasaravakkam	143 TO 155
IV Tondiarpet	34 TO 48	XII Alandur	156 TO 167
V Royapuram	49 TO 63	XIII Adyar	170 TO 182
VI Thiru. vi.ka. Nagar	64 TO 78	XIV Perungudi	183 TO 191,168,169
VII Ambattur	79 TO 93	XV Shozhinganallur	192 TO 200
VIII Anna Nagar	94 TO 108		

As per G.O.(Ms)No.136, Municipal Administration & Water Supply (election)
Dept.,dt. 12.09.11

ALL INDIA POPULATION CENSUS 2011 (PROVISIONAL)

S. No	State / UT	Persons	Male	Female
	INDIA	**1210193422**	**623724248**	**586469174**
1	Andaman & Nicobar Islands	379944	202330	177614
2	Andhra Pradesh	84665533	42509881	42155652
3	Arunachal Pradesh	1382611	720232	662379
4	Assam	31169272	15954927	15214345
5	Bihar	103804637	54185347	49619290
6	Chandigarh	1054686	580282	474404
7	Chhattisgarh	25540196	12827915	12712281
8	Dadra & Nagar Haveli	342853	193178	149675
9	Daman & Diu	242911	150100	92811
10	Goa	1457723	740711	717012
11	Gujarat	60383628	31482282	28901346
12	Haryana	25353081	13505130	11847951
13	Himachal Pradesh	6856509	3473892	3382617
14	Jammu & Kashmir	12548926	6665561	5883365
15	Jharkhand	32966238	16931688	16034550
16	Karnataka	61130704	31057742	30072962
17	Kerala	33387677	16021290	17366387
18	Lakshadweep	64429	33106	31323
19	Madhya Pradesh	72597565	37612920	34984645
20	Maharashtra	112372972	58361397	54011575
21	Manipur	2721756	1369764	1351992
22	Meghalaya	2964007	1492668	1471339
23	Mizoram	1091014	552339	538675
24	Nagaland	1980602	1025707	954895
25	NCT of Delhi	16753235	8976410	7776825
26	Orissa	41947358	21201678	20745680

27	Puducherry	1244464	610485	633979
28	Punjab	27704236	14634819	13069417
29	Rajasthan	68621012	35620086	33000926
30	Sikkim	607688	321661	286027
31	**Tamil Nadu**	**72138958**	**36158871**	**35980087**
32	Tripura	3671032	1871867	1799165
33	Uttar Pradesh	199581477	104596415	94985062
34	Uttarakhand	10116752	5154178	4962574
35	West Bengal	91347736	46927389	44420347

Source: Census of India 2011

POLICE, POPULATION AND AREA RATIO DURING THE YEAR 2010

Sl. No	States /UTs	Estimated Mid-Year Population (In Thousands)	No. of Policemen per 100 Sq. Km. of Area	No. of Policemen per 100000 of population	Area (in Sq. kms)
1	Andhra Pradesh	84129	40.0	131	275045
2	Arunachal Pradesh	1235	8.9	603	83743
3	Assam	30978	68.9	175	78438
4	Bihar	97184	65.7	64	94163
5	Chandigarh	24538	30.9	170	135191
6	Goa	1743	126.9	270	3702
7	Gujarat	58193	32.9	111	196024
8	Haryana	24590	107.4	193	44212
9	Himachal Pradesh	6687	24.4	203	55673
10	Jammu & Kashmir*	13364	76.0	576	101387
11	Jharkhand	30937	58.5	151	79714
12	Karnataka	58799	37.3	122	191791
13	Kerala	34972	104.3	116	38863
14	Madhya Pradesh*	72106	24.7	106	308245
15	Maharashtra*	110049	58.5	164	307713
16	Manipur	2702	105.4	871	22327
17	Meghalaya	2609	45.7	393	22429
18	Mizoram	1008	50.9	1065	21081
19	Nagaland	2250	60.3	445	16579
20	Orissa	40828	27.9	106	155707
21	Punjab	27268	132.4	244	50362
22	Rajasthan	67106	20.9	107	3432239
23	Sikkim	610	53.6	624	7096
24	**Tamil Nadu**	**67632**	**66.7**	**128**	**130058**

25	Tripura	3610	231.3	672	10486
26	Uttar Pradesh	199028	59.0	71	240928
27	Uttarakhand	9817	33.7	184	53483
28	West Bengal	90222	97.0	95	88752
29	A&N Islands	432	45.3	866	8249
30	Chandigarh	1125	4437.7	450	114
31	D&N Haveli	283	42.4	73	491
32	Daman & Diu	200	196.4	110	112
33	Delhi	18333	4980.6	403	1483
34	Lakshadweep	72	1037.5	461	32
35	Puducherry	1117	462.2	204	492
	All India	**1185756**	**49.9**	**133**	**3166404**

* Variation in police strength data of 2010 due to furnishing of incorrect figures in 2009 as clarified by them

Source: "Crime in India 2010" by NCRB, New Delhi

State/ UTs.	DG/ADG/IG /DIG		SSP/SP/Ad.SP/ASP /DSP		INS./SI/ ASI		BELOW ASI		TOTAL	
	Sanctioned	Actual	Sanctioned	Actual	Sanctioned	Actual	Sanctioned	Actual	Sanctioned	Actual
ANDHRA P.	74	83	751	749	15181	8004	96966	86534	112972	95370
ARUNACHAL P	6	5	71	54	599	541	2911	2906	3587	3506
ASSAM	41	41	295	295	5008	4623	24696	23735	30040	28694
BIHAR	49	50	484	333	14290	10640	52796	38892	67619	49915
CHHATTISGAR	38	24	339	287	3023	2175	22316	23560	25716	26046
GOA	3	3	35	37	422	377	3860	3621	4320	4038
GUJARAT	74	54	297	234	11054	10188	50958	38172	62383	48648
HARYANA	46	42	249	189	6537	2081	41468	40649	48300	42961
HIMACHAL P	14	39	95	93	1692	1562	8900	7977	10701	9671
J & K SS	36	35	443	439	6344	5670	44109	41715	50932	47859
JHARKHAND	49	35	230	195	7330	4756	41412	28820	49021	33806
KARNATAKA	77	68	521	494	8290	6858	68911	56269	77799	63689
KERALA	31	21	350	338	3852	3755	35470	33254	39703	37368
MADHYA P.	50	133	730	585	9049	6544	48542	45503	58371	52765
MAHRASTRA@	105	103	925	696	31245	24793	146970	140148	179245	165740
MANIPUR	26	12	142	113	2681	1342	14189	8781	17035	10249
MEGHALAYA	20	19	56	54	922	920	5461	4905	6429	5898
MIZORAM #	9	7	84	81	1133	1093	2539	2381	3765	3562
NAGALAND	22	22	78	72	519	456	5394	5087	6013	3637
ODISHA	45	43	541	338	8145	6622	24427	21932	33158	28965
PUNJAB	46	52	403	453	7344	6309	52109	41178	59902	47992
RAJASTHAN	62	46	622	757	9685	7584	56184	51221	66553	59608
SIKKIM	17	17	88	68	282	259	1793	1301	2180	1645

TAMIL NADU	**89**	**76**	**870**	**835**	**11393**	**9244**	**77764**	**62731**	**90116**	**72886**
TRIPURA	14	14	200	163	1491	1568	9492	8929	11197	10671
UTTAR P	125	117	1156	936	19948	8508	303346	101670	324575	111234
UTTARAKAND	16	13	128	98	979	909	12909	12864	14032	13884
WEST BENGAL	111	92	530	424	21527	16391	53760	46999	75928	63906
A & N ISLANDS	2	3	19	16	581	449	3124	2465	3728	2933
CHANDIGARH	2	2	18	14	626	604	5148	3804	5794	4424
D & N HAVELI			3	3	27	14	285	191	315	208
DAMAN & DIU	1	1	4	3	22	15	218	201	245	220
DELHI	50	36	368	282	12736	11566	60404	55384	73558	67268
LAKSHADWEP	2	2	2	2	85	23	469	307	556	332
PUDUCHERRY	2	2	21	20	85	23	469	307	556	332
ALL-INDIA	**1354**	**1310**	**11148**	**9753**	**224420**	**166746**	**1381276**	**1045510**	**1618198**	**1223319**

There is variation in police strength in respect of Mizoram State due to adding of non-uniform staff as clarified by them in 2010.

@ Variation in police strength over 2009 in the data of Maharashtra due to furnishing of incorrect data in 2009 as clarified by them in 2010

$$ Variation in police strength over 2009 in the data of Jammu & Kashmir due to furnishing of incorrect data in 2009 as clarified by them.

Source : "Crime in India 2010" by NCRB, New Delhi

SANCTIONED & ACTUAL STRENGTH OF CIVIL POLICE INCLUDING DIST. ARMED POLICE AS ON 31.12.2010

State/ UTs.	DG/ADG/IG /DIG		SSP/SP/Ad.SP/ASP/DSP		INS./SI/ ASI		BELOW ASI		TOTAL	
	Sanctioned	Actual	Sanctioned	Actual	Sanctioned	Actual	Sanctioned	Actual	Sanctioned	Actual
ANDHRA P.	6	11	9	5	103	103	1890	1893	2008	2012
ARUNACHAL P	0	0	0	0	15	13	52	460	67	473
ASSAM	0	0	0	0	22	22	310	164	332	186
BIHAR	0	3	0	15	4	141	101	994	105	1154
CHHATTISGAR	0	0	16	30	89	119	1012	1731	1117	1880
GOA	0	1	0	2	4	20	211	310	215	333
GUJARAT	0	2	22	8	479	315	2734	1357	3235	1682
HARYANA	0	0	0	0	323	169	2720	1749	3043	1918
HIMACHAL P	0	1	0	6	3	36	137	568	140	611
J & K SS	0	1	0	10	0	131	0	922	0	1064
JHARKHAND	0	4	0	7	0	94	0	1380	0	1485
KARNATAKA	0	NA	0	NA	0	NA	0	NA	0	NA
KERALA	0	0	1	1	95	95	2679	2643	2775	2739
MADHYA P	5	7	60	61	196	289	1509	1850	1770	2207
MAHRASTRA@	0	5	0	49	0	293	0	11671	0	12018
MANIPUR	0	0	0	0	357	156	2008	450	2365	606
MEGHALAYA	0	0	0	4	3	18	41	64	44	86
MIZORAM #	0	0	8	8	223	223	306	606	537	537
NAGALAND	0	0	2	1	6	8	87	57	95	66
ODISHA	5	5	16	16	467	467	2973	2793	3281	3281
PUNJAB	0	0	0	0	0	190	0	2144	0	2334
RAJASTHAN	2	0	35	0	116	156	1840	3507	1993	3663
SIKKIM	0	0	0	9	0	26	0	148	0	183
TAMIL NADU	6	6	109	109	1631	1631	11794	8935	13540	10681
TRIPURA	0	0	3	6	127	87	805	608	935	701
UTTAR P	4	4	67	67	338	330	2084	2005	2493	2406
UTTARAKAND	0	0	0	19	8	80	695	1203	703	1302
WEST BENGAL	0	1	1	10	387	318	2031	2005	2419	2334
A & N ISLANDS	0	0	0	0	1	20	18	254	19	274
CHANDIGARH	0	0	0	0	0	37	0	429	0	466
D & N HAVELI	0	0	0	0	2	2	7	7	9	9
DAMAN & DIU	0	0	0	0	0	0	0	0	0	0
DELHI	0	2	1	26	645	548	4003	3980	4649	4556
LAKSHADWEP	0	0	0	0	1	0	7	16	8	16
PUDUCHERRY	0	0	0	1	5	5	76	79	81	85
ALL-INDIA	28	53	350	474	5650	5142	41950	56682	47978	63348

In some States/UTs the strength of actual women police personnel is more than the sanctioned strength on account of certain specific reasons e.g. appointment of women police again general vacancy, appointment on compassionate grounds etc. as clarified by them from time to time.

There is variation in police strength in respect of Mizoram state due to adding of non uniform staff as clarified by them in 2010. @Variation in police strength over 2009 in the data of Maharashtra due to furnishing of incorrect data in 2009 as clarified by them in 2010.

$$ Variation in police strength over 2009 in the data of Jammu & Kashmir due to furnishing of incorrect data in 2009 as clarified by them in 2010.

NA – Stands for not available.

*Variation in 2010 police strength data of Jharkhand due to furnishing of incorrect data in 2009 as clarified by them in 2010

Source : "Crime in India 2010" by NCRB, New Delhi

ORGANISATIONAL SETUP AS ON 31.12.2010

Sl. No.	STATE/UT	Number of							
		Zones	Ranges	Police Districts	Sub Divisions	Circles	Rural Police Stations	Urban Police Stations	Women Police Stations
1	Andhra Pradesh	14	13	33	179	420	1274	387	27
2	Arunachal Pradesh	1	3	17	5	17	54	15	
3	Assam	2	6	30	28	45	183	130	1
4	Bihar	5	12	44	112	200	694	158	1
5	Chandigarh		5	21	66		300	101	4
6	Goa			2	8		9	16	1
7	Gujarat	14	10	31	94	85	381	138	17
8	Haryana		4	22	51		153	89	1
9	Himachal Pradesh		3	13	26		65	37	
10	Jammu & Kashmir*	2	7	29	39	26	121	63	2
11	Jharkhand	4	7	26	43	113	289	136	24
12	Karnataka		6	34	92	239	484	416	10
13	Kerala	2	4	18	54	198	311	159	4
14	Madhya Pradesh	11	15	53	142		598	346	9
15	Maharashtra	36	9	45	280		679	333	9
16	Manipur	3		10	25		83	8	9
17	Meghalaya	1	2	7	8	19	20	19	7
18	Mizoram	0	2	8	17		27	11	
19	Nagaland	1	10	11	25	17	20	30	1
20	Orissa		9	36	35	99	372	174	5
21	Punjab	4	7	25	90		202	157	5
22	Rajasthan	9	8	40		185	442	315	24
23	Sikkim	1	1	4	11		6	22	
24	Tamil Nadu≠	4	12	40	248	376	565	731	196
25	Tripura	1	2	4	22	30	39	25	1
26	Uttar Pradesh		18	72	312	393	1071	423	65
27	Uttarakhand		2	13	72	37	71	54	2
28	West Bengal	3	8	29	83	86	253	234	2

29	A&N Islands			3	5		18	3	1
30	Chandigarh				3			11	
31	D&N Haveli		1	1			1	1	
32	Daman & Diu		2	2			1	2	
33	Delhi	3	11		54			184	
34	Lakshadweep	1	1	1	1	1	9		
35	Puducherry	2	2	6	15	16	26	3	
	ALL-INDIA	**119**	**189**	**737**	**2236**	**2601**	**8811**	**4954**	**420**

@ During 2009, figure of 148 women police stations under col. 10 against Bihar was shown incorrect due to data furnished inadvertently by Bihar. Data of actual women police station in Bihar is 1 as clarified by Bihar in 2010.

As clarified by Tamil Nadu state that due to reclassification of police stations, there is variation in Rural and Urban police stations in 2010

Source : "Crime in India 2010" by NCRB, New Delhi

TOTAL EXPENDITURE ON POLICE PERSONNEL & UNIT COST ON POLICE MAN AS ON 31.12.2010

Sl. No.	State/ UTs.	Total Police expenditure (Rs.in crores) @@	Unit cost per policeman (p.a) (Rupees)	% of civil police to Total police
1	Andhra Pradesh	2185.63	198867	86.8
2	Arunachal Pradesh	159.26	213915	47.1
3	Assam	941.58	174144	53.1
4	Bihar	1400.35	226389	80.7
5	Chandigarh	605.41	144748	62.3
6	Goa	129.78	276186	85.9
7	Gujarat	1139.42	176425	75.3
8	Haryana	813.56	171290	90.5
9	Himachal Pradesh	305.34	224928	71.2
10	Jammu & Kashmir*	1405.35	182485	62.1
11	Jharkhand	1252.73	268751	72.5
12	Karnataka	1325.08	185075	89.0
13	Kerala	995.38	245470	92.2
14	Madhya Pradesh	1256.55	164999	69.3
15	Maharashtra	2720.49	151176	92.1
16	Manipur	315.75	134230	43.6
17	Meghalaya	188.00	183468	57.6
18	Mizoram	211.50	197056	33.2
19	Nagaland	498.00	497851	56.4
20	Orissa	924.18	212724	66.7
21	Punjab	1700.18	255014	72.0
22	Rajasthan	1196.01	167111	83.3
23	Sikkim	89.07	234148	43.2
24	**Tamil Nadu**	**1922.03**	**221547**	**84.0**

25	Tripura	412.13	169887	44.0
26	Uttar Pradesh	4227.99	297469	78.3
27	Uttarakhand	441.41	244630	76.9
28	West Bengal	1176.02	136592	74.2
29	A&N Islands	127.54	341107	78.4
30	Chandigarh	101.20	200040	87.4
31	D&N Haveli	7.29	350481	100.0
32	Daman & Diu	4.22	191818	100.0
33	Delhi	1490.26	201763	91.1
34	Lakshadweep	9.24	278313	100.0
35	Puducherry	7037	309455	75.7
	All India	**31748.30**	**200899**	**77.4**

@@ - BPR&D Data On Police Organisation (the data of 2009 has been used due to non-availability of 2010 data)

Source: "Crime in India 2010" by NCRB, New Delhi

ROAD ACCIDENTS IN TAMIL NADU

YEAR	Fatal		Grievous Injury		Minor Injury		Non-Injury	Total	Total Injured
	N.A.	N.P.K	N.A.	N.P.I	N.A.	N.P.I	N.A.	N.A.	GI+MI
1986	4550	4955	3309	4798	12132	20185	5856	25847	24983
1987	4850	5264	3595	5079	12528	17820	6615	27588	22899
1988	5478	5791	3936	5289	12870	20996	6297	28581	26285
1989	5761	6279	4217	5193	15030	21447	7854	32962	26640
1990	6132	6663	4329	5656	16346	23867	6916	33723	29523
1991	5978	6406	3323	4671	16354	24867	8251	33906	29538
1992	6377	7073	3417	5251	17747	26485	6706	34247	31736
1993	6528	7349	3562	5100	17957	27226	6878	34925	32326
1994	7027	7798	4199	60941	18950	28789	6861	37037	34880
1995	7974	8773	4440	6380	21661	31922	7610	41685	38302
1996	8079	9028	4471	7383	22151	31198	7493	42197	38581
1997	7947	8755	4542	6567	23362	34010	8352	44203	40577
1998	8510	9801	6562	8525	23862	33970	7789	46723	42495
1999	8734	9653	5276	7287	27231	34157	6845	48086	41444
2000	8269	9300	5278	8496	29137	44910	6239	48923	53406
2001	8579	9571	5442	8354	30963	45928	6994	51978	54282
2002	9012	9939	5830	8697	32183	46433	6478	53503	55130
2003	8393	9275	5163	8557	31600	46685	5869	51025	55242
2004	8733	9507	4875	7642	33222	49641	5678	52508	57283
2005	8843	9758	5212	7813	34652	54193	5159	53866	62006
2006	10055	11009	4630	6833	36262	57509	4198	55145	64342
2007	11034	12036	4498	6873	39494	64226	4114	59140	71099
2008	11813	12784	4426	6696	39193	63555	4977	60409	70251
2009	12727	13746	4448	6721	39676	63783	3943	60794	70504
2010	14241	15409	4613	6844	42320	68601	3822	64996	75445
2011	14359	15422	4619	6573	42766	67672	4129	65873	74245

NA=No. of Accidents   NPK=No. of persons killed   NPI=No.
of persons injured   GI=Grieviously injured   M I = Minor injured

INTERVIEW SCHEDULED
OCCUPATIONAL STRESS AND THE COPING STYLES
AMONG THE POLICE CONSTABLES IN TAMILNADU

Dear sir/madam

I am Shunmuga Sundaram pursuing Ph.D part time in Kalasalingam University. This is a Ph.D questionnaire titled **"Occupational Stress among the Police Constables"**. Yours personal details and identity are not revealed in this research. You have been randomly selected to participate in this survey; please do not mention your name in this questionnaire. I also express my hearty thanks for spending your valuable time in answering this questionnaire.

I. Demographic Characteristics:

1. Gender:

   Male   ☐   Female ☐

2. Age:

   20-29 years   ☐   30-39 years   ☐   40-49 years   ☐

   50-59 years   ☐

3. Educational Qualification:

   School level   ☐   UG   ☐   PG   ☐   Professional   ☐

   Others   _____

4. Religion:

   Hindu ☐   Muslim   ☐   Christian   ☐

5. Community:

   Other castes   ☐   Backward castes   ☐

   Most backward castes   ☐   Scheduled castes   ☐

6. Place of Residence:

   Rural   ☐   Urban   ☐

7. Marital status:

   Married   ☐   Unmarried   ☐   Divorced   ☐

   Separated   ☐

8. Number of dependents in the family:

One member ☐   Twomember ☐   Three member ☐

Four member ☐   Fivemember☐ Six member   ☐

II. Job Profile:

9. Designation Grade:

Grade II -Junior   ☐   Grade I-Promotion   ☐   Grade III-
Head Constable   ☐

10. Years of Experiences:

Less than5 years   ☐   6-10 years   ☐   11-15 years   ☐

16-20 years   ☐   More than 20 years   ☐

11. Monthly income:

Rs.5200-20200 plus grade pay   ☐

Rs.2400 Rs.5000-20000 plus grade pay   ☐

Rs.1900 Rs.5200-20200 plus grade pay Rs.2800   ☐

III. Perception about occupation:

12. Nature of stress faced by policy officials.

Sl. No	Variables	High	Low	Moderate
	Job demand			
1.	Assignment of disagreeable duties			
2.	Assignment of new or unfamiliar duties			
3.	Performing tasks not in job description			
4.	Periods of inactivity			
5.	Assignment of increased responsibility			
6.	Competition for advancement			
7.	Frequent changes from boring to demanding activities			
8.	Shift work			
9.	Delivering a death message or bad news to someone			
10.	Attending to incidences of domestic violence			
11.	Reorganization and transformation within the organization			
12.	Killing someone in the line of duty			
13.	Handling			
14.	Having to handle a large crowd/mass demonstration			
15.	A forced arrest or being physically attacked			
16.	Having to go to court			
17.	Having to deal with the media			
18.	Seeing criminals go free (for example because of lack of evidence, court leniency)			
	Lack of resources			
1.	Lack of opportunity for advancement			

2.	Fellow workers not doing their job			
3.	Inadequate support by supervisor			
4.	Lack of recognition for good work			
5.	Inadequate or poor quality equipment			
6.	Inadequate salary			
7.	Difficulty getting along with supervisor			
8.	Insufficient personnel to handle an assignment			
9.	Lack of participation in policy-making decisions			
10.	Poor or inadequate supervision			
11.	Noisy work area			
12.	Insufficient personal time (e.g., coffee breaks, lunch)			
13.	Poorly motivated co-workers			
14.	Staff shortages			
Police stresses/occupational stress				
1.	Working overtime			
2.	Dealing with crisis situations			
3.	Experiencing negative attitudes toward the organization			
4.	Making critical on-the-spot decisions			
5.	Personal insult from customer/consumer/colleague			
6.	Frequent interruptions			
7.	Excessive paperwork			
8.	Meeting deadlines			
9.	Covering work for another employee			
10.	Conflicts with other departments			
11.	Too much supervision Stressful Job-Related Events			
12.	A fellow officer killed in the line of duty			

IV. Occurrence of stress/burnout:

13. Number of days on which the event occurred during past 6 months.

Sl. No	Variables	Very frequently	Frequently	Rarely
Job demand				
1.	Assignment of disagreeable duties			
2.	Assignment of new or unfamiliar duties			
3.	Performing tasks not in job description			
4.	Periods of inactivity			
5.	Assignment of increased responsibility			
6.	Competition for advancement			
7.	Frequent changes from boring to demanding activities			
8.	Shift work			
9.	Delivering a death message or bad news to someone			
10.	Attending to incidences of domestic violence			
11.	Reorganization and transformation within the organization			
12.	Killing someone in the line of duty			
13.	Handling			

14.	Having to handle a large crowd/mass demonstration			
15.	A forced arrest or being physically attacked			
16.	Having to go to court			
17.	Having to deal with the media			
18.	Seeing criminals go free (for example because of lack of evidence, court leniency)			
Lack of resources				
1.	Lack of opportunity for advancement			
2.	Fellow workers not doing their job			
3.	Inadequate support by supervisor			
4.	Lack of recognition for good work			
5.	Inadequate or poor quality equipment			
6.	Inadequate salary			
7.	Difficulty getting along with supervisor			
8.	Insufficient personnel to handle an assignment			
9.	Lack of participation in policy-making decisions			
10.	Poor or inadequate supervision			
11.	Noisy work area			
12.	Insufficient personal time (e.g., coffee breaks, lunch)			
13.	Poorly motivated co-workers			
14.	Staff shortages			
Police stresses/occupational stress				
1.	Working overtime			
2.	Dealing with crisis situations			
3.	Experiencing negative attitudes toward the organization			
4.	Making critical on-the-spot decisions			
5.	Personal insult from customer/consumer/colleague			
6.	Frequent interruptions			
7.	Excessive paperwork			
8.	Meeting deadlines			
9.	Covering work for another employee			
10.	Conflicts with other departments			
11.	Too much supervision Stressful Job-Related Events			
12.	A fellow officer killed in the line of duty			

V. Outcome of Stress Coping strategies:
14. State the outcome of the stress

Variables	Not at all	Sometimes	Never
Loss of sexual interest or pleasure			
Thoughts of ending your life			
Poor appetite			
Crying easily			
A feeling of being trapped or caught			
Blaming yourself for things			
Feeling lonely			

Feeling lovable			
Feeling blue			
Worrying or stewing about things			
Feelings no interest in things			
Feeling hopeless about the future			
Disbelief in Others			
Quarreling with family members			
Feeling of insecurity			

15. State the stress coping strategies.

Note: 1-I usually don't do this at all, 2-I usually do this a little bit, 3-I usually do this a medium amount and 4- I usually do this a lot.

Sl. No	Variables	1	2	3	4
	Seeking social support for emotional reasons				
1.	I ask people who have had similar experience what they did				
2.	I talk t someone but how I feel				
3.	I try to get emotional support from friends or relatives				
4.	I try to get advice someone about what do to				
5.	I get sympathy and understanding from someone				
6.	I talk to someone who could do some think. About the problem				
7.	I reduce the amount of effort I putting to solving the problem				
8.	I discuss my feelings someone				
	Positive reinterpretation and growth				
1.	I force myself to wait for the right time to do something				
2.	I put aside other activities in order to concentrate on this				
3.	I think about how I might best handle the problem				
4.	I admit to myself that I can't deal with it, and quit trying				
5.	I try to see it on a different light to make it seem more positive				
6.	I try hard to prevent other thinks from interfering with my efforts at dealing with this				
7.	I do what has to be done one step at a time				
8.	I give up the attempt to get what I want				
9.	I try to come up with the strategy what to do				
10.	I focus on dealing with the problems and it necessary let other thinks slide a little				
11.	I concentrate on efforts on doing something about it				
12.	I just give up trying to reach my goal				
	Denial behaviour				
1.	I refuse to believe it has happened				
2.	I take additional action to try to get rid of the problem				
3.	I hold of doing anything about it until the situation permits				
	Acceptance of fact				
1.	I try to grow as a person as a result of the experience				
2.	I get used to the idea that it happened				
3.	I say to myself this is't real				
4.	I make sure not to make matters worse by action to soon				
5.	I make a plan of action				

6.	I learn to live with it				
7.	I take direct action around the problem				
8.	I accept that this has happened and that can't we changed				
9.	I accept the reality of the fact that it happened				
Turning to religion					
1.	I put in my trust in god				
2.	I pray more than usual				
3.	I try to find comfort in my religion				
4.	I seek god's help				
Focusing on and ventilating emotions					
1.	I sleep more than usual				
2.	I let my feelings out				
3.	I turn to work or other substitute activities to take my mind				
4.	I thought for some think good what is happing				
5.	A talk to someone to find out more about the situation				
6.	I learn shooting from experience				
7.	I think hard about what step to take				
Behavioral disengagement					
1.	I upset and let my emotion out				
2.	I restrain myself form doing anything do quickly				
3.	I go to movies or watch TV to think it				
4.	I act as though it hasn't even happened				
5.	I get upset and am really aware of it				
Mental disengagement					
1.	I drink alcohol or drink drugs, in order to think about it less				
2.	I pretended that it has not really happened				
3.	I feel a lot of emotional distress and I find myself expressing those feeling a lot				
4.	I keep myself from getting districted by other thought or activates				
5.	I daydream about thinks other than this				

15. Suggestions:

_____

_____

THANK U

Curriculum Vitae

1.Name	M. Shunmuga Sundaram
2.Designation	Research Scholar
3. Official Address	Research Scholar Department of Business Administration Kalasalingam University Krishnan Kovil-628 126
4.Phone	99942 95296
5.Email ID	sundar_sms@yahoo.com
6.Educational Qualification	M.B.A.,M.Phil.,M.B.A(INT-BUS).,PGDPM&IR.,
7.Total Teaching Experience	7 Years of Teaching
8. Research Article Published	International- 14 National- 6
9.Field of research Studies	Human Resource Management

Druck:
Canon Deutschland Business Services GmbH
im Auftrag der KNV-Gruppe
Ferdinand-Jühlke-Str. 7
99095 Erfurt